LENIN

TOWARD THE SEIZURE OF POWER

THE REVOLUTION OF 1917:
FROM THE JULY DAYS TO THE
OCTOBER REVOLUTION

BOOK I

NEW YORK
INTERNATIONAL PUBLISHERS

Copyright, 1932, by
INTERNATIONAL PUBLISHERS CO., Inc.

Printed in the U. S. A.

Composed and printed by union labor

COLLECTED WORKS

OF

V. I. LENIN

VOLUME XXI

**Completely revised, edited and annotated.
The only edition authorised by the
Marx-Engels-Lenin Institute, Moscow.**

Translated by
MOISSAYE J. OLGIN

Edited by
ALEXANDER TRACHTENBERG

THE *COLLECTED WORKS* OF V. I. LENIN
ALREADY PUBLISHED

VOLUME IV. THE ISKRA PERIOD
(1900-1902) In two books

VOLUME XIII. MATERIALISM AND EMPIRIO-CRITICISM

VOLUME XVIII. THE IMPERIALIST WAR
(1914-1916)

VOLUME XIX. WAR AND REVOLUTION
(1916-1917)

VOLUME XX. THE REVOLUTION OF 1917
(March to July, 1917) In two books

VOLUME XXI. TOWARD THE SEIZURE OF POWER
(July to November, 1917) In two books

A special subscribers' edition of the already published volumes is available.

CONTENTS

	PAGE
PREFACE TO THE ENGLISH TRANSLATION	11
FROM THE JULY DAYS TO THE KORNILOV REVOLT . . .	13-175

What Could the Cadets Count On When Leaving the Cabinet?	15
Where is Power and Where is Counter-Revolution? . . .	17
Hideous Slander by the Black Hundred Papers and Alexinsky	22
Calumny and Facts	23
Close to the Real Issue	25
Dreyfusade	26
In Refutation of Dark Rumours	28
Three Crises	29
The Question of the Bolshevik Leaders Appearing Before the Courts	34
The Political Situation	36
Letter to the Editors of the *Novaya Zhizn*	39
Letter to the Editors of the *Proletarskoye Dyelo* . . .	41
On Slogans	43
An Answer	51
On Constitutional Illusions	62
The Beginning of Bonapartism	76
Lessons of the Revolution	80
On Kamenev's Speech in the Central Executive Committee Concerning the Stockholm Conference	94
On the Question of the Party Programme	97
They Do Not See the Woods for the Trees	98
Rumours of Conspiracy	104
Political Blackmail	110
Paper Resolutions	114
On the Stockholm Conference	118
Peasants and Workers	127
On Slanderers	135
To the Central Committee of the Russian Social-Democratic Labour Party	137

CONTENTS

	PAGE
From a Publicist's Diary	140-149
The Root of the Evil	140
Serfdom and Socialism	147
On the Zimmerwald Question	150
On Violation of Democracy in Mass Organisations	151
On Compromises	152
Draft Resolution on the Political Situation	158
One of the Fundamental Questions of the Revolution	164
How is the Success of the Elections to the Constituent Assembly to be Assured?	171

THE THREATENING CATASTROPHE AND HOW TO FIGHT IT . 177-218

Famine is Approaching	179
Complete Inactivity of the Government	180
Universally Known and Easy Measures of Control	183
Nationalisation of the Banks	185
Nationalisation of the Syndicates	190
Abolition of Commercial Secrets	193
Compulsory Organisation Into Unions	197
Regulation of Consumption	200
The Destruction of the Work of Democratic Organisations by the Government	203
Financial Collapse and Measures Against It	206
Is It Possible To Go Forward While Being Afraid of Socialism?	210
The War and the Fight Against Economic Ruin	213
Revolutionary Democracy and the Revolutionary Proletariat	216

ON THE ROAD TO INSURRECTION 219-279

The Bolsheviks Must Assume Power	221
Marxism and Uprising	224
The Russian Revolution and Civil War	230
Heroes of Fraud	244
From a Publicist's Diary	249
The Tasks of the Revolution	256-264
The Tasks of the Revolution	256
Agreements With the Capitalists are Disastrous	257
Power to the Soviets	258

CONTENTS

	PAGE
Peace to the Peoples	258
Land to the Toilers	260
Struggle Against Famine and Economic Ruin	261
Struggle Against the Counter-Revolution of the Landowners and Capitalists	262
Peaceful Development of the Revolution	263
Letter to I. T. Smilga	265
Postscript to the Book *The Agrarian Programme of the Social-Democracy in the First Russian Revolution, 1905-1907*	269
The Crisis Has Matured	271
EXPLANATORY NOTES	279

PREFACE TO THE ENGLISH TRANSLATION

THE present volume covers the period from July 16 to November 6, 1917, *i.e.*, from the critical July days to the October Revolution. The major portion of this volume consists of Lenin's articles and letters written while he was obliged to seek refuge in illegality on account of the persecutions by the Kerensky government and its agents. Although the volume is large, not everything written by Lenin has been included. Many political letters addressed to the Central Committee or to its individual members, known to have been written by Lenin, are still missing, so that only a part of this highly important correspondence is to be found in this volume. A further careful study of the files of the Party press from July to November, 1917, will probably reveal that many of the unsigned articles and notes, published in these papers, were written by Lenin.

To avoid making the volume too bulky, it was considered desirable to divide it into two books. The first contains articles and letters written between July 16 and September 29; the second, his writings between the latter date and November 6. In addition, Book I includes the larger essay "The Threatening Catastrophe and How to Fight It," and Book II opens with "Will the Bolsheviks Retain State Power?" and closes with Lenin's classic "State and Revolution," which appears in a sorely needed revised translation.

All the appendices are given at the end of Book II with the exception of the explanatory notes relating to the writings included in Book I which will be found at the end of this book. The "Documents and Materials" section is larger than in the volumes hitherto published. The elucidation of the political preparation of the October uprising and the struggle against the Right opposition which fought against the uprising, demanded fuller documentation. In view of the special importance of the October 23 and 29 sessions of the Central Committee of the Party which Lenin attended and at which he made the historic speeches in support of the proposed armed uprising, it was considered advisable to include the proceedings of these sessions, even if incompletely recorded.

The preparation of the "Chronology of Lenin's Life" was fraught with difficulties. Exact information regarding Lenin's illegal existence and his peregrinations as a result of it from the outskirts of Petrograd to Helsingfors, then to Vyborg and again to Petrograd, is not available. The many reminiscences of participants are to a great extent contradictory and cannot therefore be considered trustworthy. Therefore, the dates are given only approximately.

This volume, which forms Volume XXI of Lenin's *Collected Works*—together with Volume XX, published under the title *The Revolution of 1917*—makes available in English the writings, speeches and correspondence of Lenin which cover the period from the bourgeois revolution and the overthrow of the Tsar in March, to the proletarian revolution and the establishment of the Soviet Government in November, 1917.

FROM THE JULY DAYS
TO THE KORNILOV REVOLT

WHAT COULD THE CADETS COUNT ON WHEN LEAVING THE CABINET? [1]

THIS question arises quite naturally. To correctly meet events with definite tactics, one must understand the events correctly. How, then, are we to understand the withdrawal of the Cadets? *

Spite? Disagreement, in principle, on the question of the Ukraine? Of course not. It would be ridiculous to suspect the Cadets of loyalty to principles, or the bourgeoisie of being able to do something out of spite.

No. The withdrawal of the Cadets can be understood as a result of calculations only. What is the substance of these calculations?

It is, that to govern a country that has carried out a great revolution and that is still in a state of unrest, and at that to govern it during an imperialist war of world-wide dimensions, the initiative and the vast energy of a really revolutionary class are necessary—gigantic in courage, great historically, full of boundless enthusiasm. Either suppress such a class by force—as the Cadets have been preaching since May 19—or entrust yourself to its leadership. Either be in alliance with imperialist capital; then you must take the offensive in the war, you must be the obedient servant of capital, you must put yourself under its bondage, you must throw overboard the Utopian plans of abolishing landed property without compensation (*see* Lvov's speeches, as reported in the *Birzhevka*,** against Chernov's programme); or, if you are against imperialist capital, you must immediately propose definite conditions of peace to all the peoples, because all the peoples have been tired out by the war; then you must dare to raise and know how to raise the banner of world proletarian revolution against capital, to do this not in words, but in deeds, to drive the revolution forward most decisively in Russia itself.

The Cadets are shrewd people in trade, in finance, in safeguarding capital as well as in politics. The Cadets have realised, correctly

---

* The abbreviated name of the Constitutional-Democratic Party, a party of the bourgeoisie.—*Ed.*

** Popular name of the newspaper *Birzheviye Vyedomosti* [*Stock Exchange News*].—*Ed.*

enough, that the situation is *objectively* revolutionary. They do not mind reforms; they like to share power with the reformists, the Tseretelis and Chernovs. But reforms will not help. A way of reforms leading out of the crisis, out of the war and economic ruin, does *not* exist.

From the standpoint of their class, from the standpoint of the imperialist and exploiting class, the Cadets have calculated correctly. By leaving, they say, we present an ultimatum. We know that the Tseretelis and Chernovs at present do not trust the really revolutionary class, that at present they do not wish to follow a line of really revolutionary politics. Let us frighten them, they say. To be without the Cadets, they aver, means to be without the "aid" of world-wide Anglo-American capital, means to raise the banner of revolution against the latter as well. The Tseretelis and Chernovs, they think, would not do that, they would not dare! They will yield to us!

Should it not be so, they think, then, even if a revolution against capital starts, it will not succeed and we will come back.

This is how the Cadets figure. We repeat: from the standpoint of the exploiting class, the calculation is correct.

Were the Tseretelis and the Chernovs to proceed from the standpoint of the exploited class—and not from that of the vacillating petty bourgeoisie—they would reply to these correct calculations of the Cadets by correct adherence to the political line of the revolutionary proletariat.

Written July 16, 1917.
First published in *Proletarskoye Dyelo*[2] [*Proletarian Cause*], No. 2, July 28, 1917.

WHERE IS POWER AND WHERE IS COUNTER-REVOLUTION?

THIS question is usually dismissed quite simply: there is no counter-revolution at all or we do not know where it is. But power we know quite well; it is in the hands of the Provisional Government, which is controlled by the Central Executive Committee (C.E.C.) of the All-Russian Congress of Soviets of Soldiers' and Workers' Deputies. This is the usual answer.

Yesterday's political crisis,[3] like most crises, which tear down everything conventional and shatter all illusions, has left behind as a legacy the ruins of those illusions which are expressed in the above-cited usual answers to the basic questions involved in any revolution.

There exists a former member of the Second State Duma, Alexinsky, whom the *Socialist-Revolutionaries* and *Mensheviks*, the dominant parties in the Soviets of Workers', Soldiers', and Peasants' Deputies *refused* to admit into the Executive Committee of the Soviet of Workers' and Soldiers' Deputies *before he rehabilitated himself*, i.e., before he re-established his reputation.

What was the trouble? Why did the Executive Committee publicly and formally deny its confidence to Alexinsky, demanding that he re-establish his reputation, i.e., declaring him dishonest?

Because Alexinsky had made himself so notorious with his slanders, that in Paris journalists of most diverse parties had declared him a calumniator. Alexinsky did not take the trouble to re-establish his reputation before the Executive Committee, but preferred to hide himself in Plekhanov's newspaper *Yedinstvo* [*Unity*], appearing there first under initials, and then, gaining courage, openly.

On July 17, yesterday afternoon, a few Bolsheviks were warned by friends that Alexinsky had laid before the committee of Petrograd journalists some of his new detestable slanders. The majority of those who received the warning paid absolutely no attention to it, treating Alexinsky and his "work" with disdainful contempt. But one Bolshevik, Dzhugashvili (Stalin), a member of the Central Executive Committee, who as a Georgian Social-Democrat had known Comrade Chkheidze for a long time, spoke to the latter at a meeting of the C.E.C. about this new despicable and slanderous campaign of Alexinsky's.

This happened late at night, but Chkheidze declared that the C.E.C. would not look with indifference upon the spreading of slanders by people who are afraid of an open court and an investigation by the C.E.C. In his own name, as the chairman of the C.E.C., and in the name of Tsereteli, a member of the Provisional Government, Chkheidze forthwith communicated by *telephone* with all the newspaper offices, suggesting that they *refrain from publishing Alexinsky's slanders*. Chkheidze informed Stalin that most of the papers had expressed readiness to comply with his request, that only the *Yedinstvo* and *Ryech* [*Speech*] "hesitated" for a time (we have not seen the *Yedinstvo*, but the *Ryech* has *not* printed the slanders). As a result, the calumnies appeared only on the pages of a petty, yellow, and to most intelligent people completely unknown sheet, *Zhivoye Slovo* [*Living Word*], No. 51 (404), the editor and publisher of which signs himself A. M. Umansky.[4]

The slanderers will now answer before the court. In this respect the affair is simple and not complicated.

The absurdity of the slander is quite patent: a certain ensign of the Sixteenth Siberian Rifle Regiment, Yermolenko by name, was "despatched" (?) "on May 8 to us behind the front of the Sixth Army to agitate for the speediest conclusion of a separate peace with Germany." Apparently, this is the same escaped prisoner of whom it is said in the "document" published in the *Zhivoye Slovo*: "This commission was accepted by Yermolenko on the insistence of the comrades"!!

From this alone one may judge how little faith may be put in this individual who is so dishonourable that he could accept such a "commission"! . . . The witness has no sense of honour. This is a fact.

And what is the witness's testimony?

He testified as follows: "Officers of the German General Staff, Schiditzki and Lübers, had told him that propaganda of a similar kind was being carried on in Russia by the chairman of the Ukrainian section of the Union for the Liberation of the Ukraine,[5] A. Skoropis-Yoltukhovsky, an agent of the German General Staff, and by Lenin. Lenin was commissioned to use every means in his power to undermine the confidence of the Russian people in the Provisional Government."

Thus the German officers, to induce Yermolenko to do this dishonourable thing, lied to him shamelessly about Lenin who, as is universally known, as is officially proclaimed by the *entire party* of the Bolsheviks, has always *rejected* most emphatically, consistently, and unconditionally a separate peace with Germany! The lie of these German officers is so obvious, crude, nonsensical, that not one literate person would even for a moment take it for anything but a lie. And a politically literate person would be even more certain that the coupling of Lenin with some sort of Yoltukhovsky (?) and the Union for the Liberation of the Ukraine is a particularly glaring absurdity, for both Lenin and all other internationalists have repeatedly *dissociated themselves publicly* from this suspicious social-patriotic "Union," during the war!

The crude lie told by Yermolenko, whom the Germans had bribed, or by German officers, would not deserve the slightest attention, were it not that the "document" has added some "information just received"—it is not known by whom, how, from whom, or when—according to which "money for propaganda is being received" (by whom? the "document" *is afraid* to say directly that it is Lenin who is being accused or suspected!! The document is silent as to *who* "is receiving it") "through trusted people": the "Bolsheviks" Fürstenberg (Hanecki) and Kozlovsky. It is alleged that certain data proving the transfer of money through banks are on hand, and that "the military censorship has unearthed an uninterrupted (!) exchange of telegrams of a political and financial nature between the German agents and Bolshevik leaders"!!

Again such a gross lie that its absurdity is patent. If there were even a word of truth in it, then how could one explain (1) that Hanecki had *quite recently* been allowed freely to enter Russia and just as freely to leave it? (2) that *neither* Hanecki *nor* Kozlovsky had been arrested *before* the appearance in the press of revelations concerning their crimes? Is it really possible that the General Staff, had it actually been in possession of the least bit of trustworthy information concerning the sending of money, telegrams, etc., would have permitted the publication of rumours about it through the Alexinskys and the yellow press, without first arresting Hanecki and Kozlovsky? Is it not clear that we have before us nothing more than the vulgar machinations of newspaper slanderers of the lowest category?

We may add that Hanecki and Kozlovsky are not Bolsheviks, but members of the Polish Social-Democratic Party; that we have known Hanecki, a member of its Central Committee, since the London Congress (1903) from which the Polish delegates withdrew, and so on. *No money* was ever received by the Bolsheviks from either Hanecki or Kozlovsky. All this is a lie, a most unmitigated, vulgar lie.

What is its political significance? First, it indicates that the political opponents of the Bolsheviks cannot get along without lies and libels. So low and contemptible are these opponents.

Second, it supplies us with an answer to the question put at the head of this article.

The report about the "documents" had been sent to Kerensky as early as May 29. Kerensky is a member of the Provisional Government and the Soviet, *i.e.*, of both "powers." From May 29 to July 18 is a long time. The power, if it really were power, *itself* could and should have investigated these "documents," examined the witnesses, and arrested the suspects.

The power, *both* powers—the Provisional Government and the C.E.C.—could and should have done it.

Both powers are inactive. But the General Staff is found to have some sort of relations with Alexinsky, who was not admitted to the Executive Committee of the Soviet, owing to his libelous activities! The General Staff, just at the moment of the withdrawal of the Cadets admits—probably accidentally—the handing over of their official documents to Alexinsky for publication!

The power is inactive. Neither Kerensky, nor the Provisional Government, nor the C.E.C., even thinks of arresting Lenin, Hanecki, or Kozlovsky, despite the fact that they are under suspicion. Last night, July 17, both Chkheidze and Tsereteli ask the newspapers not to print the obvious libel. But just a little later, late at night, Polovtsev sends military cadets and Cossacks to smash up the *Pravda* [*Truth*] offices, stop its publication, arrest its editors, seize its books (on the pretext of investigating whether or not suspicious financial transactions had taken place) and at the very same time, that yellow, base, filthy little sheet, *Zhivoye Slovo*, prints the foul libel to arouse the passions, bespatter the Bolsheviks, create an atmosphere of mob violence, and thus afford a plausible justification for the behaviour of Polovtsev, the military cadets and the Cossacks who wrecked the *Pravda* offices.

Whoever does not close his eyes *in order not to see the truth*, cannot remain deluded. When it is *necessary* to act, *both* powers remain inactive—the C.E.C., because it "trusts" the Cadets and is afraid of irritating them, and the Cadets are not acting as a power because they prefer to act *behind the scenes*.

Counter-revolution behind the scenes—here it is, as plain as day: the Cadets, certain circles of the General Staff ("the commanding peaks of the army," as the resolution of our party calls them) and the questionable semi-Black Hundred press. These are *not* inactive, these "work" together, hand in glove; this is the soil in which pogroms, attempted massacres, shooting of demonstrators, etc., etc., are nurtured.

Whoever does not deliberately shut his eyes, in order not to see the truth, cannot remain deluded any longer.

There is no power, and there will be none until the passing of power into the hands of the Soviets lays the foundation for the creation of such authority. Counter-revolution thrives on the absence of authority by uniting the Cadets with certain commanding peaks of the army and with the Black Hundred press. This is a sad reality, but a reality nevertheless.

Workers and soldiers! It is up to you to show firmness, steadfastness and vigilance!

Written July 18, 1917.
Pravda Bulletin,[6] July 19, 1917.

HIDEOUS SLANDERS BY THE BLACK HUNDRED PAPERS AND ALEXINSKY

THE paper *Zhivoye Slovo*, of an obviously Black Hundred character, carries in today's issue a low, filthy slander against Lenin.

The paper *Pravda* cannot appear, because its plant was wrecked by military cadets on the night of July 18. A detailed refutation of this filthy slander must therefore be postponed.

For the time being we declare that the statement of the *Zhivoye Slovo* is *nothing but slander*, that on the night of July 18 *Chkheidze rang up all the large papers*, asking them to refrain from publishing slanderous pogrom articles. The big papers complied with Chkheidze's request, and *none of them*, with the exception of the filthy *Zhivoye Slovo, published that hideous slander* on July 18.

As to Alexinsky, he is so well known as a slanderer that he *has not been admitted* to the Executive Committee of the Soviet pending his rehabilitation, *i.e.*, until he re-establishes *his standing as an honest man.*

Citizens! Do not believe the foul slanderers, Alexinsky and the *Zhivoye Slovo.*

On the face of it, the slander of the *Zhivoye Slovo* is evident as such from the following: the paper writes that on *May 29* a letter (No. 3719) accusing Lenin was sent to Kerensky from General Headquarters. Obviously it would have been the duty of Kerensky immediately to have Lenin arrested and to order a *government investigation*, had he for a single moment believed in the seriousness of these accusations or suspicions.

Written July 18, 1917.
Pravda Bulletin, July 19, 1917.

CALUMNY AND FACTS

AN immense torrent of abuse and calumny is being poured on the Bolsheviks for the demonstration of July 16 and 17.

They go so far as to accuse the Bolsheviks of "trying to seize the city," of intending to "violate" the will of the Soviets, of "encroaching on the power of the Soviets," and so on and so forth.

The facts, however, say that the Bolsheviks did not seize a single section of the city, a single building, a single institution (though they could have done so); not a single attempt at seizure was made in spite of the fact that the masses were armed.

The facts say that the only *political* instance of violence *against an institution* happened on the night of July 17, when the military cadets and Cossacks, on Polovtsev's orders, raided the *Pravda without the knowledge of the Soviet, against the will of the Soviet.*

This is a fact.

This was a premeditated and vicious use of violence against an entire establishment, an "attempt" to do "violence" not in words, but in deeds. If this attempt were lawful, then either the Provisional Government or the Soviets would have sanctioned such a step. *Neither, however, has done so.* The perpetrators of the outrage against the *Pravda have found no support* either in the Soviet or in the Provisional Government.

The Bolsheviks appealed to the soldiers who started the demonstration to act *peaceably and in an organised fashion.*

Neither the Provisional Government nor the Soviet appealed to the military cadets and Cossacks or to Polovtsev, to act peaceably and in an organised lawful fashion.

But, we are told, there was shooting.

Yes, there was shooting. But who did it? Who dares blame the shooting on anybody without an investigation?

Would you like to listen to *a witness from bourgeois quarters?*

This witness is the paper *Birzheviye Vyedomosti*, evening edition of July 17, a witness whom nobody in the world will suspect of partiality towards the Bolsheviks! This is what the witness says:

At 2 P.M. sharp, when the armed demonstrators were passing the corner of the Sadovaya and Nevsky, while the spectators, gathered in considerable numbers, were watching them quietly, *a deafening report was heard from the right side of the Sadovaya* after which disorderly rapid firing began.[7]

The witness from the bourgeois paper is compelled to admit the truth, that the shooting *began from the right side of the Sadovaya!!* Is this not clear proof that the shooting was directed *at the demonstrators?*

Is it so difficult to figure out that had the demonstrators planned or wished to use violence, *they would have concentrated on a definite institution,* as Polovtsev's military cadets and Cossacks concentrated on the *Pravda?* On the other hand, if sailors were killed, and if the witnesses from a bourgeois paper state that the shooting was started "from the right side of the Sadovaya," and at a time "when the armed demonstrators were passing, "is it not obvious that violence was intended *precisely* by the *Black Hundreds, precisely* by the *opponents* of democracy, precisely by the circles close to the Cadets?

Written July 18, 1917.
Pravda Bulletin, July 19, 1917.

CLOSE TO THE REAL ISSUE

AT the session of the Central Executive Committee on the evening of July 17th, Citizen Chaikovsky, in his speech, came unusually close to the real issue.[8]

He spoke against the seizure of power by the Soviet and, among other things, advanced the following, so to speak, "decisive" argument: we must continue the war, he said; but we cannot continue the war without money, and the English and Americans won't give any money if the power is in the hands of "Socialists"; they will give money only if the Cadets participate in the government.

This gets close to the real issue.

It is impossible to participate in the imperialist war without at the same time "participating" in the capitalist activities of subjugating the people to the capitalist gentry by means of loans.

In order really to rise against the imperialist war, it is necessary to sever *all* the ties that bind and link people to capital; fearlessly the workers and peasants must take into their hands the control of the banks and production and regulate them.

We, too, think that the English and Americans will not give any money if it is not vouched for by the Cadets. There is but one alternative: either serve the Cadets, serve capital, pile up imperialist loans (and do not pretend to the title "revolutionary" democracy, being fully content with the correct appellation of *imperialist* democracy); or break with the Cadets, break with the capitalists, break with imperialism, become revolutionists in deeds also on questions relating to the war.

Chaikovsky came very close to the real issue.

Written July 18, 1917.
Pravda Bulletin, July 19, 1917.

DREYFUSADE [9]

THE obsolete combined with the modern—this was always a method of exploitation and repression used by tsarism; thus it remains in republican Russia as well. The counter-revolutionary bourgeoisie flavours its political baiting of the Bolsheviks, the party of the international revolutionary proletariat, with the most hideous slanders, with a press "crusade" of just the same character as the campaign of the French clerical and monarchist papers in the Dreyfus case.

Dreyfus must be accused of espionage at all costs! This was then the watchword. Some Bolshevik or other must be accused of espionage at all costs! This is the watchword today. The most hideous slander, loaded dice, gross lies and artful tricks to bamboozle the reader—all these methods are being utilised by the yellow and bourgeois press generally with unusual vehemence. The net result is a mad, raging roar in which it is impossible to discern not only arguments, but at times even articulate words.

Here are a few of the methods used in our present republican Dreyfusade. First they "advanced" three main "arguments": Yermolenko, Kozlovsky's twenty million, and the implication of Parvus.

One day after this was published, the chief pogrom paper, the *Zhivoye Slovo,* already has two "corrections" to make, admitting that the "leader" of the Bolsheviks is not venal but a fanatic, and changing the twenty million into twenty thousand. At the same time another paper declares Yermolenko's testimony to be of secondary importance.

In the *Pravda Bulletin* of July 19 we showed the absolute absurdity of Yermolenko's testimony.* It has obviously become inconvenient to refer to it.

In the same *Bulletin,* there is a letter from Kozlovsky denying the allegation.[10] The story about the twenty million having been disproved, they reduce it to twenty thousand—again "round figures" instead of a definite sum.

Parvus is drawn into the fray in a furious effort to create the semblance of a connection between him and the Bolsheviks. In

* See p. 17.—*Ed.*

reality the Bolsheviks called Parvus a renegade long ago, in the Geneva *Sotsial-Demokrat* (the article on Parvus was entitled "Reaching Their Limit" *) ; the Bolsheviks ruthlessly denounced him as the German Plekhanov, and once for all eliminated every possibility of any kind of rapprochement with such social-chauvinists. It was the Bolsheviks who, in Stockholm, at a grand rally held jointly with the Swedish Left Socialists, categorically refused not only to speak to Parvus, but even to admit him in any capacity, even as a guest.[11]

Hanecki was engaged in business as an employee of the firm in which Parvus was a partner. The commercial and financial correspondence was of course censored, and is entirely accessible to examination. An effort is now made to mix these business affairs with politics, although no proof whatsoever is furnished!!

They have stooped to such a ridiculous thing as blaming the *Pravda* for the fact that its despatches to the Socialist papers of Sweden and other countries (which despatches, of course, had to pass the censor, and are fully known to him), were reprinted by the German papers, often garbled! As if the reprinting, or the vicious distortions, can be blamed on the authors!

It is a veritable Dreyfusade, a vile campaign of lies and slander upon the ground of savage political hatred. . . . How foul must be the source which spreads slander as a substitute for the clash of ideas!

Written July 19-20, 1917.
First published in the *Lenin Collection*, IV, 1926.

* See V. I. Lenin, *The Imperialist War*, *Collected Works*, Vol. XVIII, p. 364.—*Ed.*

IN REFUTATION OF DARK RUMOURS

THE *Pravda Bulletin* of July 19 carried a detailed refutation of the hideous calumny spread by the Black Hundred papers, concerning Lenin and others. A similar refutation, in a more abbreviated form, was published as a separate leaflet in the name of the Central Committee of our party.

In addition we have only to answer the following questions put to us: are the rumours concerning the arrest of Lenin, Kamenev, Zinoviev and others true? No, these rumours are *untrue*. All the Bolsheviks here named, who are particularly hounded by the hideously slanderous press, are members of the All-Russian Central Executive Committee of the Soviets of Workers' and Soldiers' Deputies. We once more request all honest citizens not to believe the filthy calumnies and dark rumours.

Written July 20, 1917.
First published in the *Lenin Collection*, VII, 1928.

THREE CRISES [12]

THE more frantic the calumnies and lies against the Bolsheviks these days, the more calmly can we, while refuting the lies and the calumnies, reflect upon the historical interrelation of events and the political, *i.e.*, *class* significance of the present course of the revolution.

In refutation of the lies and calumnies we must once more refer to the *Pravda Bulletin* of July 19, and call the particular attention of the reader to the article printed below which gives documentary evidence that on July 15 the Bolsheviks carried on propaganda *against* the demonstration (as admitted by the paper of the Socialist-Revolutionary Party); that on July 16 the sentiment of the masses had reached the highest pitch, the demonstration starting against our advice; that on July 17, in a leaflet (reprinted by the same paper of the S.-R.'s, the *Dyelo Naroda* [*People's Cause*], we called for a *peaceful* and *organised* demonstration; that on the night of July 17 we passed a decision to call off the demonstration.[13] Calumniators, continue your calumnies! You will never disprove these facts and their decisive significance in all their connection.

Let us turn to the question of the historical interrelation of events. When, as early as the beginning of April, we expressed ourselves against supporting the Provisional Government, we were attacked by both the S.-R.'s and the Mensheviks. But what has reality proven?

What has been proven by the three political crises: May 3 and 4, June 23 and July 1, and July 16 and 17?

They have proven, first, that the masses are becoming increasingly dissatisfied with the bourgeois policies of the bourgeois majority of the Provisional Government.

It is rather interesting to observe that even the organ of the ruling Socialist-Revolutionary Party, the *Dyelo Naroda*, notwithstanding its animosity towards the Bolsheviks, is compelled to admit in its issue of July 19 the deep economic and political causes of the movement of July 16 and 17.[14] The stupid, crude, hideous lie as to the artificial stimulation of this movement by the Bolsheviks and as to the Bolshevik propaganda *in favour* of that demonstration will be exposed more and more every day.

The common cause, the common origin, the deep common root of all three above-mentioned political crises are evident, especially if we look upon them and their interrelation in the way science demands that politics be looked upon. It is foolish even to think that three such crises could be produced artificially.

Second, it is instructive to establish what each one of these crises had in common with the others, and what was its individual feature.

What is common to all is a mass dissatisfaction overflowing all bounds, a mass resentment against the bourgeoisie and its government. Whoever forgets, or leaves unmentioned, or minimises *this essence of the matter*, renounces the elementary truths of Socialism concerning the class struggle.

The class struggle in the Russian Revolution! Let this be thought of by those who call themselves Socialists, who know something about the class struggle in European revolutions.

What is individual in each of these crises is the way it manifests itself. The first one (May 3-4) was stormy and spontaneous, altogether unorganised; it led to Black Hundred elements' firing at the demonstrators and to preposterous and lying accusations against the Bolsheviks. After the outburst came a political crisis.

In the second case the demonstration was called by the Bolsheviks and called off after a stern ultimatum and a direct veto by the Congress of Soviets; then followed a general demonstration on July 1 which rallied a clear majority to the Bolshevik slogans. As the S.-R.'s and Mensheviks themselves admitted on the evening of July 1, a political crisis would certainly have broken out, had it not been arrested by the offensive at the front.

The third crisis broke out spontaneously on July 16 despite the efforts of the Bolsheviks to check it on July 15; it reached its climax on July 17, and on July 18 and 19 it caused a furious outburst of counter-revolution. There were vacillations among the S.-R.'s and Mensheviks, Spiridonova and a number of other S.-R.'s expressing themselves in favour of the passing of power to the Soviets, and the Menshevik-internationalists, previously opposed to it, also joining in this demand.

The last, and, perhaps, the most instructive conclusion to be drawn from the consideration of the events as a whole is that *all* three crises manifest some form of demonstration, of a more complicated type that is new in the history of our revolution, a type where the movement appears in waves, a sudden fall following a rapid rise, revolution and counter-revolution becoming more acute and the middle elements being "washed out" for a more or less prolonged period of time.

In all three crises the movement took the form of a *demonstration*. An anti-government demonstration would be the most fitting description of the events, formally speaking. But the fact of the matter is that it is not an ordinary demonstration; it is something considerably more than a demonstration and less than a revolution. It is an outburst of revolution and counter-revolution *together;* it is a rough, sometimes sudden "washing out" of the middle elements, while the proletarian and bourgeois elements make a stormy appearance.

In this respect it is highly characteristic that, for *each one* of these movements, the middle elements blame *both* of the definite class powers—the proletarian as well as the bourgeois. Look at the S.-R.'s and Mensheviks. They are ready to leap out of their skins shouting frantically that, by their extremism, the Bolsheviks are helping the counter-revolution; at the same time, however, they admit that the Cadets (with whom they form a bloc in the government) are counter-revolutionists. "We must draw a line," said the *Dyelo Naroda* yesterday, "we must dig a deep trench between ourselves and all the elements to the Right, including the lately turned militant *Yedinstvo*" (with whom, we may note in passing, the S.-R.'s formed a bloc during the elections); "this is our urgent task." [15]

Compare with this today's issue of the *Yedinstvo* (July 20), in which Plekhanov, in an editorial, is compelled to state an indisputable fact, namely, that the Soviets (*i.e.*, the S.-R.'s and Mensheviks) will "weigh the matter for two weeks," and that, if power were to pass to the Soviets, "it would be tantamount to a victory of the Leninists." "If the Cadets do not adhere to the idea that the worse, the better," says Plekhanov, "they will be compelled to admit that they made a big mistake" (in leaving the cabinet) "because this facilitated the work of the Leninists." [16]

Is this not characteristic? The middle elements blame the Cadets for facilitating the work of the Bolsheviks and the Bolsheviks for facilitating the work of the Cadets! Is it so difficult to realise that, if we substitute class designations for political ones, we have before us the dreams of the petty bourgeoisie as to the disappearance of the class struggle between the proletariat and the bourgeoisie? That it is the complaint of the petty bourgeoisie against the class struggle between the proletariat and the bourgeoisie? Is it so difficult to see that no Bolsheviks in the world would be able to "call forth" a single "movement of the people," not to speak of three movements, if the proletariat were not motivated by the deepest economic and political causes? That no Cadets and monarchists combined would be able to call forth any movement "from the Right" if it were not for the fact that equally deep causes create the counter-revolutionary attitude of the bourgeoisie as a class?

Both we and the Cadets were blamed for the May 3-4 movement; we were blamed for instability, extremism, and for intensifying the situation; the Bolsheviks were even accused (absurd as it may be) of the firing on the Nevsky; but when the movement was over, those same S.-R.'s and Mensheviks, in their common and official organ, the *Izvestiya* * [*News*], wrote that the "movement of the people" had "swept away the imperialist Milyukov, et al., *i.e.*, they *praised* the movement!! Is this not characteristic? Is it not perfectly obvious that the petty bourgeoisie does not understand the mechanism and the essence of the class struggle between the proletariat and the bourgeoisie?

The objective situation is this. A tremendous majority of the country's population is petty-bourgeois by its living conditions and more so by its ideas. But big capital rules the country, primarily through banks and syndicates. There is in this country an urban proletariat strong enough to go its own way, but not yet able to draw at once to its side the majority of the semi-proletarians. Out of this fundamental class fact follows the inevitability of such crises as the three we are now examining, as well as their forms.

The forms of the crises may, of course, change in the future, but the substance of the issue will remain even if, for instance, the S.-R. Constituent Assembly convenes in October. The S.-R.'s have promised the peasants (1) to abolish private property in land; (2) to transfer the land to the toilers; (3) to confiscate the landowners' lands and transfer them to the peasants without compensation. These great reforms can never be realised without the most decisive revolutionary measures against the bourgeoisie, measures that can be undertaken *only* when the poorest peasantry joins the proletariat, *only* when the banks and syndicates are nationalised.

The gullible peasants, who for a time believed that these beautiful

---

* The official organ of the Soviet.—*Ed.*

things can be achieved by compromising with the bourgeoisie, will inevitably be disappointed and . . . "dissatisfied" (mildly speaking) with the sharp class struggle of the proletariat against the bourgeoisie for the actual realisation of the promises of the S.-R.'s. Thus it was, and thus it will be.

Written July 20, 1917.
Published in the magazine *Rabotnitsa* [*Woman Worker*], No. 7, August 1, 1917.

THE QUESTION OF THE BOLSHEVIK LEADERS APPEARING BEFORE THE COURTS [17]

JUDGING by private conversations, there are two opinions on this question.

Comrades yielding to the "Soviet atmosphere" are often inclined towards appearing before the courts.

Those who are closer to the working masses apparently incline towards not appearing.

In principle, the question reduces itself to an estimation of what are commonly called constitutional illusions.

If one thinks that a *just* government and *just* courts are possible in Russia, that the convocation of the Constituent Assembly is probable, then he may arrive at the conclusion that it is necessary to appear.

But such an opinion is thoroughly erroneous. The latest events, especially after July 17, have shown in the most flagrant fashion that the convocation of the Constituent Assembly is improbable (without a new revolution), that no just government or just court exists, or can exist (at present) in Russia.

The court is an organ of power. The liberals sometimes forget this. It is a sin for a Marxist to forget it.

Where, then, is the power? Who constitutes the power?

There is no government. It changes daily. It is inactive.

The power that is active is the military dictatorship. Under such conditions it is ridiculous even to speak of "the courts." It is not a question of "courts," but of *an episode in the civil war*. This is what those in favour of appearing before the courts unfortunately do not want to understand.

Pereverzev and Alexinsky as initiators of the "case"—is it not ridiculous to speak of a court in such a case? Is it not naïve to think that, under such conditions, any court can examine, investigate, establish anything?

Power is in the hands of a military dictatorship. Without a new revolution this power can only become stronger for a while, first of all for the duration of the war.

"I have done nothing unlawful. The courts are just. The courts will examine the case. The trial will be public. The people will understand. I shall appear."

This reasoning is childishly naïve. Not a trial but a campaign of persecution against the internationalists, this is what *the authorities need*. To seize them and hold onto them is what Messrs. Kerensky and Co. need. Thus it was (in England and France), thus it will be (in Russia).

Let the internationalists work underground as far as it is in their power, but let them not commit the folly of voluntarily appearing before the courts!

Written July 21, 1917.
First published in the magazine *Proletarskaya Revolyutsiya* [*Proletarian Revolution*], No. 1 (36), 1925.

THE POLITICAL SITUATION [18]

THE counter-revolution has become organised and consolidated, and has actually taken state power into its hands.

The full organisation and consolidation of the counter-revolution consists in a combination of the three main forces of the counter-revolution, a combination excellently conceived and already carried out in practice: (1) the party of the Constitutional-Democrats, *i.e.*, the real leaders of the organised bourgeoisie, by leaving the cabinet, confronted it with an ultimatum, thus clearing the ground for the overthrow of this cabinet by the counter-revolution; (2) the army headquarters and the commanding peak of the army, with the conscious or semi-conscious aid of Kerensky, whom even the most prominent Socialist-Revolutionaries now call a Cavaignac, have seized actual state power and proceeded to shoot down the revolutionary sections of the army at the front, disarm the revolutionary army sections and the workers in Petrograd and Moscow, suppress and forcibly quell unrest in Nizhni-Novgorod,[19] arrest the Bolsheviks and suppress their papers not only without trial but even without a governmental order. Fundamentally, state power in Russia is at present actually a military dictatorship. This fact is still obscured by a number of institutions, revolutionary in words, but powerless in practice; but it is, nevertheless, such a real and fundamental fact that without understanding it, it is impossible to understand the political situation at all; (3) the Black Hundred monarchist and bourgeois press, having progressed from hounding the Bolsheviks to hounding the Soviets, the "incendiary" Chernov, etc., has proven with the utmost clarity that the real meaning of the now prevailing policy of military dictatorship, supported by the Cadets and monarchists, is preparation for disbanding the Soviets. Many of the leaders of the S.-R.'s and Mensheviks, *i.e.*, the present majority of the Soviets, have already recognised this fact and have recently openly admitted it, but like real petty bourgeois they shake off this imminent reality with sonorous, empty phrases.

The leaders of the Soviets as well as of the Socialist-Revolutionary and Menshevik Parties, with Tsereteli and Chernov at their head, have definitely betrayed the cause of the revolution by placing it in the hands of the counter-revolutionists and transforming themselves, their parties and the Soviets into fig-leaves of the counter-revolution.

This is proven by the fact that the Socialist-Revolutionaries and the Mensheviks have betrayed the Bolsheviks, and have tacitly agreed to the destruction of their papers, not even daring directly and openly to tell the people that they are doing so and why. Having sanctioned the disarming of the workers and the revolutionary regiments, they have deprived themselves of all real power. They have turned into the most empty chatterers who help the reaction to "engage" the attention of the people until it has accomplished all the preparations for disbanding the Soviets. Without understanding this complete and final bankruptcy of the Socialist-Revolutionary and Menshevik Parties and their present majority in the Soviets, without understanding the complete fictitiousness of their "Directory" and other masquerades, it is impossible to understand anything about the present political situation.

All hopes for a peaceful development of the Russian Revolution have definitely vanished. The objective situation is this: either a victory of the military dictatorship with all it implies, or a victory of the decisive struggle of the workers, possible only when it comes together with a deep mass upheaval against the government and the bourgeoisie as a result of economic ruin and the prolongation of the war.

The slogan of all power passing to the Soviets was a slogan of a peaceful development of the revolution, possible in April, May, June, and up to July 18-22, *i.e.*, up to the time when actual power passed into the hands of the military dictatorship. Now this slogan is no longer correct, as it does not take into account this already accomplished passing of power and the real complete betrayal of the revolution by the S.-R.'s and Mensheviks. Neither adventurous undertakings, nor insurrections, nor partial resistance, nor hopeless sporadic attempts to oppose reaction can remedy the situation. What can help is a clear understanding of the situation, the endurance and steadfastness of the workers' vanguard, preparation of forces for the decisive struggle, for whose victory conditions at present are terribly difficult, but still possible, if the facts and trends here enumerated coincide. No constitutional or republican illusions of any kind; no more illusions of a peaceful way; no sporadic actions; no yielding *now* to the provocation of the Black Hundreds and Cossacks; but gather the forces, reorganise them, and steadfastly prepare for the decisive struggle, if the course of development permits it on a real mass, national scale. The transfer of the land to the peasants is impossible at present without a decisive struggle, since the counter-revolution, having taken power, has completely united with the landowners as a class.

The aim of the struggle can be only the passing of power into the hands of the proletariat, supported by the poorest peasantry, in order to carry out in practice the programme of our party.

The party of the working class, not abandoning open existence, but never for a moment exaggerating its importance, must *combine* open with underground work, as it did in 1912-1914.

Do not miss a single hour of open work. But do not cherish any constitutional and "peaceful" illusions. (Organise immediately underground organisations or nuclei everywhere for the publication of leaflets, etc. Reorganise immediately, consistently, steadfastly, all along the line. Act as we did in 1912-1914 when we managed to speak about overthrowing tsarism by a revolution, without at the same time losing our legal base in the State Duma, in the insurance societies, in the trade unions, etc.)

Written July 23, 1917.
First published in the *Lenin Collection*, IV, 1926.

LETTER TO THE EDITORS OF THE *NOVAYA ZHIZN* [*NEW LIFE*] [20]

PERMIT us, comrades, to resort to your hospitality because of the forced suspension of our party paper. Papers of a certain kind have started a furious baiting campaign against us, accusing us of espionage or of communicating with the enemy government. The extraordinary . . . light-mindedness (an inappropriate and much too weak a word) with which this baiting is conducted may be seen from the following plain facts:

The *Zhivoye Slovo* first published a statement declaring that Lenin was a spy; then, in a "correction" which did not correct anything, it declared that he was not accused of espionage. First it comes out with Yermolenko's testimony, then it is compelled to admit that it is downright awkward and shameful to use the testimony of such a person as an argument. The name of Parvus is dragged in without mention being made that no one denounced Parvus as sharply and mercilessly even in 1915 as did the Geneva *Sotsial-Demokrat*, which we edited and which, in an article entitled "Reaching Their Limit," branded Parvus as a renegade licking Hindenburg's boots,* etc. Every literate person knows, or can easily find out, that there can be absolutely no political or other relations between ourselves and Parvus. The name of one Sumenson is dragged in, a person with whom we not only never had anything to do, but never even met. A business enterprise of Hanecki and Kozlovsky is also dragged in, but not a single fact is mentioned as to where, how and when the business was a screen for espionage. Not only have we never participated directly or indirectly in commercial enterprises, but we have never received from the above comrades a single kopeck either for ourselves personally or for the party.

They go so far as to blame us for the fact that the *Pravda* despatches were reprinted in the German papers in distorted fashion, but forgot to mention that the *Pravda* issues German and French bulletins abroad, and that the reprinting of material from these bulletins is entirely free.[21]

---

* See V. I. Lenin, *The Imperialist War, Collected Works*, Vol. XVIII, p. 364.—*Ed.*

And all this is done with the participation, and even at the initiative, of Alexinsky, who has not been admitted to the Soviets, who, in other words, has been recognised as a notorious slanderer!! Is it really possible not to understand that *such* methods against us are tantamount *to legal assassination?* The Central Executive Committee's discussion of the conditions under which the members of the Central Executive Committee could be brought before the courts undoubtedly introduces an element of orderliness. Will the Socialist-Revolutionary and Menshevik Parties want to participate in an attempt at legal murder? To put us on trial without even indicating whether we are accused of espionage or mutiny, to put us on trial without any precise indictment at all? To stage an obviously unfair trial which may handicap their own candidates in the elections of the Constituent Assembly? Will those parties, on the eve of the convocation of the Constituent Assembly in Russia, stage the beginning of a Dreyfusade on Russian soil? The near future will give an answer to these questions which we deem it the duty of the free press to raise openly.

We are not talking about the bourgeois press. Of course, Milyukov believes in our espionage or in our acceptance of German money about as much as Markov and Zamyslovsky believed that Jews drink children's blood.

But Milyukov and Co. know what they are doing.

N. Lenin.
G. Zinoviev.
L. Kamenev.

Novaya Zhizn, No. 71, July 24, 1917.

LETTER TO THE EDITORS OF THE
PROLETARSKOYE DYELO [22]

Comrades:

We have changed our minds about submitting to the decree of the government ordering our arrests, for the following reasons.

From the letter of Pereverzev, the former Minister of Justice, published on Sunday in the paper *Novoye Vremya* [*New Times*], it is apparent that the espionage case of Lenin and others was quite deliberately framed up by the party of the counter-revolution.[23]

Pereverzev has openly admitted that he took advantage of unconfirmed rumours to arouse the wrath of the soldiers (*sic!*) against our party. This is admitted by the Minister of Justice of yesterday, a man who only yesterday called himself a Socialist. Pereverzev is gone, but whether the new Minister of Justice will hesitate to adopt Pereverzev's and Alexinsky's methods, nobody can venture to say.

The counter-revolution tries to create a new Dreyfus affair. The counter-revolution believes in our espionage as much as the leaders of the Russian reaction, the creators of the Beilis case,* believed that Jews drink children's blood. There are no guarantees of justice in Russia at present.

The Central Executive Committee, which considers itself the plenipotentiary organ of Russian democracy, did appoint a commission to investigate the espionage charges, but under the pressure of the counter-revolutionary forces, the commission has been dismissed. The Central Executive Committee refrained from either confirming or revoking the order for our arrest. It washed its hands of the case, thus really delivering us to the counter-revolution.

The charges of conspiracy and moral inciting to insurrection preferred against us are of a very definite nature, but no precise indictment of our alleged crime is brought either by the government or by the Soviet, both of which know very well that it is simply nonsense to speak of conspiracy in referring to a movement like that of July 16-18. The leaders of the Mensheviks and S.-R.'s are simply trying to appease the counter-revolution that is already bearing down on them, and for this reason they deliver a number of our

---

* A famous ritual murder case in Russia in 1913.—*Ed.*

party members to the counter-revolution, in compliance with the latter's request. There can be at present no legal basis in Russia, not even such constitutional guarantees as exist in the bourgeois, Social-Democratic, orderly countries. To deliver oneself at present into the hands of the authorities would mean to deliver oneself into the hands of the Milyukovs, Alexinskys, Pereverzevs, into the hands of rampant counter-revolution, which looks upon all the charges against us as a simple episode in the civil war.

After the things that happened on July 19-21, not a single Russian revolutionist can harbour constitutional illusions any longer. Revolution and counter-revolution are coming to grips in a decisive fashion. We shall, as heretofore, struggle on the side of the former.

We shall, as heretofore, aid the revolutionary struggle of the proletariat with all our strength. The Constituent Assembly alone, if it convenes, and if its convocation is not the work of the bourgeoisie, will have full authority to pass upon the decree of the government ordering our arrest.

N. LENIN.
G. ZINOVIEV.

Proletarskoye Dyelo, No. 2, July 28, 1917.

ON SLOGANS

It happens only too often that, when history makes a sharp turn, even the most advanced parties cannot get used to the new situation for some time, and repeat slogans that were correct yesterday, but have no more meaning today, having lost it as "suddenly" as the sharp turn in history "suddenly" occurred.

Something like this may, apparently, repeat itself with the slogan of all state power passing to the Soviets. This slogan was correct during that period of our revolution, say between March 12 and July 17, that has now vanished irrevocably. This slogan has obviously ceased to be correct at present. Without understanding this, it is impossible to understand anything about the urgent questions of the present moment. Every single slogan must be deducted from the sum total of the peculiarities of a given political situation. The political situation in Russia is now, after July 17, radically different from the situation of March 12-July 17.

During that period of our revolution now past, there prevailed in the state the so-called "dual power" which both materially and formally expressed the indefinite and transitory character of state power. Let us not forget that the question of power is the fundamental question of every revolution.

At that time, power was in a state of flux. It was shared, under a voluntary agreement, by the Provisional Government and the Soviets. The Soviets represented delegations from the mass of free workers and soldiers, *i.e.*, such as are not subject to any force from without. The workers and soldiers were armed. Arms in the hands of the people, and the absence of an outside force over the people—this is what the situation was *in essence*. This is what opened and guaranteed a peaceful road of development for the whole revolution. The slogan, "All power passing to the Soviets" was the slogan of the next step, which could be immediately made along this peaceful road of development. It was the slogan of a peaceful development of the revolution, possible between March 12 and July 17 and, of course, most desirable, but at present absolutely impossible.

It seems that not all the adherents of the slogan, "All power passing to the Soviets" have given sufficient thought to the circumstance that it was a slogan of a peaceful development of the revolution. We say peaceful, not only because nobody, no class, no single force of importance was then (between March 12 and July 17) able to resist or to prohibit the transfer of power to the Soviets. This alone is not the whole story. Peaceful development would then have been possible even in the sense that the struggle of classes and parties *within* the Soviets could—provided full state power had passed to the latter in due time—have taken the most peaceful and painless forms.

This latter side of the case has not yet been given sufficient attention. According to their class composition, the Soviets were organs of the movement of workers and peasants, the ready form of their dictatorship. Had they had full power, then the main shortcoming of the petty-bourgeois circles, their main fault, namely, their confidence in the capitalists, would have been overcome in practice, would have been refuted by the experience of their own measures. The classes and parties which had power could have succeeded each other peacefully inside of the Soviets as the only body possessing all power; the contact between all the Soviet parties and the masses could have remained firm and unimpaired. One must not forget for a single moment that only such a very close contact, freely growing in extent and depth, between the Soviet parties and the masses, would have helped the peaceful outgrowing of the illusions of petty-bourgeois compromise with the bourgeoisie. The passing of power to the Soviets would not and could not in itself have changed the interrelation of classes; it would have changed nothing in the petty bourgeois nature of the peasantry. It would, however, have made a long step towards breaking the peasantry away from the bourgeoisie, towards bringing it closer to the workers, and finally uniting it with them.

Things could have followed this course had power in due time passed to the Soviets. It would have been most easy, most advantageous for the people. Such a course would have been the most painless, and it was therefore necessary to fight for it most energetically. At present, however, this struggle, the struggle for the passing of power to the Soviets in due time, is finished. The peaceful course of development has been rendered impossible. The non-peaceful, the most painful road has begun.

The turning point of July 17 consisted just in this, that after it the objective situation changed abruptly. The fluctuating state of power ceased, the power having passed at a decisive point into the hands of the counter-revolution. The development of the parties on the basis of a compromise between the petty-bourgeois Socialist-Revolutionaries and Mensheviks and the counter-revolutionary Cadets, has brought about a situation where both these petty-bourgeois parties have in practice proved the aiders and abettors of counter-revolutionary atrocities. The unconscious confidence of the petty bourgeoisie in the capitalists has led the former, in the course of the development of party struggle, to a conscious support of the counter-revolutionists. The cycle of development of party relations has been completed. On March 12, all classes found themselves united against the monarchy. After July 17, the counter-revolutionary bourgeoisie, hand in hand with the monarchists and the Black Hundreds, has attached to itself the petty-bourgeois Socialist-Revolutionaries and Mensheviks, partly by intimidating them, and has given over actual state power into the hands of the Cavaignacs, into the hands of a military clique that shoots down the insubordinate soldiers at the front, while it raids the Bolsheviks in Petrograd.

The slogan of the power passing to the Soviets would at present sound quixotic or mocking. Objectively, this slogan would be a deception of the people. It would spread among it the illusion that to seize power, the Soviets even *now* have only to wish or to decree it; that there are still parties in the Soviet which have not been tainted by aiding the hangmen; that one can undo what has happened.

It would be the deepest error to think that the revolutionary proletariat is capable of "refusing" to support the Socialist-Revolutionaries and Mensheviks out of "revenge" for their actions in raiding the Bolsheviks, in shooting down soldiers at the front and in disarming the workers. Such a statement of the question would mean, first, to ascribe to the proletariat philistine conceptions of morality (*for the good of the cause* the proletariat will support not only the vacillating petty bourgeoisie but also the big bourgeoisie); second—and this is the main thing—it would mean to substitute philistine "moralising" for an analysis of the political essence of the matter.

This essence of the matter is that at present power can no longer be seized peacefully. It can be obtained only after a victory in a decisive struggle against the real holders of power at the present moment, namely, the military clique, the Cavaignacs, who rely on the reactionary troops brought to Petrograd, on the Cadets and on the monarchists.

The essence of the matter is that those new holders of state power can be defeated only by the revolutionary masses of the people, whose movement depends not only on their having a proletarian leadership but also on their turning away from the Socialist-Revolutionary and Menshevik Parties, which have betrayed the cause of the revolution.

Those who bring into politics philistine morals reason this way: assuming, they say, that the Socialist-Revolutionaries and the Mensheviks have committed an "error" in supporting the Cavaignacs, who are disarming the proletariat and the revolutionary regiments. Still, they say, one must give them a chance to "rectify" their error; one must not "make it difficult" for them to rectify their "error"; one must make it easier for the petty bourgeoisie to incline towards the side of the workers. Such reasoning is childishly naïve or simply stupid, if it is not a new deception of the workers. For the vacillating petty-bourgeois masses to incline towards the workers would mean this, and this only, that those masses have turned their backs on the Socialist-Revolutionaries and Mensheviks. For the Socialist-Revolutionary and Menshevik Parties to rectify their "errors" would mean only this, that they declare Tsereteli and Chernov, Dan and Rakitnikov to be abettors of the hangmen. We are fully and unconditionally in favour of such a "rectifying" of their error. . . .

The basic question of the revolution, we said, is the question of power. We must add that it is the revolution that at every step reveals any beclouding of the question as to the holders of real power; that it is the revolution that reveals any discrepancy between formal and real power. This is one of the main characteristics of every revolutionary period. In March and April, 1917, one did not know whether real power was in the hands of the government or in the hands of the Soviets.

Now, however, it is especially important that the class-conscious workers should look soberly at the basic question of the revolution, namely, in whose hands is the state power at the present moment. Think of its material manifestations; do not take phrases for deeds; then the answer will not be difficult to find.

The state consists, first of all, of detachments of armed men with material appendages like jails, wrote Friedrich Engels.[24] Now it consists of military cadets, reactionary Cossacks purposely brought to Petrograd; it consists of those who keep Kamenev and others in jail; who have shut down the newspaper *Pravda;* who have disarmed the workers and a definite section of the soldiers; who are shooting down an equally definite section of soldiers; who are shooting down an equally definite section of troops in the army. Those hangmen are the real power. The Tseretelis and the Chernovs are Ministers without power; they are marionette Ministers; they are the leaders of parties that support hangmen's actions. This is a fact. Tsereteli or Chernov may, personally, "not approve" of the hangmen's actions; their papers may timidly disavow those actions; this, however, does not change the fact; a modification of the political cloak does not change the substance.

The organ of 150,000 Petrograd voters was suppressed; the military cadets killed (July 19) the worker Voinov for carrying the *Pravda Bulletin* from the print shop; are these not hangmen's actions? Is this not the work of Cavaignacs? Neither the government nor the Soviets are "guilty" of this, they will tell us.

So much the worse for the government and the Soviets, we answer, for that means that they are zeros, they are marionettes; real power is not in their hands.

First of all, and most of all, the people must know the *truth*— in whose hands state power really is. We must tell the people the whole truth, namely, that power is in the hands of a military clique of Cavaignacs (Kerensky, some generals, officers, etc.) who are supported by the bourgeoisie as a class, with the Constitutional-Democratic Party at its head, and with all the monarchists acting through all the Black Hundred papers, through the *Novoye Vremya,* the *Zhivoye Slovo,* etc., etc.

This power must be overthrown. Without this all phrases about fighting counter-revolution are empty phrases, are "self-deception and deception of the people."

This power is now supported both by Ministers Tsereteli and Chernov, and by their parties. We must make clear to the people their hangman's rôle; we must make it clear that such a *finale* of those parties was inevitable after their "errors" of May 4, May 18, June 22 and July 17, after their approval of the policy of the offensive at the front, which policy predetermined nine-tenths of the Cavaignac victory in July.

All the agitation among the people must be reshaped so as to take into account the concrete experience of the present revolution, and particularly the July Days, *i.e.*, so as to clearly point out the real enemy of the people, the military clique, the Constitutional-Democrats and the Black Hundreds, and so as definitely to unmask those petty-bourgeois parties, the Socialist-Revolutionary and the Menshevik Parties, who have played and are playing the rôle of hangmen's aides.

All the agitation among the people must be reshaped so as to make it clear that it is absolutely hopeless for the peasants to obtain the land as long as the power of the military clique has not been overthrown, as long as the Socialist-Revolutionary and the Menshevik Parties have not been exposed and deprived of the people's confidence. This would be a very long and difficult process under "normal" conditions of capitalist development, but the war and economic ruin will hasten the process tremendously. These are such "hasteners" that a month or even a week with them is equal to a year otherwise.

Against the above, two arguments could probably be advanced: first, that to speak now of a decisive struggle means to encourage sporadic actions which would help only the counter-revolution; second, that its overthrow would still mean the passing of power to the Soviets.

In reply to the first argument, we say: the workers of Russia are already enlightened enough not to yield to provocation at a moment which is clearly unfavourable for them. Nobody denies that to organise workers' actions and to offer resistance at the present moment would mean to aid the counter-revolution. Neither does any one deny that a decisive struggle is possible only with a new revolutionary upsurge from the very depths of the masses. However, it is not enough to speak about a revolutionary upsurge, or about the aid of the western workers, etc., in general; it is necessary to draw a definite conclusion from our past, to take into account our own lessons. And this consideration will yield the slogan of a decisive struggle against the counter-revolution which has usurped power.

The second argument also reduces itself to substituting abstract reasoning for concrete truths. The bourgeois counter-revolution cannot be overthrown by any one, by any force but the revolutionary proletariat. It is the revolutionary proletariat which, as a result of the experience of July, 1917, must independently take state power, for outside of this there *cannot be* a victory of the revolution. Power in the hands of the proletariat, support of the proletariat by the poorest peasantry or by the semi-proletarians—this is the only way out, and we have already pointed out the circumstances that can hasten it enormously.

Soviets can and must appear in this new revolution, but *not* the present Soviets, not organs of compromise with the bourgeoisie, but organs of a revolutionary struggle against it. That even then we shall be in favour of building the whole state after the Soviet type, is true. This is not a question of Soviets in general, it is a question of struggle against the *present* counter-revolution and against the *treachery* of the *present* Soviets.

To substitute the abstract for the concrete is one of the main faults, one of the most dangerous faults in a revolution. The present Soviets have fallen through, have suffered a total collapse because they were dominated by the Socialist-Revolutionary and Menshevik Parties. At this moment, those Soviets resemble a flock of sheep brought to the slaughter-house, pitifully bleating when placed under the knife. The Soviets, *at present*, are powerless and helpless against the counter-revolution that has gained and is still gaining victories. The slogan of the power passing to the Soviets might be construed as a "simple" call to let power pass into the hands of the present Soviets, and to say so, to appeal for this, would at present mean to deceive the people. Nothing is more dangerous than deception.

The cycle of the development of class and party struggle in Russia from March 12 to July 17 is completed. A new cycle begins, into which enter not the old classes, not the old parties, not the old Soviets, but such as have been renovated in the fire of struggle, hardened, enriched with knowledge, re-created in the course of the struggle. We must look not backward but forward. We must operate not with old but with new, post-July, class and party categories. We must, at the beginning of the new cycle, proceed from the bourgeois counter-revolution that is victorious, that has become victorious thanks to the S.-R.'s and Mensheviks becoming reconciled to it, and that can be vanquished only by the revolutionary proletariat. Of course, there are still going to be many and various stages in this new cycle, before the final victory of the counter-revolution, before the final defeat (without a struggle) of the S.-R.'s and Mensheviks and the new upsurge of a new revolution. All this, however, can be discussed later on when these stages have each appeared. . . .

   Written in the middle of July, 1917.
   Published as a pamphlet by the Cronstadt Committee of the R.S.-D.L.P.

AN ANSWER

I

On August 4, the papers printed the communication issued by the "Public Prosecutor of the Petrograd Supreme Court" about the inquiry into the events of July 16-18, and about the summoning before the Court of a group of Bolsheviks, myself included, charged with treason and the organisation of an armed uprising.[25]

The government was forced to make public this communication because this heinous case has become too scandalous and appeared to all intelligent persons as an obvious forgery, perpetrated with the aid of the slanderer Alexinsky, in fulfilment of the persistent desires and demands of the counter-revolutionary Cadet Party.

But by the publication of this communication, the government of Tsereteli and Co. disgraced itself the more, for now the grossness of the forgery, particularly, stares one in the face.

I left Petrograd on Thursday, July 12, on account of illness, and I only returned on Tuesday morning, July 17. But of course I assume full and unequivocal responsibility for all steps and measures taken by the Central Committee of our party, as well as by our party as a whole. I call attention to my absence to account for my lack of information concerning some details and for my alluding mainly to documents which have appeared in the press.

It is obvious that documents precisely of this nature, particularly if they appeared in papers inimical to the Bolsheviks, should have been the first to be carefully collected, put in order, and analysed by the Prosecutor. But the "republican" Prosecutor, who is carrying out the policies of the "Socialist" Minister Tsereteli, was loath to discharge this most basic obligation.

The government newspaper, *Dyelo Naroda*, stated definitely soon after July 17 that on July 15 the Bolsheviks had publicly agitated in the Grenadier Regiment against demonstrations.

Had the Prosecutor a right to suppress this document? Had he any grounds for not taking into account the testimony of such a witness?

And this testimony establishes the very important fact that the movement developed spontaneously and that the Bolsheviks endeavoured to delay rather than to hasten the demonstrations.

Moreover, the same newspaper printed a still more important document, namely, the text of the proclamation which had been signed by the Central Committee of our party, and which had been composed on the night of July 16.[26] This proclamation was written and handed over to the printer after the movement, despite our efforts to check it, or, more correctly, to regulate it, had swept away all barriers—after the demonstration had become a fact.

All the baseness and vileness, all the treachery of the Tsereteli Prosecutor, are most manifest in this beating about the bush, in this ignoring of the question as to just when, on what day and hour, whether before the Bolshevik proclamation or after it, the demonstration began.

The text of this proclamation stresses the necessity of giving the movement a peaceful and organised character.

Can one imagine anything more ridiculous than the accusation of "organising an armed uprising" laid at the door of the party which on the eve of the seventeenth, *i.e.*, on the eve of the decisive day, had issued a proclamation advising a "peaceful and organised demonstration"? Another question: what is the difference between the Prosecutors in the case of Dreyfus and Beilis, and the "republican" Prosecutor of the "Socialist" Minister Tsereteli, a Prosecutor who silently evades this proclamation?

Further, the Prosecutor does not mention that on the night of July 17, the C.C. of our party got out a proclamation calling off the demonstration, and printed this proclamation in the *Pravda*, the offices of which were wrecked by a detachment of counter-revolutionary soldiers on that very night.

Further, the Prosecutor does not mention that on July 17, Trotsky and Zinoviev, in a series of speeches delivered before the workers and soldiers who were marching towards the Tauride Palace, urged them to disperse after they had made their will manifest.

These speeches were heard by hundreds and thousands of people. Now, let every honest citizen who does not want his country to be disgraced by another "Beilis case" take the trouble to see to it that irrespective of their party affiliations, those who heard the speeches make written declarations to the Prosecutor (keeping copies for themselves), stating whether the speeches of Trotsky and Zinoviev contained an appeal to disperse. A decent Prosecutor would himself have turned to the population with such a request, but how can one imagine decent Prosecutors in the cabinet of Kerensky, Yefremov, Tsereteli and Co.? And is it not high time that the Russian citizens themselves take care that "Beilis cases" become impossible in their country?

Incidentally, I, personally, owing to illness, delivered only one speech on July 17, from the balcony of Kshesinskaya's house.* The Prosecutor mentions it, attempts to give its contents, but not only does he not mention any witnesses, he even suppresses the testimony of witnesses which was published in the press. I am far from having a complete set of the newspapers, but I have seen two references in the press: first, in the Bolshevik paper, *Proletarskoye Dyelo* (Cronstadt), and second, in the official Menshevik paper, *Rabochaya Gazeta* [*Workers' Gazette*].[27] Why not verify the contents of my speech by these documents and by public appeals to the population?

The entire speech consisted of the following: first, an apology for confining myself to only a few words on account of illness; second, a greeting to the revolutionary Cronstadtians in the name of the Petrograd workers; third, an expression of confidence that our slogan "All Power to the Soviets" must, and will, conquer, despite all the zigzags of the path of history; fourth, an appeal for "firmness, steadfastness and vigilance."

I dwell on these particulars in order not to pass by that insignificant, but really factual material, which was so hastily, perfunctorily, and loosely touched upon—hardly touched upon—by the Prosecutor.

But of course the main thing is not the details, but the general picture, the general significance of July 17. The Prosecutor proved completely incapable of even thinking about this.

On this question, we first of all have the most valuable testimony in the press of a vehement foe of Bolshevism, a person who invariably pours upon us a flood of invectives and vituperation—the correspondent of the official *Rabochaya Gazeta*. This correspondent published his personal observations shortly after July 17.[28] The facts definitely established by him may be reduced to the following: the observations and the experiences of the author are divided into two sharply differentiated halves; the author distinguishes the second from the first by saying that it took a "favourable turn" for him.

* The house of a well-known dancer, occupied by the Bolsheviks and used as their headquarters.—*Ed.*

The first half of the author's experiences comprises his efforts to defend the Ministers before the turbulent crowd. He is subjected to insults, violence, and finally to detention. The author hears all kinds of cries and slogans, extremely vehement, of which he recalls one in particular: "Death to Kerensky" (because he ordered an offensive, "laid down forty thousand lives," etc.).

The second half of the author's experiences, the one which he considers a "favourable turn," begins at the moment when the riotous crowd leads him "before the tribunal" into Kshesinskaya's house. There the author is immediately released.

These are the facts which serve the author as a pretext for disgorging a torrent of abuse upon the Bolsheviks. Abuse coming from a political opponent is natural, particularly if the opponent is a Menshevik who feels that the masses, weighed down by capital and an imperialist war, are not with him, but against him. But abuse does not change the facts, which, even according to the account of this most violent enemy of the Bolsheviks, prove that the aroused masses got to the point of shouting "Death to Kerensky," that the organisation of the Bolsheviks supplied the movement with the slogan "All Power to the Soviets," and that this organisation was the only one to maintain moral authority over the masses, urging it to abandon violence.

These are the facts. Let the voluntary and the involuntary servants of the bourgeoisie shout and howl at us, accusing the Bolsheviks of "aiding and abetting the elemental movement," etc., etc.

We, as representatives of the party of the revolutionary proletariat, maintain that our party always has been and always will be with the oppressed masses, when the masses express their thousand-times-justified and legitimate indignation against the high cost of living, against the lethargy and treachery of the "Socialist" Ministers, against the imperialist war and its prolongation. Our party did its imperative duty by going together with the justly indignant masses on July 17, and by trying to give their movement, their demonstrations, as much of a peaceful and organised character as possible. For on July 17 a peaceful passing of power to the Soviets was still possible, a peaceful development of the Russian Revolution was still realisable.

How stupid the Prosecutor's fairy tale about the "organisation of an armed uprising" is, may be seen from the following. No one denies that among the armed soldiers and sailors who on July 17 crowded the streets of Petrograd the vast majority were on the side of our party. Our party had every opportunity to commence the unseating and arrest of hundreds of officials, to occupy dozens of government and official buildings and institutions, etc.

Nothing of this sort was done. Only people who have become so confused that they repeat all kinds of fairy tales disseminated by counter-revolutionary Cadets can remain blind to the ridiculous absurdity of the assertion that on July 16 and 17 the "organisation of an armed uprising" took place.

The first question which should have been put forward by the investigation, if it were anything like a real investigation, is, "Who began the shooting?" The next question is, "How many killed and wounded were there on each side, and under what circumstances did each killing and wounding take place?"

If the investigation were anything like a real investigation (and not like the claptrap printed in the papers of the Dans, the Alexinskys, etc.), it would be the investigators' duty to arrange an open, public examination of the witnesses and then immediately to publish the minutes of the examination.

This is the way investigating committees always acted in England when England was a free country. This, or approximately this, is the way that the Executive Committee of the Soviets felt obliged to act at the very beginning, when fear of the Cadets had not yet completely numbed its conscience. It is known that the Executive Committee, in the press at that time, promised to publish two bulletins daily on the work of its investigating committee. It is also known that the Executive Committee (*i.e.*, the Socialist-Revolutionaries and the Mensheviks) deceived the people by not fulfilling the promise it made. But the text of that promise has remained in history as an admission from our enemies, an admission as to how an honest investigator should have acted.

It is instructive at any rate to note that one of the first bourgeois papers which supplied information about the shooting on July 17 was the rabidly anti-Bolshevik paper, the evening *Birzhevka* of the same date. And it is precisely from the information supplied by this paper that we gather that the shooting was not begun by those who took part in the demonstration, but that the first shots were aimed at them!! Of course, the "republican" Prosecutor of the "Socialist" cabinet preferred to remain silent on this testimony of the *Birzhevka!!* And yet this evidence given by the *Birzhevka*, an organ absolutely hostile to Bolshevism, is in full accord with the general picture of the event given by our party. If this event had been an armed uprising, then, of course, the insurgents would not have started out by shooting into their opponents; they would first have surrounded certain barracks, certain buildings, they would have wiped out certain sections of the army, etc. On the other hand, if the event was a demonstration against the government, and the counter-demonstration was made up of defenders of the government, then it was quite natural that the counter-revolutionists, angered by the enormous mass of people in the demonstration, and partly with a provocative purpose, should have started the shooting, and that the people in the demonstration should have met shots with shots.

Lists of those killed, though probably not very complete, were printed nevertheless in a few papers (I think in the *Ryech* and in the *Dyelo Naroda*).[29] The first and immediate duty of the investigation was to verify, complete, and officially publish these lists. To refuse to do this meant to hide the evidence of the fact that the shooting was begun by the counter-revolutionists.

Indeed, a cursory examination of the printed lists shows that the two main and outstanding groups, the Cossacks and the sailors, had each about the same number killed. Would such a thing be possible, if the ten thousand sailors who arrived in Petrograd on July 17 and combined with the workers and soldiers, particularly with the machine gunners, who had many machine guns, had pursued the aims of an armed uprising?

It is obvious that in that case the number of killed among the Cossacks and the other opponents of the insurrection would have been ten times as great, for no one denies that the predominance of the Bolsheviks among the armed people on the streets of Petrograd, on July 17, was enormous. A great deal of testimony given by opponents of our party and printed in the press is at hand, and any sort of honest investigation would doubtless have collected and published all this evidence.

If the number of those killed is approximately the same on each side, this proves that the shooting was actually begun by the counter-revolutionists, and that those who were in the demonstration merely retaliated. Otherwise there could not have been the same number killed on each side.

Finally, of the information published in the press, the following is exceedingly important: on July 17, Cossacks were killed; this happened during an open fusillade between those in the demonstration and those in the counter-demonstration. Such shooting takes place even in non-revolutionary times, when the population gets sufficiently excited; for instance, they are not infrequent in the Latin countries, particularly in the south. The murder of the Bolsheviks, however, is known to have occurred even after July 17, when there was no encounter between two excited factions, when the killing of an unarmed person by an armed one was really assassination. Such was the killing of the Bolshevik Voinov on Shpalernaya Street on July 19.

What kind of an investigation is it which does not collect in full even the material which has appeared in the press—the number killed on each side, the time and circumstances of each case where death resulted? This is not an investigation, but a travesty.

The investigation being of such a nature, it stands to reason that it is futile to expect from it even an attempt at an historical evaluation of July 17. Yet such an evaluation is indispensable to any one who wants to maintain an intelligent attitude towards politics.

Whoever would attempt historically to evaluate July 16 and 17 cannot shut his eyes to the identity of the origin of this movement with that of May 3 and 4.

In both cases there were spontaneous outbursts of popular indignation.

In both cases armed masses went into the streets.

In both cases the shooting back and forth resulted in a certain (approximately equal) number of victims on each side.

In both cases the anti-government demonstrations were connected with deep and protracted crises of power.

In both cases there were extremely sharp outbursts in the struggle between the revolutionary masses and the counter-revolutionary elements of the bourgeoisie, while the elements which were in the middle, neither here nor there, ready to acquiesce, were temporarily pushed aside from the field of action.

The difference between the two movements is that the second was much more intense than the first, and that the Socialist-Revolutionary and Menshevik Parties, neutral on May 3 and 4, have since then become involved in their dependence on the counter-revolutionary Cadets (because of the coalition Cabinet and the policy of an offensive), and so found themselves on July 16 and 17 on the side of the counter-revolution.

The counter-revolutionary Cadet Party brazenly lied after the events of May 3 and 4, shouting, "Those who did the shooting on the Nevsky were Leninists," and clown-like, they demanded an investigation. The Cadets and their friends then constituted the majority in the government; the investigation was therefore wholly in their hands. It was begun, but abandoned, and nothing was published.

Why? Evidently because the facts did not in the least bear out what the Cadets wanted. In other words, the investigation of May 3 and 4 was "smothered," because the facts proved that the firing had been begun by the counter-revolutionists, the Cadets and their friends. This is clear.

The same thing apparently happened on July 16 and 17, and this accounts for the crude and glaring falsification of Mr. Prosecutor, who in order to please Tsereteli and Co. has mocked all the rules of any half-way decent investigation.

The movement on July 16 and 17 was the last attempt to induce the Soviets, by way of demonstrations, to take power. From that moment on, the Soviets, *i.e.*, the S.-R.'s and Mensheviks in control of them, virtually handed over power to the counter-revolution, represented by the Cadets and supported by the S.-R.'s and Mensheviks. A peaceful development of the Russian Revolution has now become impossible. History puts the question thus: either complete victory for the counter-revolution, or a new revolution.

II

The accusation of espionage and of relations with Germany, another Beilis case, deserves but cursory notice. Here the "investigation," after a particularly crude perversion of the facts, simply parrots the slanders of the notorious calumniator Alexinsky.

It is untrue that in 1914 Zinoviev and I were arrested by the Austrian authorities. I alone was arrested.

It is untrue that I was arrested as a Russian subject. I was arrested on suspicion of spying. The local gendarme mistook the diagrams of agrarian statistics in my notebook for "plans"! Clearly, the Austrian gendarme was right on a level with Alexinsky and the *Yedinstvo* group. It seems, however, that I have broken the record in my pursuit after internationalism, for I have been persecuted by *both* the warring coalitions as a spy—in Austria by the gendarme, and in Russia by Alexinsky, the Cadets and Co.

It is not true that Hanecki played a part in my release from the Austrian prison. A part was played by Victor Adler, who put the Austrian authorities to shame. A part was played by the Poles, who were ashamed that such a despicable arrest of a Russian revolutionist could take place in their country.

It is a contemptible lie that I had relations with Parvus, that I visited military camps, etc. Nothing of the kind happened, or could ever happen. Upon the appearance of the very first numbers of Parvus's magazine, the *Kolokol* [*Bell*], our paper, the *Sotsial-Demokrat*,* branded Parvus as a renegade and a German Plekhanov. Parvus is just as much of a social-chauvinist on the side of Germany as Plekhanov is on the side of Russia. As revolutionary internationalists we had and could have nothing in common with any German, Russian, or Ukrainian (Union for the Liberation of the Ukraine) social-chauvinist.

Steinberg is a member of the emigrant committee in Stockholm. The first time I met him was in Stockholm. About May 3, or a bit later, Steinberg came to Petrograd and, if I remember correctly, tried to obtain a subsidy for the emigrants' society. The Prosecutor could have verified it quite easily, if he had wanted to verify it.

The Prosecutor plays up the fact that Parvus is connected with Hanecki, and that Hanecki is connected with Lenin. But this is simply the trick of a swindler, for every one knows that Hanecki had financial dealings with Parvus, while I and Hanecki had not.

Hanecki, as a tradesman, worked for Parvus; they conducted business together. There are a great many emigrants who have admitted in the press that they have worked in establishments and undertakings belonging to Parvus.

The Prosecutor brings out the point that commercial correspondence might serve as a screen for relations of an espionage nature. It would be interesting to know how many Cadets, Mensheviks and S.-R.'s could be accused, according to this wonderful prescription, for commercial correspondence.

But if the Prosecutor is in possession of a series of telegrams from Hanecki to Sumenson (these telegrams have been published); if the Prosecutor knows in which bank, when, and how much money

---

* See V. I. Lenin, *The Imperialist War, Collected Works*, Vol. XVIII, p. 364.—*Ed.*

Sumenson had (and the Prosecutor has published a few figures of this nature), then why should he not summon two or three office and business employees to take part in the investigation? In two days they would put at his disposal a complete abstract of all the commercial and bank records.

Hardly anything reveals the nature of this "Beilis case" so well as the fragmentary figures cited by the Prosecutor: "Within half a year Sumenson drew 750,000 rubles; she has 180,000 rubles left on her account." If you do publish figures, why not publish them in full? Exactly when, exactly from whom did Sumenson receive money "within half a year," and to whom did she pay it out? Exactly when, and exactly what consignments of goods were received?

What is easier than to gather such complete data? In two or three days this could and should have been done. This would have uncovered the whole cycle of commercial dealings between Hanecki and Sumenson. It would have left no room for obscure innuendoes for the Prosecutor to manipulate!

Alexinsky's vilest and meanest slanders, paraphrased to sound like a "state" document by the officials of the Cabinet of Tsereteli and Co.—this is how low the S.-R.'s and Mensheviks have fallen!

III

Of course, it would be extremely naïve to regard the "judicial cases" instituted by the Cabinet of Tsereteli, Kerensky and Co. against the Bolsheviks as actual judicial cases. It would be an absolutely unpardonable constitutional illusion.

The S.-R.'s and Mensheviks, having entered into a coalition with the counter-revolutionary Cadets on May 19 and having adopted a policy of offensive warfare, *i.e.*, the renewal and continuation of the imperialist war, inevitably found themselves captives of the Cadets.

As captives, they were forced to participate in the filthiest Cadet deals, in their basest and most slanderous plots.

The "case" of Chernov is rapidly beginning to enlighten even the most backward, that is, it proves the correctness of our views. Besides Chernov, the *Ryech* is beginning to denounce Tsereteli as a "hypocrite" and a "Zimmerwaldist."

AN ANSWER

Now the blind shall see, and stones shall speak.

The counter-revolution is closing its ranks. The Cadets are at the bottom. The staff, the military leaders, and Kerensky are in their grip; the Black Hundred press is at their service. Such are the allies of the bourgeois counter-revolution.

The despicable slandering of political opponents will help the proletariat sooner to understand where the counter-revolution is, and to sweep it away in the name of freedom, peace, bread for the hungry, land for the peasants.

N. LENIN.

Rabochy i Soldat [*Worker and Soldier*], Nos. 3 and 4, August 8 and 9, 1917.

ON CONSTITUTIONAL ILLUSIONS [30]

BY constitutional illusions is meant a political error which consists in people accepting the normal, juridic, regulated, legally controlled, in brief, "constitutional," order as existing, although in reality it does not exist. It may seem at first glance that in present-day Russia, in July, 1917, when no constitution has yet been evolved, one cannot speak of the appearance of constitutional illusions. But this is a profound error. In reality the crux of the present political situation in Russia consists in the very large masses of the population being permeated with constitutional illusions. Without understanding this, one cannot understand anything of the present political situation in Russia. Not a single step towards a correct outline of tactical tasks can be made in present-day Russia without making it one's first and foremost business to expose constitutional illusions systematically and mercilessly, to uncover all their roots, to re-establish a correct political perspective.

Let us take the three opinions that are most typical by way of present-day constitutional illusions, and analyse them more carefully.

First opinion: our country is on the eve of a Constituent Assembly; this is why everything that is going on at present has a temporary, a passing, a not very essential, not decisive character, since everything will soon be revised and definitely established by the Constituent Assembly. Second opinion: certain parties—like the Socialist-Revolutionaries or the Mensheviks, or an alliance of the two—have an obvious undoubted majority among the people or among the "most influential" institutions like the Soviets, and therefore the will of these parties and these institutions, as well as the will of the majority of the people generally, cannot be dodged, even less violated by republican, democratic, revolutionary Russia. Third opinion: a certain measure, like the suppression of the paper *Pravda*, has not been legalised either by the Provisional Government or by the Soviets; therefore it is only an episode, a chance occurrence; by no means can it be looked upon as anything decisive.

Let us analyse each one of these opinions.

I

The convocation of the Constituent Assembly was promised by the first Provisional Government. To lead the country to the Constituent Assembly was recognised by that government as its main task. The second Provisional Government fixed October 13 as the date for the convocation of the Constituent Assembly. The third Provisional Government most solemnly reaffirmed the same date after July 17.

Still, there are ninety-nine chances out of a hundred that the Constituent Assembly will not be convoked on that date. Were it to be convoked on that date, there are ninety-nine chances out of a hundred that it will be as feeble and useless as was the First Duma, until the second revolution wins in Russia. In order to realise this, it is sufficient to turn for one minute from the hubbub of phrases, promises and petty affairs of the day which are cluttering up the brains of the people, and to cast a glance at the thing that is fundamental and all-determining in public life—the class struggle.

That the bourgeoisie in Russia has most closely united with the landowners is clear. This is proven by the entire press, by all the elections, all the policies of the Cadets and the parties to the Right of them, all the actions of the "congresses" of "interested" persons.

The bourgeoisie understands perfectly well what the petty-bourgeois chatterers from among the Socialist-Revolutionaries and "Left" Mensheviks fail to understand, namely, that it is *impossible* to abolish private property in land in Russia, and with no compensation at that, without a gigantic economic revolution, without placing the banks under the control of all the people, without nationalising the syndicates, without a number of the most merciless revolutionary measures against capital. The bourgeoisie understands this perfectly well. At the same time it cannot fail to know, to see, to feel that an overwhelming majority of the peasants in Russia will at present not only express themselves in favour of confiscating the landowners' lands, but will prove also much more to the Left than Chernov. For the bourgeoisie knows more than we do how many partial concessions were made by Chernov, let us say, from May 19 to June 15, as regards delaying and narrowing down the various peasants' demands, as well as how much effort it cost the *Right* Socialist-Revolutionaries (Chernov being considered the "Centre" among the S.-R's!) at the Peasant Congress and in the Executive Committee of the All-Russian Soviet of Peasant Deputies to "quiet" the peasants and to feed them with promises.

The bourgeoisie differs from the petty bourgeoisie in that it has learned from its economic and political experience to understand the conditions under which it can retain "order" (*i.e.*, the slavery of the masses) under the capitalist system. The bourgeois are men of affairs, men of large-scale commercial schemes; they are wont to approach political questions in a strictly business-like manner, with a mistrust for words and a readiness to seize the bull by the horns.

The Constituent Assembly in present-day Russia will yield a majority to peasants that are more Left than are the S.-R.'s. The bourgeoisie knows this. Knowing this, it cannot fail to fight most decisively against a speedy convocation of the Constituent Assembly. To wage the imperialist war in the spirit of the secret treaties concluded by Nicholas II, to defend land proprietorship or compensation for it is a thing impossible or incredibly difficult under a Constituent Assembly. The war will not wait. The class struggle will not wait. This was strikingly proven even in the brief span of time between March 13 and May 4.

Two views on the Constituent Assembly took shape from the very beginning. The S.-R.'s and the Mensheviks, permeated with constitutional illusions, viewed the matter with the naïve confidence of a petty bourgeois unwilling to heed the class struggle. The Constituent Assembly has been proclaimed, they said, the Constituent Assembly will be—and that's enough! All the rest, they said, is of the devil. The Bolsheviks, on the contrary, said: only in proportion as the power and the authority of the Soviets grow, will the convocation and the success of the Constituent Assembly be guaranteed. With the Mensheviks and the S.-R.'s the centre of gravity was shifted to the legal act of declaring, promising, proclaiming the convocation of the Constituent Assembly. With the Bolsheviks the centre of gravity was shifted to the class struggle: if the Soviets win, they said, the Constituent Assembly will be assured; if not, it will not be assured.

This is exactly what happened. The bourgeoisie has waged against the convocation of the Constituent Assembly a struggle that was at times covert and at times overt, but all the time unceasing and relentless. This struggle expressed itself in a wish to delay its convocation to the end of the war. This struggle expressed itself in postponing the date of the convocation of the Constituent Assembly several times. When at last, after July 31, more than a month after the formation of the coalition cabinet, the date for the convocation of the Constituent Assembly was fixed, a Moscow bourgeois paper declared that that had been done under the influence of Bolshevik propaganda. The *Pravda* published a verbatim quotation from that paper.[31]

After July 17, when the servility and the dismay of the S.-R.'s and the Mensheviks gave a "victory" to the counter-revolution, a brief but highly characteristic expression slipped into the *Ryech:* a reference to the "speediest possible" convocation of the Constituent Assembly!! And on July 29, a note appeared in the *Volya Naroda* [*People's Will*] and in the *Russkaya Volya* [*Russian Will*] saying that the Cadets demanded the postponement of the convocation of the Constituent Assembly under the pretext that it was "impossible" to convoke it in such a "short" time; according to the same note, the Menshevik Tsereteli, doing lackey service to the counter-revolution, had agreed to postpone it till December 3![32]

Such a note, undoubtedly, could slip in only against the wish of the bourgeoisie. Such "revelations" are not to the advantage of the latter. But murder will out. The counter-revolution, becoming brazen after July 17, blurts out the truth. The first seizure of power by the counter-revolutionary bourgeoisie after July 17 is immediately followed by a measure (a very earnest measure at that) *against* the convocation of the Constituent Assembly.

This is a fact. And this fact reveals all the futility of constitutional illusions. Unless a new revolution takes place in Russia, unless the power of the counter-revolutionary bourgeoisie (primarily the Cadets) is overthrown, unless the people withdraw their confidence from the Socialist-Revolutionary and Menshevik Parties as parties of conciliation with the bourgeoisie, the Constituent Assembly will either not be convoked at all, or it will be a "Frankfort talkfest," * a feeble and useless collection of petty bourgeois mortally frightened by the war and by the prospect of the bour-

---

* Reference is here made to the National Assembly held at Frankfort during the 1848 Revolution. While the delegates were talking about the various liberties they were going to include in the proposed constitution, the monarchy reorganised its forces and defeated the revolution.—*Ed.*

geoisie "boycotting the government," helplessly torn between attempts to rule without the bourgeoisie and the fear of doing without the bourgeoisie.

The Constituent Assembly question is *subordinated* to the question as to the course and the outcome of the class struggle between the bourgeoisie and the proletariat. Some time ago the *Rabochaya Gazeta* dropped the remark that the Constituent Assembly would be like the Convention.[33] This is one of the examples of how our Menshevik lackeys of the counter-revolutionary bourgeoisie brag in a vain, miserable, contemptible way. In order not to be a "Frankfort talkfest" or a First Duma, in order to be a Convention, one must dare, know how, and have power to deal merciless blows to the counter-revolution, not to compromise with it. For this purpose it is necessary that power should be in the hands of the most advanced, most determined, most revolutionary class of the present epoch. For this purpose it is necessary that that class should be supported by the whole mass of the city and village poor (the semi-proletarians). For this purpose it is necessary first of all to deal mercilessly with the counter-revolutionary bourgeoisie, *i.e.*, first of all with the Cadets and the top leadership of the army. Such are the real, the class, the material conditions for a Convention. It is sufficient to enumerate those conditions precisely and clearly, to realise how ridiculous the bragging of the *Rabochaya Gazeta* is, how infinitely foolish the constitutional illusions of the S.-R.'s and Mensheviks are as regards a Constituent Assembly in present-day Russia.

II

In castigating the petty-bourgeois "Social-Democrats" of 1848, Marx branded with especial fury their unbridled phrase-mongering as to the "people" and the majority of the people generally.[34] It is timely to recall this when we analyse the second opinion regarding the constitutional illusions about a "majority."

Definite conditions of reality are needed in order that the majority may actually decide in matters of state. Namely, there must be established, on the one hand, a state order, a state power which would make it possible to decide matters by a majority and would guarantee the transformation of this possibility into a reality. On the other hand, this majority, by its class composition, by the interrelation of classes inside that majority (and outside of it) must *be able* harmoniously and successfully to pull the chariot of state. It is clear for every Marxist that these two conditions of reality play a decisive rôle as regards the majority of the people and the course of state affairs in accord with the will of this majority. Still, all the political literature of the S.-R.'s and the Mensheviks, and more so their political behaviour, reveal an absolute lack of understanding of these conditions.

A state in which political power is in the hands of a class whose interests coincide with the interests of the majority can be ruled in actual accord with the will of the majority.

If, however, political power is in the hands of a class whose interests are in conflict with the interests of the majority, then any majority rule inevitably turns into a deception or a suppression of that majority. Every bourgeois republic shows us hundreds and thousands of examples of this kind. In Russia, the bourgeoisie rules, both economically and politically. Its interests, particularly during an imperialist war, are in sharpest conflict with the interests of the majority. Therefore the whole essence of the question, from a materialist, Marxist, and not a formal, legal formulation of it, consists in exposing this conflict, in fighting against the deception of the masses by the bourgeoisie.

Our Socialist-Revolutionaries and Mensheviks, on the contrary, have fully shown and proven their actual rôle as an instrument for the deception of the masses (the "majority") by the bourgeoisie, as conductors and abettors of such deception. No matter how sincere individual S.-R.'s and Mensheviks may be, their fundamental political ideas—as though it is possible to get out of an imperialist war and arrive at a "peace without annexations and indemnities" without a dictatorship of the proletariat and a victory of Socialism, as though it is possible to have the land pass to the people without compensation and to have "control" over production in the interests of the people without the above condition—these fundamental political (and, of course, also economic) ideas of the S.-R.'s and Mensheviks represent, objectively, nothing but a petty-bourgeois self-deception or, what is the same, a deception of the masses (the "majority") by the bourgeoisie.

This is our first and foremost "amendment" to the manner in which the majority question is approached by the petty-bourgeois democrats, the Socialists of the Louis Blanc type, the S.-R.'s and

Mensheviks. What value is there, in practice, to a "majority," we ask, if the majority itself is only a formal factor, while materially, in actual reality, this majority is the majority of the parties carrying into effect the deception of this majority by the bourgeoisie?

And, of course, this deception can be correctly understood only—and here we approach the second "amendment," the second of the above indicated fundamental conditions—when we make clear its class roots and its class meaning. This is not a personal deception, not (speaking bluntly) a "swindle"; it is a deceptive idea flowing from the economic situation of a class. The petty bourgeois finds himself in such an economic situation, the conditions of his life are such, that he cannot help deceiving himself, that he must inevitably and against his will gravitate alternately towards the bourgeoisie and towards the proletariat. It is *economically impossible* for him to have an independent "line."

His past draws him towards the bourgeoisie, his future towards the proletariat. His judgment gravitates towards the latter, his prejudice (using a well known expression of Marx) towards the former. In order that the majority of the people should become an actual majority ruling the state, actually serving the interests of the majority, actually safeguarding its rights, etc., a certain condition in the life of the classes is required. This condition is that the majority of the petty bourgeoisie should, at least at the decisive moment and in the decisive place, join the revolutionary proletariat.

Barring this, the majority is a fiction which may last a while, glitter, shine, vociferate, gather the laurels, but is absolutely and inevitably doomed to collapse. Such has been, let us note in passing, the collapse of the majority enjoyed by the S.-R.'s and Mensheviks, as revealed in the Russian Revolution in July, 1917.

A revolution, furthermore, is distinguished from the "normal situation" in a state in that the controversial state questions are decided directly by the struggle of classes and masses, including the armed uprising. It cannot be otherwise, once the masses are free and armed. It follows from this fundamental fact that, in revolutionary times, it is not sufficient to make clear the "will of the majority"; that at the decisive moment and in the decisive place you *must prove the stronger one,* you must *be victorious.* Beginning with the Peasant War in the Middle Ages in Germany, through all the large-scale revolutionary movements and epochs up to 1848 and 1871, and further up to 1905, we see innumerable examples of how the more organised, more class-conscious, better armed minority forces its will upon the majority and is victorious over it.

Friedrich Engels particularly emphasised the lessons of the experiences which to some degree make the peasant uprising of the sixteenth century identical to the 1848 Revolution in Germany, namely, the desultory character of the actions, the absence of centralisation among the oppressed masses, which is due to their petty-bourgeois status in life.[35] Approaching the matter from this angle we arrived at the same conclusion. A plain majority of the petty-bourgeois masses decides nothing, and can decide nothing, for the atomised millions of rural petty proprietors can get organisation, political consciousness of action, and centralisation (which is necessary for victory) *only* when they are led either by the bourgeoisie or by the proletariat.

It is well known that in the long run the problems of social life are decided by the class struggle in its bitterest, sharpest form, namely, in the form of civil war. And in this war, as in any other war—a fact also well known and in principle not disputed by any one—it is the economic factors that decide. It is highly characteristic and ominous that neither the S.-R.'s nor the Mensheviks, while not denying this "in principle" and perfectly well realising the capitalist character of present-day Russia, dare soberly to look the truth in the face. They are afraid to admit the truth, namely, that every capitalist country, including Russia, is fundamentally divided into three basic and main forces: the bourgeoisie, the petty bourgeoisie, and the proletariat. The first and the third are spoken of by all, they are recognised by all. As to the second—that is, the *majority* in numbers!—no one wants to appraise it soberly either from the economic, the political, or the military point of view.

The truth is too strong for the naked eye; this is why the Socialist-Revolutionaries and Mensheviks are afraid of understanding themselves.

III

When we started writing this little article, the suppression of the *Pravda* was only an "accidental" fact as yet; the action was not yet confirmed by the state. Now, after July 29, the state power has formally suppressed the *Pravda*.

If we look at this suppression historically, if we take it as a whole, if we take the whole process of preparing and carrying out this measure, it sheds an unusually clear light on the "essence of the constitution" in Russia and on the danger of constitutional illusions.

It is well known that, beginning from April, the Cadet Party, with Milyukov and the paper *Ryech* at its head, have demanded repressions against the Bolsheviks. This demand for repressions, voiced in various forms, from "statesmanlike" articles in *Ryech* to Milyukov repeatedly exclaiming, "Arrest them" (Lenin and other Bolsheviks), has been one of the major, if not the major component part of the political programme of the Cadets during the revolution.

Long before Alexinsky and Co. invented and fabricated, in June and July, the hideously calumnious charge that the Bolsheviks were German spies or were receiving German money; long before they were accused of "armed uprisings" or of "mutiny"—an accusation just as calumnious and contrary to generally known facts and published documents—long before that the Cadet Party systematically, uninterruptedly and relentlessly demanded repressions against the Bolsheviks. If this demand has now been realised, what opinion must one have about the honesty or the intelligence of people who forget, or make believe that they forget, the actual class and party source of this demand? How, then, shall we characterise the action of the S.-R.'s and the Mensheviks—who now try to present the case as if they believed that this was an "accidental," an "isolated" cause for repressive measures against the Bolsheviks, a "cause" making its appearance only on July 17—how can we not characterise it as the most palpable falsification or the most incredible political obtuseness? After all, there must be some limits to the distortion of undisputed historic truths!

It is sufficient to compare the May 3-4 movement with that of July 16-17 to realise at once their similar character: an elemental outburst of dissatisfaction; impatience and indignation of the masses; provocative shots from the right; persons killed on the Nevsky; calumnious cries on the part of the bourgeoisie and the Cadets to the effect, particularly, that "the Leninists fired shots on the Nevsky"; extreme bitterness and a sharpening of the struggle between the proletarian masses and the bourgeoisie; complete confusion on the part of the petty-bourgeois parties, the S.-R.'s and Mensheviks; a tremendous range of vacillations in their policy generally and in their approach to the question of state power—all these objective facts characterise both movements. June 22-23 and July 1 show us in another form the identical class picture.

The course of events is as clear as can be: the dissatisfaction, the impatience and the indignation of the masses grow more and more; the struggle between the proletariat and the bourgeoisie becomes more and more sharpened, particularly because they are fighting for influence over the petty-bourgeois masses; in connection with this two very important historic events take place which prepare the dependence of the S.-R.'s and Mensheviks upon the counter-revolutionary Cadets. These events are, first, the formation on May 19 of a coalition cabinet in which the S.-R.'s and Mensheviks find themselves in the rôle of servants of the bourgeoisie getting more and more entangled in deals and agreements with it, rendering it a thousand "services" and delaying the most necessary revolutionary measures; second, the advance at the front. The advance inevitably proved to be a renewal of the imperialist war, a gigantic increase in the influence, the weight, the rôle of the imperialist bourgeoisie, an unusually wide dissemination of chauvinism among the masses, and, last but not least, a transfer of power, first military, then state power generally, to the counter-revolutionary leaders of the army.

Such is the course of historic events which, between May 3-4 and July 16-17, deepened and sharpened class contradictions, and which, after July 17, allowed the counter-revolutionary bourgeoisie to realise that which already on May 3-4 had become clearly outlined as its programme and tactics, its immediate task and the "nice" little means which were supposed to lead it to its goal.

There is nothing more meaningless from an historical point of view, there is nothing more pitiful theoretically and more ridiculous practically than the philistine lamentations over July 17 (which, by the way, are being repeated by L. Martov) to the effect that the Bolsheviks "managed" to inflict a defeat upon themselves, that their defeat was caused by their "adventurism," and so on and so forth. All these lamentations, all this reasoning to the effect that we "should not have" participated (in the attempt to give a "peaceful and organised" character to the highly justified dissatisfaction and indignation of the masses!!), are in the last analysis either renegadism when they come from Bolsheviks or an expression of the state of fright and confusion that is usual for a petty bourgeois. In reality the July 16-17 movement grew out of the May 3-4 movement with the same inevitability with which summer follows spring.

It was the absolute duty of the proletarian party to remain with the masses, in an attempt to give their just actions a peaceful and organised character, and not to move aside, not to wash one's hands, Pilate fashion, on the pedantic grounds that the masses were not organised to the last man and that there were excesses in their action (as if there were no excesses on May 3-4! as if there has been a single serious movement of the masses in history without excess!).

As to the defeat of the Bolsheviks after July 17, it followed with historic necessity from the entire previous course of events precisely because on May 3-4 the petty-bourgeois masses and their leaders, the S.-R.'s and Mensheviks, had not yet been bound by the advance at the front and had not yet been entangled by little deals with the bourgeoisie in the "coalition cabinet," while about July 17 they had already been so bound and entangled that they could not fail to say, "We are ready to co-operate with the counter-revolutionary Cadets" (in repressions, in calumnies, in hangmen's work). On July 17 the S.-R.'s and Mensheviks finally sank into the garbage pit of counter-revolution, because they had been continually rolling down into that pit in May and June, in the coalition cabinet and in the matter of approving the policy of advance at the front.

It looks as if we have deviated from our subject, which is the question of the closing of the *Pravda*, and shifted to the question of an historical analysis of July 17. But it only seems so; in reality it is impossible to understand one thing without the other. We have seen that the closing of the *Pravda*, the arrests of Bolsheviks and other measures of persecution against them, represent, if the core of the matter and the connection between events is considered, nothing but a carrying out of an old programme by the counter-revolution and by the Cadets in particular.

It is highly instructive now to see *who* it was that realised this programme, and by what methods.

Let us look at the facts. On July 15 and 16 the movement is growing, the masses are seething with indignation over the government's inactivity, over the high cost of living, the economic ruin, the offensive at the front. The Cadets leave, playing a game of seeming defeat and confronting the S.-R.'s and Mensheviks with an ultimatum, leaving it to these parties that are bound to power, but have no power, to pay for the defeat and the indignation of the masses.

On July 15 and 16 the Bolsheviks kept the masses from action. This has been acknowledged *even* by a witness from the *Dyelo*

Naroda, who has told what happened in the Grenadier Regiment on July 15.[86] In the evening of July 16, the movement overflows its bounds and the Bolsheviks write an appeal advocating the necessity of giving the movement a "peaceful and organised" character. On July 17, the provocative shots from the right increase the number of victims of the fighting on either side. We must emphasise that the promise of the Executive Committee to investigate the events, to issue bulletins twice a day, etc., etc., has remained an idle promise! Nothing at all has been done by the S.-R. and Mensheviks; not even a complete list of the dead on either side has been published by them!!

In the night of July 17, the Bolsheviks wrote an appeal advocating the cessation of action, and during the same night it was printed in the *Pravda*. But there began on the same night, first, the arrival in Petrograd of counter-revolutionary troops (apparently called by the S.-R.'s and Mensheviks, by their Soviets, or with their consent—a "delicate" point over which, of course, they keep a sternly guarded silence even to the present time, when the last necessity of secrecy has disappeared!). Secondly, raids on the Bolsheviks, carried out by the military cadets and similar elements acting according to instructions of the military commander Polovtsev and the general staff, began on the same night. In the night between July 17 and 18, the *Pravda* was raided. On July 18 and 19, the printing plant of the *Trud* [Labour] was raided, a workingman by the name of Voinov was killed in broad daylight for carrying the *Pravda Bulletin* from that printing plant, house searches and arrests were made among the Bolsheviks, and the revolutionary regiments were disarmed.

Who started to do all this? Not the government and not the Soviet, but a counter-revolutionary military band concentrated around the general staff, acting in the name of the "intelligence service" and coming out with the fabrication of Pereverzev and Alexinsky in order to "arouse the ire" of the army, and so forth.

The government is absent; the Soviets are absent; they are shivering over their own fate; they are continually being informed that the Cossacks may come and raid them. The Black Hundred and Cadet press, which has succeeded in its hounding of the Bolsheviks, begins to hound the Soviets.

The S.-R.'s and Mensheviks had bound themselves hand and foot by all their policies. Being bound, they called (or tolerated the calling of) counter-revolutionary troops to Petrograd. This bound them still more. They sank to the very bottom of the hideous counter-revolutionary garbage pit. In a cowardly fashion they dismissed their own commission appointed to investigate the Bolsheviks' "case." Ignominiously they surrendered the Bolsheviks to the counter-revolution. Humbly they participated in the demonstration connected with the funeral of the murdered Cossacks, thus kissing the hand of the counter-revolutionists.

They are bound; they are at the bottom of the pit.

They are frantic; they give a portfolio to Kerensky; they surrender to the Cadets; they organise a "Zemsky Sobor" or a "coronation" of the counter-revolutionary government in Moscow.[37] Kerensky dismisses Polovtsev.

But all these tossings remain but tossings, without changing the *essence of the matter*. Kerensky dismisses Polovtsev and at the same time he gives shape and legality to Polovtsev's *measures*, to his policy; he suppresses the *Pravda*, he introduces capital punishment for soldiers, he forbids meetings at the front, he continues the arrests of the Bolsheviks (even Kollontai!) in accord with Alexinsky's programme.

The "essence of the constitution" in Russia is revealed with striking clarity. The advance at the front, and the coalition with the Cadets in the rear, put the S.-R.'s and Mensheviks in the pit of counter-revolution. In *reality*, state power is passing into the hands of the counter-revolution, into the hands of the military band. Kerensky and the government of Tsereteli and Chernov are *only a screen for it*; they are compelled to give *post factum* legal standing to its measures, its steps, its policies.

The haggling that is going on between Kerensky, Tsereteli, Chernov and the Cadets is of secondary significance, if not entirely insignificant. Whether the Cadets will win out in this haggling or whether Tsereteli and Chernov will still hold out "by themselves," does not change the essence of the matter; the turn of the S.-R's and Mensheviks towards counter-revolution (a turn necessitated by all their policies after May 19) remains the fundamental, the main decisive fact.

The cycle of party development has been completed. The S.-R.'s and Mensheviks were rolling down, step by step, from "confidence" in Kerensky on March 13 and May 19, which bound them to the counter-revolution, down to July 18 when they fell to the very bottom.

A new period is beginning. The victory of the counter-revolution is causing the masses to become disappointed in the Socialist-Revolutionary and Menshevik Parties, and is opening the road for their coming over to the policy of supporting the revolutionary proletariat.

Written August 8, 1917.
Rabochy i Soldat,[38] Nos. 11 and 12, August 17 and 18, 1917.

THE BEGINNING OF BONAPARTISM

Now that the Cabinet of Kerensky, Nekrasov, Avksentyev and Co.[39] has been formed, the most fatal error the Marxists could make would be to take words for deeds, deceptive appearances for reality, or generally for something serious.

Let us leave this business to the Mensheviks and Socialist-Revolutionaries, who simply perform the part of mountebanks around the Bonapartist Kerensky. Indeed, is it not buffoonery, when Kerensky, obviously controlled by the Cadets, forms something in the nature of a secret conclave consisting of himself, Nekrasov, Tereshchenko and Savinkov; passes over in silence the Constituent Assembly and the declaration of July 22; [40] proclaims in his addresses to the people the sacred union of all the classes; concludes an agreement, on conditions known to no one, with Kornilov, who presented a most brazen ultimatum; continues the policy of scandalous, outrageous arrests, while the Chernovs, the Avksentyevs, and the Tseretelis are busy posing and phrase-mongering?

Is it not buffoonery, when in a time like this Chernov is occupied with challenging Milyukov to appear before a court of arbitration; when Avksentyev declaims upon the futility of a narrow, class point of view, when Tsereteli and Dan push through the Central Executive Committee of the Soviets most vapid resolutions, stuffed with meaningless phrases, reminding one of the Cadet First Duma during its worst period of impotence in the face of tsarism?

Just as the Cadets of 1906 prostituted the first assembly of the people's representatives in Russia, reducing it to a pitiful talking-shop in face of the growing tsarist counter-revolution, so have the S.-R.'s and Mensheviks of 1917 prostituted the Soviets, reducing them to a pitiful talking-shop in face of the growing Bonapartist counter-revolution.

Kerensky's Cabinet is indubitably the first step towards Bonapartism.

We see the basic historical symptom of Bonapartism: the manœuvring of the state power, which relies on the military (on the worst elements of the army), between two conflicting classes and forces which more or less balance each other.

THE BEGINNING OF BONAPARTISM

The class struggle between the bourgeoisie and the proletariat has reached its extreme limit: on May 3 and 4, as well as on May 16 and 18, the country was on the verge of civil war. Does not this socio-economic condition form the classical soil for Bonapartism? And this condition is combined with others, fully akin to it; the bourgeoisie rants and raves against the Soviets, but it is *as yet* powerless to disperse them, while the Soviets, prostituted by Messrs. Tsereteli, Chernov and Co., are *already* powerless to offer serious resistance to the bourgeoisie.

The landlords and peasants also live as on the eve of civil war; the peasants demand land and freedom, they can be kept in check, if at all, only by a Bonapartist government capable of making the most unscrupulous promises to all classes without keeping any of them.

Add to this the fact of military defeat brought about by a foolhardy offensive, when phrases about saving the fatherland are bandied about (concealing the desires of the bourgeoisie to save its imperialist programme), and you have before you a perfect picture of the social and political setting for Bonapartism.

Let us not be deceived by phrases. Let us not be led into the belief that we have before us only the first steps of Bonapartism. It is these first steps that we must be able to apprehend, so that we may not find ourselves in the laughable predicament of the dull philistine, who groans over the second step though he himself has helped along with the first.

Constitutional illusions, such as, for instance, that the present Cabinet is more Left than all the preceding ones (see *Izvestiya*), or that well-meaning criticism by the Soviets could rectify the errors of the government, or that the arbitrary arrests and suppression of newspapers were isolated occurrences, which, it is to be hoped, will never take place again, or that Zarudny is an honest man and that in republican and democratic Russia a fair trial is possible, and therefore every one must appear, and so on and so forth, would under the present circumstances be nothing less than stupid philistinism.[41]

The stupidity of these constitutional philistine illusions is too obvious, and we need not bother to refute them.

No, the struggle with the bourgeois counter-revolution demands soberness and the ability to see and describe things as they are.

Bonapartism in Russia is not an accident, but the natural product of the evolution of the class struggle in a petty-bourgeois country with a considerably developed capitalism and a revolutionary proletariat. Historical stages like those of May 3-4, May 19, June 22-23, July 1-2, July 16-18, are landmarks which show clearly the preparation for Bonapartism. It would be the greatest error to think that Bonapartism is precluded by a democratic setting. On the contrary, it is exactly in such a setting (the history of France confirmed it twice) that it evolves under certain interrelations of classes and the struggle between them.

However, to recognise the inevitability of Bonapartism does not at all mean to forget the inevitability of its downfall.

If we should say *only* that in Russia a temporary triumph of the counter-revolution is noticeable, it would be a mistake.

If we analyse the inception of Bonapartism and, fearlessly looking the facts in the face, tell the working class and the whole people that the beginning of Bonapartism is a fact, we would by this very means lay the basis for a serious and stubborn struggle for the overthrow of Bonapartism, a struggle which would be conducted on a broad political scale, and would rest on deep class interests.

Russian Bonapartism of 1917 differs from the beginnings of French Bonapartism—in 1799 and 1849—in a number of respects, for instance, the fact that here not one basic problem of the revolution has been settled. The struggle for the solution of the agrarian and the national questions is only now becoming a burning question.

Kerensky and the counter-revolutionary Cadets who use him as a pawn can neither convoke the Constitutent Assembly on the appointed date, nor postpone it, without in either case deepening the revolution. And the catastrophe brought on by continuing the imperialist war keeps on approaching with even greater force and speed than before.

The advance detachments of the Russian proletariat have managed to emerge from our June and July days without serious loss of blood. The party of the proletariat has every opportunity of choosing such tactics and such a form or forms of organisation as, under all circumstances, would keep sudden (or would-be sudden) Bonapartist persecutions from cutting short its existence and its systematic messages to the people.

Let the party loudly and clearly proclaim to the people the whole truth: that we are experiencing the beginnings of Bonapartism; that the "new" government of Kerensky, Avksentyev and Co. is merely a screen to conceal the counter-revolutionary Cadets and military clique which have power in their hands; that the people will not get peace, the peasants will not get the land, the workers will not get the eight-hour day, the hungry will not get bread, without complete liquidation of the counter-revolution. Let the party say it, and each step in the march of events will confirm the correctness of its position.

With remarkable speed, Russia has gone through a whole epoch since the majority of the people placed their faith in the petty-bourgeois parties of the S.-R.'s and the Mensheviks. And now the majority of the labouring masses have to pay heavily for their trustfulness. All signs seem to indicate that the march of events continues at an accelerated pace and that the country is approaching the next epoch, when the majority of the labouring masses will be forced to entrust their fate to the revolutionary proletariat. The revolutionary proletariat will take the power, will start a Socialist revolution, will draw into it—despite all the difficulties and possible zigzags of evolution—the proletarians of all the advanced countries, and will vanquish war and capitalism.

Rabochy i Soldat, No. 6, August 11, 1917.

LESSONS OF THE REVOLUTION

EVERY revolution means a sharp turn in the life of the great masses of the people. If this turn has not matured, no real revolution can take place. And in the very same way as a turn in the life of any person teaches him a great deal, compelling him to go through and to feel a great deal, so also a revolution gives to every people in a brief time the richest and most valuable lessons.

During a revolution millions and tens of millions of people learn each week more than they do in a year of the usual somnolent life. For at a sharp turn in the life of a whole people it becomes particularly clear which classes of the people pursue which aims, what force they possess, by what means they act.

Every class-conscious worker, soldier and peasant must ponder the lessons of the Russian Revolution, particularly now, at the end of July, when it has become obvious that the first period of our revolution has ended in failure.

What indeed were the masses of workers and peasants striving for when they made the revolution? What did they expect of the revolution? It is known that they expected freedom, peace, bread, land.

But what do we see now?

Instead of freedom the former rule of wilfulness begins to be re-established. Capital punishment is being introduced for the soldiers at the front. The peasants are being placed on trial for seizing the landowners' land on their own initiative. The printing plants of the workers' papers are being raided. Workers' papers are being suppressed without trial. The Bolsheviks are being arrested, often without any charges or with obviously calumnious charges.

One may perhaps argue that the persecution of the Bolsheviks does not constitute a violation of freedom, for only certain persons are persecuted on certain charges. But this argument is an avowed and obvious untruth, for how can one raid a printing press and suppress a paper for the crimes of individual persons even if those charges are proven and recognised by the court? It would be quite different if the government had legally declared the whole party of the Bolsheviks, their very line, their views, to be criminal. But everybody knows that the government of free Russia could not and did not do anything of the kind.

The main thing to be considered at present is that the papers of the landowners and the capitalists furiously swore at the Bolsheviks for their struggle against the war, against the landowners and against the capitalists, and demanded open arrests and persecution of the Bolsheviks even at a time when not a single charge had been invented against a single Bolshevik. The people want peace. The revolutionary government of free Russia has again started waging a war of conquest on the basis of the very same secret treaties which former Tsar Nicholas II concluded with the English and French capitalists in order that the Russian capitalists might rob other peoples. These secret treaties have remained unpublished to the present day. The government of free Russia has used subterfuges; it has failed to offer to all the peoples a just peace.

There is no bread. Famine is looming again. Everybody sees that the capitalists and the rich are shamelessly deceiving the treasury in the matter of military contracts (the war now costs the people fifty million rubles daily), that they make unheard-of profits through high prices, but the workers have done nothing by way of earnestly keeping account of the production and distribution of goods. The capitalists are becoming more and more brazen every day, throwing the workers into the streets at a time when the people are suffering from a goods famine. A tremendous majority of the peasants have loudly and clearly declared at a long series of congresses that they proclaim the landowners' property in land to be unjust and predatory, yet the government, which calls itself revolutionary and democratic, keeps on leading the peasants by the nose for months and deceiving them by delays and procrastination. For months Minister Chernov was not allowed by the capitalists to issue laws prohibiting the purchase and sale of land. And when finally this law was issued, the capitalists started a hideous campaign of vilification against Chernov; this campaign is continued even to the present day.

So far has the government gone in brazenly defending the landowners, that it begins to put the peasants on trial for seizing land "wilfully."

The peasants are being led by the nose, they are being persuaded to wait for the Constituent Assembly. Yet the convocation of this assembly is being postponed more and more. Now, when, under the influence of the Bolsheviks' demands, the date has been set for October 13, the capitalists cry openly that this is an "impossibly" short period, and they demand the postponement of the convocation of the Constituent Assembly. The most influential members of the party of capitalists and landowners, the "Cadets" or "People's Freedom" Party, such as Panina, openly advocate the postponement of the convocation of the Constituent Assembly to the end of the war.

Let us wait with the land till we have the Constituent Assembly. Let us wait with the Constituent Assembly till the end of the war. Let us wait with ending the war till we have complete victory. This is what it comes to. The capitalists and the landowners, having their own majority in the government, are simply mocking the peasantry.

But how could this happen in a free country after the tsarist power was overthrown?

In an unfree country, a Tsar and a handful of landowners, capitalists, officials not elected by anybody, rule over the people.

In a free country, only those who have been elected rule over the people. At the elections the people are divided into parties, and usually each class of the population forms its own party; for instance, the landowners, the capitalists, the peasants, the workers form separate parties. This is why the people are ruled in free countries by means of an open struggle of the parties and a free agreement among them.

After the overthrow of the tsarist power on March 12, 1917, Russia for about four months was ruled like a free country, namely, by means of an open struggle among freely formed parties and a free agreement among them. Consequently, to understand the development of the Russian Revolution, it is most necessary to study what the main parties were, what class interests they defended, and what the interrelations among all these parties were.

After the overthrow of the tsarist power, state power passed into the hands of the first Provisional Government. It consisted of representatives of the bourgeoisie, *i.e.*, capitalists who were joined by the landowners. The party of the "Cadets," the main party of the capitalists, occupied the foremost place as the ruling and governmental party of the bourgeoisie.

Power fell into the hands of this party not by accident, although not the capitalists, of course, but the workers and the peasants, the soldiers and the sailors were those who had fought the tsarist troops and shed their blood for freedom. Power fell into the hands of the party of the capitalists because that class possessed the power of wealth, organisation, and knowledge. During the time after 1905, and particularly during the war, the class of the capitalists, and that of the landowners associated with it, made the greatest progress in Russia by way of organising itself.

The Cadet Party always was monarchist, both in 1905 and between 1905 and 1917. After the victory of the people over tsarist tyranny, that party declared itself to be republican. The experience of history shows that, after the people have conquered the monarchy, the parties of the capitalists have always agreed to be republican if only that has enabled them to retain the privileges of the capitalists and their supreme power over the people.

In words, the Cadet Party stands for "people's freedom." In deeds it stands for the capitalists, and it was immediately joined by all the landowners, all the monarchists, all the Black Hundreds. The press and the elections are proof of this. All the bourgeois papers and all the Black Hundred press began to sing in unison with the Cadets after the revolution. Not daring to appear openly, all the monarchist parties supported the Cadet Party during elections, as for instance in Petrograd.

Having obtained state power, the Cadets bent every effort to continue the predatory war of conquest begun by Tsar Nicholas II who had concluded secret predatory treaties with the English and French capitalists. By these treaties the Russian capitalists were promised the seizure of Constantinople, Galicia, Armenia, etc., in case of victory. As to the people, the government of the Cadets put it off by idle pretexts and promises, referring all great matters necessary for the workers and peasants to the Constituent Assembly and not setting a date for its convocation.

The people, using their freedom, began to organise independently. The chief organisations of the workers and peasants, who form the overwhelming majority of the population of Russia, were the Soviets of Workers', Soldiers', and Peasants' Deputies. Those Soviets began to be formed even during the February Revolution; a few weeks later, all the class-conscious, advanced members of the working class and the peasantry, in most of the large cities of Russia and in many counties, were united in Soviets.

The Soviets were elected with absolute freedom. The Soviets were real organisations of the masses of the people, the workers and the peasants. The Soviets were real organisations of a tremendous majority of the people. The workers and the peasants, dressed in soldiers' uniforms, were armed.

It goes without saying that the Soviets could and should have taken into their hands all state power. There ought to have been no other power in the state outside of the Soviets, pending the convocation of the Constituent Assembly. Only thus would our revolution have become a real people's revolution, a real democratic revolution. Only thus could the labouring masses that are really striving for peace, that are really not interested in a war of conquest, have begun decisively and firmly to carry out in life a policy that would have put an end to the war of conquest and would have led to peace. Only thus could the workers and peasants have checked the capitalists, who are making insane profits "on the war" and have brought the country to ruin and famine. In the Soviets, however, a minority of the deputies were on the side of the party of revolutionary workers, the Social-Democrats-Bolsheviks, who demanded that all state power should be given over to the Soviets. The majority of the deputies in the Soviets were on the side of the parties of the Social-Democrats-Mensheviks and Socialist-Revolutionaries, who were against the power being given over to the Soviets. Instead of removing the government of the bourgeoisie and replacing it by a government of the Soviets, these parties insisted on supporting the government of the bourgeoisie and making agreements with it, on forming a common government with it. This policy of agreements with the bourgeoisie on the part of the Socialist-Revolutionary and Menshevik Parties, trusted by a majority of the people, forms the main content of the entire course of the development of the revolution for the five months that have passed since it began.

Let us first of all see how this policy of agreements between the Socialist-Revolutionaries and Mensheviks on the one hand and the bourgeoisie on the other was progressing, and then let us look for an explanation of the fact that the majority of the people trusted them.

The policy of agreements between the Mensheviks and S.-R.'s

on the one hand and the capitalists on the other was carried on during all the periods of the Russian Revolution, either in one form or another.

At the beginning of March, 1917, as soon as the people won and the tsarist power proved overthrown, the Provisional Government of the capitalists included Kerensky among its members as a "Socialist." In reality Kerensky had never been a Socialist, he had only been a Trudovik;* he began to count himself among the "Socialist-Revolutionaries" only in March, 1917, when to do so was already both safe and advantageous. Through Kerensky as vice-president of the Petrograd Soviet, the Provisional Government of the capitalists from the very beginning made an attempt to attach to itself and to tame the Soviet. The Soviet, *i.e.*, the S.-R.'s and Mensheviks predominating in it, allowed itself to be tamed by agreeing, immediately after the formation of the Provisional Government of the capitalists, to "support it," "in so far" as it carried out its promises.

The Soviet looked upon itself as supervising, controlling the actions of the Provisional Government. The leaders of the Soviet established a so-called "contact commission," *i.e.*, a commission for contact, for relations with the government. In this contact commission the S.-R. and Menshevik leaders of the Soviet continually negotiated with the capitalists' government, serving in fact, as Ministers without portfolios, as unofficial Ministers.

This state of affairs continued throughout March and almost all of April. The capitalists resorted to delays and pretexts, trying to gain time. Not a single more or less earnest step for developing the revolution did the capitalists' government take during that time. It did absolutely nothing even to carry out its direct task, the convocation of the Constituent Assembly; it did not raise the question locally; it did not even organise a central commission to prepare the solution of the problem. The government was concerned with one thing only: how to renew secretly the predatory international treaties which the Tsar had concluded with the capitalists of England and France; how to thwart the revolution most carefully and unostentatiously; how to promise everything without fulfilling anything. The S.-R.'s and Mensheviks played in the "contact commission" the rôle of fools; they were fed by high-

* Labourites—a group of Duma deputies, primarily representatives of peasant districts.—*Ed.*

sounding phrases and promises. Like the crow in the famous fable, the S.R.'s and Mensheviks yielded to flattery, listening as they did with pleasure to the assertions of the capitalists that they valued the Soviets highly and were not taking a single step without them.

In reality, time passed and the government of the capitalists did absolutely nothing for the revolution. On the other hand, it managed during this time to renew the secret predatory treaties, directed against the revolution, or, more correctly, to confirm and "vitalise" them by conducting new and no less secret negotiations with the diplomats of Anglo-French imperialism. During this time it managed to lay the foundations for a counter-revolutionary organisation (or at least for a rapprochement) of the generals and officers of the army directed against the revolution. It managed to start organising against the revolution the industrialists, the manufacturers, the mill owners, who, under the onslaught of the workers, were compelled to give one concession after the other, yet, at the same time, were beginning to sabotage production and to prepare to stop it, only looking for an opportune moment.

The organisation of the advanced workers and peasants in the Soviets, however, proceeded apace. The best men of the oppressed classes felt that, notwithstanding the agreement between the government and the Petrograd Soviet, notwithstanding the oratory of Kerensky, notwithstanding the "contact commission," the government remained an enemy of the people, an enemy of the revolution. The masses felt that if the resistance of the capitalists were not broken, the cause of peace, the cause of freedom, the cause of the revolution was bound to be lost. Impatience and bitterness were growing among the masses.

It led to an outburst on May 3-4. The movement flared up in an elemental way; nobody prepared it. The movement was so obviously directed against the government that one of the regiments even came out fully armed, and it marched to the Mariinsky palace to arrest the Ministers. It became clearly evident to everybody that the government could not remain in power. The Soviets could (and should) have taken power into their hands without meeting with the least resistance from any quarter. Instead, the S.-R.'s and the Mensheviks supported the collapsing government of the capitalists; they entangled themselves by more agreements with it;

they made more fateful steps leading to the downfall of the revolution.

The revolution teaches all classes with a rapidity and thoroughness unknown in normal, peaceful times. The capitalists, better organised, more experienced in the affairs of the class struggle and of politics, learned faster than the others. Seeing that the situation of the government was untenable, they resorted to a measure which, for a number of decades after 1848, had been practised by the capitalists of other countries to fool, divide and weaken the workers. This measure is the so-called "coalition" government, *i.e.*, a united cabinet composed of members of the bourgeoisie and of renegades from Socialism.

In those countries where freedom and democracy have existed side by side with the revolutionary labour movement longer than in other countries, namely, in England and France, the capitalists have used this method many times and with great success. The "Socialist" leaders, having entered a bourgeois Cabinet, inevitably proved to be pawns, puppets, screens for the capitalists, instruments for deceiving the workers. The "democratic and republican" capitalists of Russia resorted to this very method. The S.-R.'s and Mensheviks let themselves be fooled outright, and on May 19 a "coalition" Cabinet with the participation of Chernov, Tsereteli and Co. came into being.

The fools from the Socialist-Revolutionary and Menshevik Parties were jubilant, bathing as they did self-admiringly in the rays of the ministerial glory of their leaders. The capitalists gleefully rubbed their hands, having found in the "Soviet leaders" assistants for their activity against the people and having exacted from them a promise to suport "aggressive actions at the front," *i.e.*, to renew the imperialist predatory war that had been stopped for a while. The capitalists knew very well that these leaders were puffed-up weaklings; they knew that the promises on the part of the bourgeoisie—concerning control or even organisation of production, concerning peace policies, etc.—would never be fulfilled.

This is exactly what happened. The second period in the development of the revolution, from May 19 to June 22 or July 1, fully bore out the calculations of the capitalists on the ease with which the S.-R.'s and Mensheviks could be fooled.

While Plekhanov and Skobelev were fooling themselves and the people by high-sounding phrases to the effect that 100% of the profits would be taken away from the capitalists, that their "resistance was broken," etc., the capitalists continued to fortify themselves. Nothing, absolutely nothing was undertaken during that time to curb the capitalists. The Ministers, renegades from Socialism, proved to be talking machines intended to distract the attention of the oppressed classes while the entire apparatus of state administration really remained in the hands of the bureaucracy (the officials) and the bourgeoisie. The notorious Palchinsky, Assistant Minister of Industry, was a typical representative of that apparatus, thwarting all possible measures against the capitalists. The Ministers chatted, and everything remained as before.

Minister Tsereteli was particularly singled out by the bourgeoisie to fight against the revolution. He was sent to "quiet" Cronstadt when the local revolutionists dared to remove an appointed commissar. The bourgeoisie launched in its papers an incredibly noisy, vicious and furious campaign of lies, calumnies and slander against Cronstadt, accusing it of wishing "to secede from Russia," repeating this and similar absurdities in a thousand ways, and frightening the petty bourgeoisie and the philistines. A typical representative of thick-headed, frightened philistinism, Tsereteli swallowed the bait with more devotion than all the others; he "sacked and subdued" Cronstadt more ardently than the others, without understanding his own rôle as a lackey of the counter-revolutionary bourgeoisie. It appeared that he was instrumental in carrying through an "agreement" with revolutionary Cronstadt whereby the commissar for Cronstadt was not appointed by the government directly and simply, but was to be elected locally and *confirmed* by the government. On such miserable compromises was wasted the time of the Ministers who had run over from Socialism to the bourgeoisie.

Wherever a bourgeois Minister could not have appeared with a defence of the government, for instance, before the revolutionary workers or the Soviets, a "Socialist" Minister, Skobelev, Tsereteli, Chernov, etc., appeared (or, more correctly, was sent by the bourgeoisie), faithfully working for the bourgeois cause, creeping out of his skin in defending the Cabinet, whitewashing the capitalists, fooling the people by repeating promises, promises, promises, by counseling them to wait, wait, wait.

Minister Chernov was particularly busy bargaining with his bourgeois colleagues; up to July, up to the new "governmental crisis" which began after the movement of July 16-17, up to the time when the Cadets left the Cabinet, Minister Chernov was continually engaged in the useful, interesting, and deeply popular work of "persuading" his bourgeois colleagues, of inducing them to agree at least to a decree prohibiting purchase and sale of land. This measure had been most solemnly promised to the peasants at the All-Russian Congress (Soviet) of Peasant Deputies in Petrograd. Still, the promise remained nothing but a promise. Chernov proved unable to carry it through either in May or in June, until the revolutionary tide, the elemental outburst of July 16-17, coinciding with the Cadets' leaving the Cabinet, made it possible to enact this measure. But even so it remained isolated and unable materially to improve the struggle of the peasantry against the landowners for the land.

At the front, the counter-revolutionary imperialist task of going on with the imperialist predatory war, a task which Guchkov, a Minister hateful to the people, had been unable to carry out, was being simultaneously carried out, successfully and splendidly, by the "revolutionary-democratic" Kerensky, this fresh-baked member of the Socialist-Revolutionary Party. He was intoxicated by his own eloquence; incense was burned in his honour by the imperialists who used him as a pawn; he was flattered; he was worshipped; —all because he devotedly and faithfully served the capitalists, persuading the "revolutionary army" to agree to resume the war which was being fought to carry out the treaties concluded by Tsar Nicholas II with the capitalists of England and France, a war fought in order that the Russian capitalists might get Constantinople and Lemberg, Erzerum and Trebizond.

In this way the second period of the Russian Revolution, from May 19 to June 22, passed. The counter-revolutionary bourgeoisie became strengthened, became consolidated, shielded and defended as it was by the "Socialist" Ministers; it prepared an offensive both against the enemy without and against the enemy within, *i.e.*, the revolutionary workers.

On June 22, the party of the revolutionary workers, the Bolsheviks, organised a demonstration in Petrograd with the aim of giving an organised expression to the relentlessly growing dissatisfaction and the indignation of the masses. The S.-R. and Menshevik leaders, entangled in agreements with the bourgeoisie, bound by the imperialist policy of an offensive at the front, became frightened, feeling that they were losing their influence among the masses. A howl went up against the demonstration, a general howl in which this time the counter-revolutionary Cadets united with the S.-R.'s and the Mensheviks. Under their leadership, and as a result of their policy of conciliation with the capitalists, it became fully evident, it stood out in bold relief that the petty-bourgeois masses were turning towards an alliance with the counter-revolutionary bourgeoisie. Therein lies the historic significance of the crisis of June 22; therein lies its class meaning.

The Bolsheviks called the demonstration off because they did not wish to lead the workers into a desperate fight against the united Cadets, S.-R.'s and Mensheviks. The latter, however, in order to retain at least a remnant of the confidence of the masses, were compelled to call a general demonstration for July 1. The bourgeoisie was beside itself with rage, rightly seeing therein a swing of petty-bourgeois democracy towards the proletariat; it decided to paralyse the action of democracy by an advance at the front.

July 1 won a substantial victory for the slogans of the revolutionary proletariat, the slogans of Bolshevism, among the Petrograd masses; on July 2 the bourgeoisie and the Bonapartist * Kerensky solemnly declared that the advance at the front had begun on the very day of July 1.

The advance at the front meant in fact resuming the predatory war undertaken in the interests of the capitalists and against the will of an overwhelming majority of the toilers. This is why the advance at the front was inevitably combined on the one hand with a great increase in chauvinism and with a passing of military (consequently also state) power to the military clique of Bonapartists; on the other hand, with the beginning of oppressive measures against the masses, with persecutions against the internationalists, with the abolition of the freedom of propaganda, with the imprisoning and shooting of those who were against the war.

May 19 tied the S.-R.'s and Mensheviks to the chariot of the bourgeoisie with a rope; July 1 bound them, as servants of the capitalists, with a chain.

* By the word Bonapartism (after the names of the two French emperors, Bonaparte) we designate a government which tries to appear non-partisan, utilising the exceedingly acute struggle between the parties of the capitalists and of the workers. In reality serving the capitalists, such a government fools the workers most of all, with promises and petty grants.

The bitterness of the masses, due to the continuance of the predatory war, naturally grew still faster and stronger. On July 16-17 came an outburst of their indignation, an outburst which the Bolsheviks attempted to restrain and which, of course, they were bound to attempt to lead into the best organised channels.

The S.-R.'s and Mensheviks, as slaves of the bourgeoisie chained by their master, agreed to everything: to the bringing of reactionary army units to Petrograd; to the re-introduction of capital punishment; to the disarming of the workers and the revolutionary army units; to arrests and persecution; to the suppression of newspapers without trial. Power which the bourgeoisie, sitting in the cabinet, was unable fully to seize, which the Soviets did not wish to seize, fell into the hands of the military clique, of the Bonapartists, who of course were fully supported by the Cadets and the Black Hundreds, by the landowners and capitalists.

So it went from step to step. Once having set foot on the inclined plane of conciliation with the bourgeoisie, the S.-R.'s and Mensheviks rolled down with irresistible force till they reached the bottom. On March 13 they promised, in the Petrograd Soviet, conditional support to the bourgeois government. On May 19 they saved it from collapse and allowed themselves to be made into its servants and defenders by agreeing to an advance at the front. On June 22 they united with the counter-revolutionary bourgeoisie in a campaign of furious viciousness, lies and calumnies against the revolutionary proletariat. On July 2 they approved the resuming of the predatory war. On July 16 they agreed to summoning the reactionary army units; this was the beginning of their final surrender of power to the Bonapartists. Down, from step to step.

This shameful finale of the Socialist-Revolutionary and Menshevik Parties is no accident; it is a result of the economic situation of the small owners, the petty bourgeoisie, as repeatedly corroborated by the experience of Europe.

Everybody has had a chance to observe how the petty owners bend every effort, how they strain themselves, to reach "easy street," to become real masters, to rise to the position of an "established" business man, a real bourgeois. As long as capitalism rules, there is no way out for the small owner; he must either become a capitalist (which is at best possible for one out of a hundred small owners) or become a ruined owner, a semi-proletarian and then a proletarian. The same thing is repeated in politics; petty-bourgeois democracy, especially its leadership, follows in the wake of the bourgeoisie. The leaders of petty-bourgeois democracy console their masses with promises and assertions as to a possible agreement with the large-scale capitalists; for a short time they, at best, receive from the capitalists some concessions for a small upper stratum of the toiling masses, while in every decisive problem, in every important matter, petty-bourgeois democracy always proves to be at the tail-end of the bourgeoisie, to be a feeble appendage of the bourgeoisie, an obedient tool in the hands of the financial kings. The experience of England and France has proven this many times.

The experience of the Russian Revolution from February to July, 1917, when events, particularly under the influence of the imperialist war and the very deep crisis created by it, were developing with unusual rapidity, confirmed most strikingly and palpably the old Marxist truth about the unstable position of the petty bourgeoisie.

This is the lesson of the Russian Revolution: there is no escape for the masses from the iron grip of war, famine, enslavement to the landowners and capitalists, unless they fully break with the Socialist-Revolutionary and Menshevik Parties, unless they clearly recognise their treacherous rôle, unless they renounce all kinds of agreements with the bourgeoisie and decisively join the side of the revolutionary workers. The revolutionary workers alone, when supported by the poorest peasants, will be able to break the resistance of the capitalists, to lead the people to the conquest of the land without compensation, to full freedom, to victory over famine, to victory over the war, to a just and lasting peace.

Postscript

This article, as is apparent from the text, was written at the beginning of August.

The history of the revolution during August fully confirmed what was said in this article. Later, at the beginning of September, Kornilov's revolt created a new turn in the revolution, having shown clearly to all the people that the Cadets in alliance with the counter-revolutionary generals were striving to disperse the Soviets and to re-establish the monarchy. How strong this new phase of the revolution is, and whether it will be able to put an end to the destructive policy of conciliation with the bourgeoisie, the near future will show.

The article was written at the beginning of August; the postscript, September 19, 1917. The article was published in *Rabochy*,[42] Nos. 8 and 9, September 12 and 13, 1917, and the postscript in the pamphlet *Lessons of the Revolution* published by the *Priboi* publishing house.

ON KAMENEV'S SPEECH IN THE CENTRAL EXECUTIVE COMMITTEE CONCERNING THE STOCKHOLM CONFERENCE [43]

COMRADE KAMENEV's speech of August 6 in the Central Executive Committee concerning the Stockholm Conference cannot fail to arouse resentment from all Bolsheviks who are loyal to their party and their principles.

In the first sentence of his speech, Comrade Kamenev made a declaration of a formal nature which renders his speech positively monstrous. Comrade Kamenev declared that he spoke for himself personally; that "our fraction has not discussed this question."

Since when have individual members of an organised party begun to speak on important questions "for themselves personally"? Since the fraction has not discussed the question, Comrade Kamenev had no right to bring it up. This is the first conclusion to be drawn from his own words.

Second, what right had Comrade Kamenev to forget that there is a decision of the Central Committee of the party against participating at Stockholm? If this decision has not been abrogated by a congress or by a new decision of the Central Committee, it is law for the party. If it has been abrogated, Comrade Kamenev ought to have said so, and ought not to have spoken in the past tense: "We Bolsheviks have hitherto maintained a negative attitude towards the Stockholm Conference."

The conclusion again to be drawn is that not only had Kamenev no right to make this speech, but that he directly violated the decision of the party; he spoke directly against the party; he violated its will by not saying a word about the Central Committee's decision, which is binding for him. Yet this decision was in due time published in the *Pravda*, with an addendum saying that the representative of the party would leave the Zimmerwald Conference should it express itself in favour of participating at Stockholm.*

The arguments in favour of the "hitherto" negative attitude of the Bolsheviks towards participating at Stockholm were quoted by

---

* See V. I. Lenin, *The Revolution of 1917, Collected Works*, Vol. XX, Book II, p. 73.—*Ed.*

Kamenev incorrectly. He did not mention that the Stockholm Conference will include social-imperialists, that it is shameful for a revolutionary Social-Democrat to have anything to do with such people.

Sad as it may be to admit it, we must admit that Starostin, often much confused, has expressed the point of view of revolutionary Social-Democracy a thousand times better, more correctly, with more dignity, than Kamenev. To go to confer with social-imperialists, with Ministers, with hangmen's aides in Russia—this is a shame and a betrayal. In such a case, one doesn't talk about internationalism.

Kamenev's arguments in favour of "changing" our view on Stockholm are ridiculously weak.

> It has become evident to us—Kamenev said—that from this [??] moment Stockholm ceases [??] to be a blind tool in the hands of imperialist governments.

This is not true. There is not a single fact to back this, and Kamenev was not able to quote anything substantial. If the Anglo-French social-imperialists do not join the conference, while the Germans do, is this any fundamental change?? Is this really any change from the standpoint of an internationalist? Can Kamenev already have "forgotten" the decision of our party conference (May 12) concerning a perfectly analogous case, that of a Danish social-imperialist? *

> Over Stockholm—Kamenev is reported by the papers as saying—a broad revolutionary banner is beginning to wave, under which the forces of the world proletariat are being mobilised.

This is the emptiest declamation in the spirit of Chernov and Tsereteli. This is a glaring untruth. Not a revolutionary banner, but a banner of deals, compromises, forgiveness for social-imperialists, bankers' negotiations concerning the division of annexations—this is the banner which is really beginning to wave over Stockholm.

It is intolerable that a party of internationalists responsible before the whole world for revolutionary internationalism should compromise itself by flirting with the schemes of Russian and German social-imperialists, with the negotiations among the Ministers of the

---

* See V. I. Lenin, *The Revolution of 1917, Collected Works,* Vol. XX, Book II, p. 401.—*Ed.*

bourgeois-imperialist government, the Chernovs, Skobelevs, and Co.

We have decided to build the Third International. We must accomplish this in spite of all difficulties. Not a step backward to deals with social-imperialists and renegades from Socialism!

Proletary,[44] No. 5, August 29, 1917.

ON THE QUESTION OF THE PARTY PROGRAMME

COMRADE BUKHARIN'S note in *Spartak*, to the effect that a "small" congress is being called to adopt a programme, shows how urgent this question is.[45]

The question is really pressing.

Our party stands at the fore of the other internationalist parties; this is now a fact.

It is therefore obliged to take the initiative, to come out with a programme that *answers* the questions of imperialism.

It will be a scandal and a shame if we do not do this.

I propose that the Central Committee decide:

"*Every* organisation of the party is immediately to appoint one or several commissions to prepare the programme; it *obliges* them, as well as all theoreticians and writers, etc., to give *precedence* to this matter, and to present either their own draft, or changes and amendments to drafts of others, not later than within 3 to 7 days."

This is perfectly realisable with steady work.

To collect and print those drafts or to send them to the main organisations in typewritten form will require a couple of weeks.

Then *immediately* announce the calling of a *small* congress (one delegate to four or five thousand members) *within a month*—for the purpose of adopting the programme.

Our party is obliged to come forward with a programme—only *thus* shall we *advance* the cause of the Third International not in words but in deeds.

All the rest is phrases, promises, postponements to the Greek Calends. When we take the initiative, we shall hasten the work in every respect, and only then shall we prepare the programme of the Third International.

Written August 26-31, 1917.
First published in the *Lenin Collection*, VII, 1928.

THEY DO NOT SEE THE WOODS FOR THE TREES

At the session of the Central Executive Committee of the Soviets on August 17, L. Martov said (we quote from the report in the *Novaya Zhizn*) that "Tsereteli's criticism is too mild," that "the government does not offer resistance to counter-revolutionary attempts on the part of the military" and that "it is not our aim to overthrow the present government or to undermine confidence in it. . . ." "The correlation of forces is in reality such," Martov continued, "that there is no ground for demanding the passing of power to the Soviets. This could come up only in the course of a civil war, which at present is inadmissible." "It is not our intention to overthrow the government," Martov concludes, "but we must remind it that there are forces in the country other than the Cadets and the military. Those are the forces of revolutionary democracy, and on them the Provisional Government must rely." [46]

These ideas of Martov's are remarkable, and it is worth while to dwell on them most attentively. They are remarkable in that they reproduce with unusual boldness the most widespread, the most pernicious, the most dangerous political errors of the petty-bourgeois mass, its most typical superstitions. Of all the representatives of this mass, Martov, as a publicist, is surely one of the most "Left," one of the most revolutionary, one of the most enlightened and clever. It is therefore much more useful to analyse his ideas than those of a Chernov, who parades with empty verbiage, or those of a stupid Tsereteli, etc. In analysing Martov's ideas, we analyse what is at present most reasonable in the ideas of the petty bourgeoisie.

Extremely characteristic are, first of all, Martov's vacillations as regards the passing of power to the Soviets. Prior to July 17, Martov was *against* this slogan. After July 17, he is *for* it. Early in August, he is again against it, and note how monstrously illogical, how amusing his argumentation is from the point of view of Marxism. He is against it because, he says, "The correlation of forces is in reality such that there is no ground for demanding the passing of power to the Soviets. This could come up only in the course of a civil war, which at present is inadmissible."

98

What confusion! It appears, first, that prior to July 17 such transfer of power was possible *without* a civil war (sacred truth!), but it was just then that Martov was against such transfer of power. . . . Second, it appears that after July 17, when Martov was *for* the passing of power to the Soviets, such transfer would have been possible without civil war; which is an obvious, glaring and flagrant untruth, because the facts are that on the night of July 17-18 the Bonapartists, supported by the Cadets, and lackey-fashion aided by the Chernovs and Tseretelis, brought the counter-revolutionary troops into Petrograd. To seize power peacefully under such conditions would have been absolutely impossible.

Third and last, it appears, according to Martov, that a Marxist or even a plain revolutionary democrat has a right to reject a slogan that correctly expresses the interests of the people and the interests of the revolution, on the ground that that slogan can be realised "only in the course of a civil war. . . ." This is an obvious absurdity, an obvious renunciation of all class struggle, all revolution. For who does not know that the history of all revolutions the world over reveals, not an accidental, but an inevitable transformation of class struggle into civil war? Who does not know that it is precisely *after* July 17 that we see in Russia the beginning of civil war on the part of the counter-revolutionary bourgeoisie, disarming of regiments, executions at the front, murder of Bolsheviks? It appears, don't you see, that civil war is "inadmissible" for revolutionary democracy just at a time when the course of events has, by sheer necessity, brought about a situation where civil war is started by the counter-revolutionary bourgeoisie.

Martov became confused in a most unbelievable, amusing, helpless fashion.

Disentangling the confusion introduced by Martov, one must say:

It was before July 17 that the slogan of power passing into the hands of the then existing Soviets was the only correct one. At that time such passing of power was possible in a peaceful way, without civil war, because at that time there had been no systematic acts of violence against the masses, against the people, as there were after July 17. At that time this slogan guaranteed a peaceful forward development of the whole revolution and particularly made it possible to eliminate peacefully the class struggle of parties *within* the Soviets.

After July 17, the passing of power to the Soviets became impossible without civil war, since, on July 17-18, power passed to a military Bonapartist clique supported by the Cadets and the Black Hundreds. It follows from this that all Marxists, all adherents of the revolutionary proletariat, all honest revolutionary democrats *must* now make clear to the workers and the peasants the radical change in the situation, a change which necessitates a new path for the passing of power to the proletarians and semi-proletarians.

Martov has advanced no arguments in defence of his "idea" of the inadmissibility of civil war "at present," in defence of his declaration that it is not his intention "to overthrow the present government." This opinion, particularly when expressed without motivation at a meeting of defensists, inevitably smacks of the defensist argument that civil war within is inadmissible while the enemy threatens from without.

We do not know whether Martov would have the courage to advance such an argument openly. Among the mass of the petty bourgeoisie this argument is one of the most popular. It is, of course, one of the cheapest. The bourgeoisie was not afraid of revolution and civil war at moments when the enemy threatened from without, as was the case in September, 1870, in France, or in February, 1917, in Russia. The bourgeoisie was not afraid to seize power at the price of civil war at moments when the enemy threatened from without. Just as little will the revolutionary proletariat reckon with this "argument" of liars and lackeys of the bourgeoisie.

One of the most flagrant theoretical errors committed by Martov, an error also highly typical of the whole circle of political ideas of the petty bourgeoisie, consists in confusing tsarist and monarchist counter-revolution generally with bourgeois counter-revolution. Here we have the specific narrowness or specific stupidity of a petty-bourgeois democrat who cannot break away from economic, political and ideological dependence upon the bourgeoisie, who grants it priority, who sees in it an "ideal," who trusts its cries about the danger of a "counter-revolution from the Right."

This circle of ideas, or, more correctly, this thoughtlessness of the petty bourgeoisie, was voiced by Martov in his speech when he said: "To counterbalance the pressure exerted on it [the government] from the Right, we must organise a counter-pressure."

Here is a sample of philistine credulity and forgetfulness of the class struggle. It appears that the government is something above classes and above parties; that "pressure" is being brought to bear upon it too strongly from the Right, therefore one must press more strongly from the Left. Oh, wisdom worthy of Louis Blanc, Chernov, Tsereteli, and all that despicable crew! How infinitely useful this philistine wisdom is for the Bonapartists; how they long to present the situation to "the foolish little peasants" in such a light as to make them believe that the present government is fighting both against the Right and Left, against the extremes only, in the meantime organising the state on a firm basis, introducing in practice real democracy—whereas in reality this Bonapartist government is a government of the counter-revolutionary bourgeoisie!

It is profitable for the bourgeoisie (and necessary for the perpetuation of its domination) to deceive the people by depicting the situation as if the bourgeoisie represented "the revolution in general, while counter-revolution threatens from the Right, from the Tsar." It is only through the infinite stupidity of the Dans and Tseretelis, through the infinite conceit of the Chernovs and Avksentyevs, that this idea, nurtured by the conditions of life of the petty-bourgeoisie, is current among "revolutionary democracy."

Any one who has learned anything from history or from Marxist doctrine, however, will have to admit that the cornerstone of a political analysis must be the question of *classes:* in behalf of what class is the revolution we speak of? In behalf of what class is the counter-revolution?

The history of France shows us that the Bonapartist counter-revolution emerged at the end of the eighteenth century (and then a second time in 1848-1852) on the basis of a counter-revolutionary bourgeoisie, and in turn it paved the way for the restoration of a legitimate monarchy. Bonapartism is the form of government which grows out of a counter-revolutionary bourgeoisie where democratic transformations and a democratic revolution are taking place.

One must purposely shut his eyes not to see how, in our very presence, Bonapartism is growing in Russia under very similar conditions. The tsarist counter-revolution is at present utterly insignificant; it has not a shadow of political importance; it plays no political rôle. The bugaboo of a tsarist counter-revolution is purposely put forward and made a fuss over by charlatans to frighten fools, to treat philistines to a political sensation, to distract the attention of the people from the real and serious counter-revolution. It is impossible to read without laughing the reasonings of a

Zarudny, who makes a great point of worrying about the counter-revolutionary rôle of a back-yard organisation named "Holy Russia" while "not noticing" the counter-revolutionary rôle of the organisation of the entire bourgeoisie of Russia called the Cadet Party.

The Cadet Party is the main political force of the bourgeois counter-revolution in Russia. This force has splendidly consolidated around it all the Black Hundred elements, both at the elections [47] and (which is still more important) in the apparatus of the military and civil administration and in the press campaign of lies, calumny, and baiting—directed primarily against the Bolsheviks, *i.e.*, the party of the revolutionary proletariat, and then against the Soviets.

Slowly but surely the present government is following the political line which the Cadet Party has been systematically preaching and preparing since March, 1917. It has renewed and is prolonging the imperialist war; it has stopped the peace "prattle"; it has given the Ministers the right to suppress newspapers, to disperse conferences, to make arrests and send into exile; it has restored capital punishment and executions of soldiers at the front; it is disarming the workers and the revolutionary regiments; it has flooded the capital with counter-revolutionary troops; it has begun to arrest and persecute the peasants for unauthorised "seizures"; it is shutting down factories and organising lock-outs—here is a far from complete list of measures which give the clearest picture of the bourgeois counter-revolution of Bonapartism.

And what about the postponed convocation of the Constituent Assembly and the coronation of Bonapartist politics with a *Zemsky Sobor* in Moscow—this step leading to the postponement of the Constitutent Assembly to the end of the war? Is this not a gem of Bonapartist politics? And Martov does not see where the main headquarters of the bourgeois counter-revolution is located. . . . Really, they do not see the woods for the trees.

What an infinitely dirty lackey's rôle the Central Executive Committee of the Soviets, *i.e.*, the S.-R.'s and Mensheviks who dominate it, played in the question of postponing the convocation of the Constituent Assembly! The Cadets struck the keynote; they advanced the idea of postponement; they started a campaign in the press; they engineered a *Cossack Congress* to demand postponement. (A Cossack Congress! How could the Libers, Avksentyevs, Chernovs and Tseretelis refrain from acting as lackeys!) The Mensheviks and

S.-R.'s ran after the Cadets like cockerels, they crawled at their master's whistle like a dog threatened with a whip.

Instead of giving the people a plain statement of the facts showing how brazenly, how shamelessly the Cadets have been delaying and hindering the convocation of the Constitutent Assembly since March; instead of exposing the lying evasions and the assertions that it was impossible to convoke the Constituent Assembly at the appointed time, the Bureau of the Central Executive Committee promptly put aside all the "doubts" expressed even by Dan (even by Dan!) and despatched two lackeys of this collegium of lackeys, Bramson and Bronzov, to the Provisional Government with a report "on the necessity of postponing the elections to the Constituent Assembly till November 10-11...." A splendid prelude to the coronation of the Bonapartists by a *Zemsky Sobor* in Moscow. Whoever has not become altogether vile must join the party of the revolutionary proletariat. Without the victory of the revolutionary proletariat, peace for the people, land for the peasants, bread for the workers and all the toilers, *cannot be secured.*

N. KARPOV.*

Proletary, No. 6, September 1, 1917.

* One of Lenin's pseudonyms.—*Ed.*

RUMOURS OF CONSPIRACY

The note printed under the above title in No. 103 of the *Novaya Zhizn,* August 30, deserves very serious attention; it must be dwelt on (over and over again), even though what is brought up in the note as something serious, is not serious at all.

Its contents may be put as follows: on August 27 a rumour was spread in Moscow to the effect that some Cossack units were moving towards Moscow from the front and that at the same time "certain military groups, enjoying the sympathy of certain circles of society in Moscow," were organising "decisive counter-revolutionary actions." It was further alleged that the military authorities had notified the Moscow Soviet of Workers' and Soldiers' Deputies, and "with the participation of representatives of the Central Executive Committee" (*i.e.,* Mensheviks and Socialist-Revolutionaries) had taken steps to inform the soldiers of the necessity of guarding the city, etc. "The representatives of the Moscow Bolsheviks," the note concludes, "were also invited to participate in these preparations, since they have influence in many military units, and access to these was given them on this occasion." [48]

This last phase is intentionally framed in an obscure and equivocal manner. If the Bolsheviks have influence in many military units (which is undisputable and generally known), then how and by whom *could* "access" to these units be given to the Bolsheviks? This is an obvious absurdity. If, however, "on this occasion," "access" was really given to the Bolsheviks (by whom? Obviously by the Mensheviks and S.-R.'s!) to *any kind* of military units, that means that a certain *bloc,* an alliance, an agreement on "defence against counter-revolution" was reached between the Bolsheviks and the defensists.

This circumstance gives serious import to a note that is not at all serious, and requires of all the class-conscious workers a most attentive attitude towards the facts mentioned.

The rumours spread by the defensists, *i.e.,* by the Mensheviks and S.-R.'s, are obviously absurd, and the filthy and hideous political scheme of spreading these rumours is quite evident. The real counter-revolutionist is that very Provisional Government which the defensists claim they want to defend. Cossack troops were actually recalled from the front to the capitals, for instance to Petrograd on July 16, by none other than the Provisional Government and the "Socialist" Ministers, as was formally confirmed by the Cossack General Kaledin at the Moscow counter-revolutionary imperialist conference. This is a fact.

This fact, exposing the Mensheviks and S.-R.'s, and proving their betrayal of the revolution, *their alliance* with the counter-revolutionists, *their alliance* with the Kaledins—this fact the Mensheviks and S.-R.'s would like to cover up, to hush up, to eradicate from people's memory with the aid of "rumours" to the effect that the Cossacks are moving on Moscow against the will of Kerensky, Tsereteli, Skobelev, Avksentyev, that the Mensheviks and the S.-R.'s are "defending the revolution," and the like. The little political scheme of the Menshevik and defensist traitors is as clear as can be; they wish to deceive the workers, to pose as revolutionists, to learn something about the Bolsheviks (in order to transmit it to the secret service, of course), to patch up their reputation! The scheme is as vile as it is clumsily done! At small expense, by concocting a stupid little "rumour," they hope to gain "access" to the Bolshevik military units and to strengthen the confidence in the Provisional Government generally by assuring naïve people that it is this government that the Cossacks wish to overthrow, that it is *not* in collusion with the Cossacks, that it is "defending the revolution," and so on, and so forth.

The little scheme is obvious. The rumours, of course, are absurd and fabricated. But confidence in the Provisional Government they expect to get in cold cash, and what is more, they expect to draw the Bolsheviks into a "bloc" with them!

It is difficult to believe that there can be found among the Bolsheviks fools and scoundrels willing to enter into a bloc with the defensists at present. It is difficult to believe, first, because there is a direct resolution of the Sixth Congress of the Russian Social-Democratic Labour Party [49] which says (*cf. Proletary*, No. 4) that "the Mensheviks have definitely gone over to the camp of the enemies of the proletariat." There can be no agreements, no blocs with people who have definitely gone over to the camp of the enemy. "The primary task of revolutionary Social-Democracy," continues the same resolution, "is to isolate them" (the Menshevik defensists) "completely from all more or less revolutionary elements of the working class." It is obviously against this isolation that the Mensheviks and S.-R.'s are fighting by spreading absurd rumours. It is obvious that both in Moscow and in Petrograd the workers are turning away more and more from the Mensheviks and S.-R.'s, realising ever more clearly the treacherous counter-revolutionary nature of their policies, and it is to "improve conditions" that the defensists are compelled to resort to every available trick.

The resolution of the congress being what it is, the Bolsheviks who would enter into a bloc with the defensists with the purpose of "giving access" or indirectly expressing confidence in the Provisional Government (which supposedly must be defended against the Cossacks)—such Bolsheviks would of course immediately and deservedly be expelled from the party.

There are, however, other reasons why it is difficult to believe that there can be found, in Moscow or elsewhere, Bolsheviks capable of entering into a bloc with the defensists, of forming with them anything like common, albeit temporary bodies, of entering into any kind of agreement, etc., with them. Let us imagine a circumstance most favourable for such rather unlikely Bolsheviks: let us assume that, in their naïveté, they actually believe in the rumours they hear from the Mensheviks and S.-R.'s; let us even assume that, to imbue them with confidence, they were given certain, also invented, "facts." It is obvious that, even under such conditions, not a single honest Bolshevik, or one who has not entirely lost his senses, would enter into any bloc with these defensists, would make any agreements about "giving access," etc. Even under such conditions this is what a Bolshevik would say: "Our workers and soldiers will fight against the counter-revolutionary troops if they start an offensive against the Provisional Government; they will *not* defend this government which called for Kaledin and Co. on July 16, but they will independently defend the revolution while pursuing their own aims, the aims of securing a victory for the workers, a victory for the poor, a victory for the cause of peace, and not a victory for the imperialists, for Kerensky, Avksentyev, Tsereteli, Skobelev and Co." Even under the exceptionally unlikely circumstances here assumed, a Bolshevik would say to the Mensheviks: "Of course we shall fight, but we shall not agree to the smallest political alliance with you, nor to the least expression of confidence in you—we shall fight in the very same way as the Social-Democrats fought against tsarism in March, 1917, together with the Cadets, without entering into any alliance with the Cadets or trusting them for a single second. The least confidence in the Mensheviks would be as much of a betrayal of the revolution now as confidence in the Cadets would have been in 1905-1917."

A Bolshevik would say to the workers and soldiers: "Let us fight, but not a shadow of confidence in the Mensheviks, if you do not want to be deprived of the fruits of victory."

It is all too advantageous for the Mensheviks to spread false rumours and allegations to the effect that the government they are supporting is saving the revolution, while in reality it has *already formed a bloc* with the Kaledins, it is *already* counter-revolutionary, it has *already* taken a great number of steps, and is daily taking new steps, to fulfil the conditions of this bloc with Kaledin.

To believe in these rumours, to support them directly or indirectly, would mean, on the part of the Bolsheviks, to betray the cause of the revolution. The chief guarantee of the success of the revolution at present is that the masses should clearly realise the treachery of the Mensheviks and S.-R.'s and completely break with them, and that all sections of the revolutionary proletariat should boycott them as absolutely as they boycotted the Cadets after the experience of 1905.

I request that several copies of this article be typed, so that it may be sent to several party papers and magazines to be printed, and at the same time be put before the Central Committee in my behalf with the following postscript:

I request that this article be considered as a report of mine to the Central Committee, with the added proposal that the Central Committee order an official investigation in which Moscow comrades who are not members of the Central Committee are to participate, in order to establish the fact whether the Bolsheviks had common institutions with the defensists on this basis, whether there were blocs and agreements, what they consisted of, etc. It is necessary to investigate the facts and the details officially, to learn all details. If the fact of the existence of the bloc is confirmed, it is necessary to suspend the members of the Central Committee or of the Moscow Committee from work and, pending the convocation of the congress, to place the question of their formal suspension before the next plenum of the Central Committee. For it is *now*, after the Moscow

Conference, after the strike, after July 16-18, that Moscow is acquiring, or can acquire, the significance of a *centre*. In this tremendous proletarian centre, which is larger than Petrograd, the growth of a movement similar to that of July 16-18 is fully possible. At that time the task in Petrograd was to give the movement a peaceful and organised character. This *was* a correct slogan. The task *now* in Moscow is entirely different; the old slogan would be absolutely incorrect at present. The task now would be for the workers to *seize power* themselves and to declare themselves the government in the name of peace, land to the peasants, convoking the Constituent Assembly at the time agreed upon with the peasants locally, etc. It is quite possible that such a movement will flare up in Moscow, owing to unemployment, famine, a railroad strike, economic ruin, etc. It is highly important to have "at the helm" in Moscow persons who will not swerve to the Right, who are incapable of forming blocs with the Mensheviks, who, in case the movement rises, will understand the *new* tasks, the *new* slogan of seizing power, the *new* ways and means leading to it. This is why an "investigation" of the bloc case, censure of the bloc-ist Bolsheviks, if there are any, and their suspension, are necessary not only for the sake of discipline, not only for the purpose of correcting the foolishness already committed, but for the sake of the most essential interests of the *future* movement. The strike of August 25 in Moscow proved that the *active* proletariat is for the Bolsheviks, notwithstanding the fact that the Duma elections yielded a majority to the S.-R.'s. This is very similar to the situation in Petrograd prior to July 16-18, 1917. But the difference in the situation is that at that time Petrograd could not even seize power physically, and had it done so physically, it could not have retained it politically, for Tsereteli and Co. had not yet sunk to the level of supporting the hangman. This is why *at that time*, on July 16-18, 1917, in Petrograd, the slogan of seizing power would have been *incorrect*. At that time even the Bolsheviks did not have and could not have the conscious determination to treat Tsereteli and Co. as counter-revolutionists. At that time neither the soldiers nor the workers could have had the experience the month of July brought them.

Now the situation is entirely different. Now, if a spontaneous movement flares up in Moscow, the slogan must be nothing but seizure of power. This is why it is highly important, unusually important, that the movement in Moscow be led by persons fit for the task, who have *fully* grasped and thoroughly assimilated this slogan. This is why it is necessary over and over again to insist on an investigation and suspension of the guilty.

Written August 31-September 1, 1917.
First published in the *Lenin Collection*, VII, 1927.

POLITICAL BLACKMAIL

BLACKMAIL is the extortion of money under the threat of exposing certain facts or invented "stories" which may be unpleasant to the person concerned, or under the threat of causing him some other discomfiture.

Political blackmail is the threat of exposing, or the actual exposing, of real, or more often invented, "stories" with the aim of causing political damage, of calumniating, of depriving an opponent of, or of making it difficult for him to carry on political activity.

Our republican (excuse me for using this expression), even our democratic bourgeois and petty bourgeois manifested themselves as the heroes of political blackmail when they started a "campaign" of defamation, lies and slander against the parties and the political leaders they dislike. Tsarism persecuted crudely, savagely, bestially. The republican bourgeoisie persecutes *filthily*, striving to besmirch the reputation of the hated proletarian revolutionist and internationalist by means of slander, lies, insinuations, defamation, rumours, etc., etc.

The Bolsheviks in particular have had the honour of experiencing these methods of persecution used by republican imperialists. In general, the Bolshevik might apply to himself the well-known words of the poet:

> He hears the voice of approbation
> Not in the dulcet sounds of praise,
> But in the roar of irritation! [50]

Frenzied cries of indignation against the Bolsheviks appeared on the pages of all the bourgeois and nearly all the petty-bourgeois press almost *immediately* after the beginning of the Russian Revolution. And the Bolshevik, the internationalist, the supporter of the proletarian revolution, may justly hear in these frenzied cries of indignation the sound of approbation; for the wrathful hatred of the bourgeoisie is often the best proof of correct and honest service to the proletariat on the part of the slandered, hounded, persecuted.

The blackmailing character of the slanderous tactics of the bourgeoisie may be most clearly illustrated by an example which does *not* concern our party—the example of the Socialist-Revolutionary Chernov. Some members of the Cadet Party, notorious slanderers headed by Milyukov and Hessen, in order to intimidate or expel Chernov, started a campaign against him for his alleged "defeatist" articles abroad, and for his connection with persons alleged to have received money from the agents of German imperialism. The baiting campaign began to spread. It was taken up by the entire bourgeois press.

But the Cadets and the S.-R.'s "made peace," agreeing to a certain composition of the Cabinet. And—oh, wonder!—the Chernov "affair" vanished! Without trial, without examination, without publishing of documents, without questioning of witnesses, without experts' conclusions, the "affair" disappeared in a few days. When the Cadets were dissatisfied with Chernov, a slanderous "affair" arose. When the Cadets had made political peace with Chernov, at least temporarily, the "affair" disappeared.

Here is a clear case of political blackmail. Baiting in the press, slander, insinuations serve in the hands of the bourgeoisie and such scoundrels as the Milyukovs, Hessens, Zaslavskys, Dans, etc., as a weapon of political struggle and political revenge. The political aim is attained, and the "affair" against X or Y "disappears," proving the filthy meanness of character, the base dishonesty, the blackmailing nature of those who started the "affair."

For it is obvious that those who do not practice blackmail, those who are moved by honest motives, would not discontinue their revelations no matter what political changes took place; on the contrary, they would, under all circumstances, bring the revelations to a conclusion, to a court verdict; they would fully acquaint the public with the case, collect and publish *all* the documents, or openly and directly admit that an error or a misunderstanding had occurred.

Chernov's example clearly demonstrates the real essence of the blackmailing campaign against the Bolsheviks by the bourgeois and petty-bourgeois press. When the political aim of those knights and henchmen of capital seemed to them to have been reached, when the Bolsheviks had been arrested and their papers suppressed, then the blackmailers *said nothing!* Having in their possession every means of bringing out the truth—the press, money, aid of the foreign bourgeoisie, aid of the "public opinion" of all bourgeois Russia, friendly support of the state power of one of the largest states in the world—having in their possession all this, the heroes of the crusade against the Bolsheviks, the Milyukovs and Hessens, the Zaslavskys and Dans, *said nothing!*

It becomes clear to every honest person, as it immediately became clear to the class-conscious workers whose entire life prepares them for a quick understanding of the methods of the bourgeoisie, that the Milyukovs and Hessens, the Zaslavskys and Dans, etc., etc., are *political blackmailers*. It is necessary to fix this in the minds of the masses, to explain this to the masses, to write about it every day in the papers, to collect documents about it for a pamphlet, to boycott the blackmailers, etc., etc. Against slander and blackmail, these are the methods of struggle worthy of the proletariat!

One of the latest to suffer from blackmail was our comrade Kamenev. He has "refrained from public activity" until his case is tried.[51] We think this is a mistake. This is exactly what the blackmailers needed. They do not want to try his case. It would have been sufficient for Kamenev to contrast the dastardly attack with the confidence of *his own* party—and let the dogs of the *Ryech, Birzhevka, Dyen, Rabochaya Gazeta,* and other vile sheets bark.

Should our party consent to the suspension of public activities of its leaders because they were slandered by the bourgeoisie, the party would suffer terribly; harm would be caused to the proletariat; and its enemies would rejoice. For the bourgeoisie has many papers; it has even more blackmailing, venal pens (like those of Zaslavsky and Co.); it would be too easy for it to "suspend" our party workers. The bourgeoisie is not interested in examining the case, in a search for truth.

No, comrades! Let us not yield to the critics of the bourgeois press! Let us not give satisfaction to the blackmailing scoundrels, the Milyukovs, Hessens, Zaslavskys. Let us rely on the verdict of the proletarians, of the class-conscious workers in our party, numbering 240,000 internationalists. Let us not forget that throughout the whole world the internationalists are persecuted by the bourgeoisie, in league with the defensists, by means of lies, slander, blackmail.

Let us be unswerving in branding the blackmailers. Let us unhesitatingly submit our smallest doubts to the tribunal of class-conscious workers, to the court of our party; in it we trust; in it we see the intelligence, the honour and the conscience of our epoch; in a world-wide alliance of revolutionary internationalists we see the only guarantee of the movement for emancipation of the working class.

No yielding to the "public opinion" of those who sit in one Cabinet with the Cadets, who shake hands with the Milyukovs, Dans, Zaslavskys.

Down with the political blackmailers! Boycott and scorn them! Incessantly expose their vile names to the working masses! We must unswervingly follow our own way, safeguard the working power of our party, guard its leaders from even wasting their time on mud-slingers and their filthy slander.

Proletary, No. 10, September 6, 1917.

PAPER RESOLUTIONS

Mr. Tsereteli is one of the most talkative "Socialist" Ministers and leaders of philistinism. It is hard to make oneself read through his innumerable speeches, so empty and vulgar are those really "ministerial" orations which say nothing, commit him to nothing, have no serious meaning whatever. These eloquent "manifestations" of Tsereteli's (which, thanks to their emptiness, must have made him popular with the bourgeoisie) are rendered particularly intolerable by the boundless conceit of the orator, and it is difficult to decide whether extraordinary stupidity or cynical political shrewdness are hidden underneath those glib, smooth and sugary phrases.

The more empty Tsereteli's speech, the more energetically must we emphasise an absolutely incredible, extraordinary thing that happened to this orator at the plenary session of the Petrograd Soviet on August 31. It is incredible, but it is a fact: Tsereteli let slip a plain, clear, reasonable, truthful word. He let slip a word which adequately expresses a deep and earnest political truth, with a meaning not accidental, but characterising the entire political situation of the present in its essential, fundamental traits, in its very foundations.

According to the report of the *Ryech* (the reader will of course remember that Tsereteli was opposed to the resolution abolishing capital punishment), Tsereteli said:

... None of your resolutions will help. What is needed is not paper resolutions but concrete actions....[52]

What is true is true. It is a pleasure to hear a sensible idea....

Of course, with this truth Tsereteli first of all and most of all hits himself. For it was he, as one of the most prominent leaders of the Soviet, who helped prostitute this institution, reduce it to the pitiful rôle of some kind of a liberal gathering destined to bequeath to the world an archive of typically impotent nice little wishes. Tsereteli, who has sponsored hundreds of "paper resolutions" in a Soviet castrated by the Socialist-Revolutionaries and Mensheviks, is less than anybody entitled to complain about "paper resolutions" when it comes to a resolution that hits himself very hard. Tsereteli has placed himself in the highly ridiculous position of a parliamentarian who more than anybody else has fussed about "parliamentary" resolutions, more than anybody else has extolled their significance, more than anybody else has busied himself with them, but who, when he meets with a resolution directed *against himself*, begins to shout that "the grapes are sour," that strictly speaking, it is a paper resolution.

Still, a truth, even when uttered by a fraud, and on a false note, remains a truth.

The resolution is a paper resolution, not for the reason declared by the former Minister Tsereteli, who thinks that capital punishment is necessary (no joking!) for the defence of the revolution. It is a paper resolution because it repeats in stereotype fashion the formula that has been learned by heart and mechanically repeated ever since March, 1917: "The Soviet demands from the Provisional Government." Being accustomed to "demand," they repeat it out of habit, without noticing that the situation has changed, that power has gone and that a "demand" not based on force is ridiculous.

Moreover, a "demand" repeated in stereotype fashion spreads among the masses the illusion that the situation has not changed, that the Soviet is a power, that in proclaiming its "demand," the Soviet has accomplished something and can go to sleep with the easy conscience of a "revolutionary" (pardon me!) "democrat" who has done his duty.

A reader may ask: was it not necessary for the Bolsheviks, who are for a sober political understanding, for examining social forces and against empty phrases, not to vote for the resolution?

No. It was necessary to vote for it, if only for the reason that one of the paragraphs of the resolution (§ 3) contains the true and splendid thought (fundamental, main, decisive) that capital punishment is a weapon against the *masses* (it would be different if it were a question of a weapon against the landowners and capitalists).[53] It was necessary to vote for it, even though the philistine S.-R.'s mutilated Martov's text by rejecting the reference to the "imperialist aims alien to the interests of the people," adopting instead the "defence of the fatherland and the revolution" which is a thoroughly lying phrase, deceiving the people and camouflaging the predatory war.

It was necessary to vote for the resolution, at the same time emphasising disagreement with certain parts, and making the following declaration: "Workers! Do not think that the Soviet is at present in a position to demand anything from the Provisional Government. Do not yield to illusions. Know that the Soviet has *already* lost power to demand, that the *present* government is completely captive in the hands of the counter-revolutionary bourgeoisie. Think hard of this bitter truth." Nobody could have prevented the Soviet members from voting *for* the resolution with such reservations in one form or another.

Then the resolution would have ceased being a "scrap of paper."

And then we would have evaded the question of Tsereteli, who, provocateur-fashion, asked the Soviet members whether they wished to "overthrow" the Provisional Government (Tsereteli did this in exactly the same fashion as did Katkov under Alexander III when he asked the Liberals whether they wished to "overthrow" the autocracy). We could have answered the ex-Minister: "Beloved citizen, you have just published a penal law against those who 'make attempts' or even make preparations 'to overthrow' the government (which was formed by an agreement of the landowners and capitalists with the petty-bourgeois traitors to democracy). We understand fully that the whole bourgeoisie would appreciate you even more if you could 'fit' a few Bolsheviks under this pleasant law (pleasant for you). Do not be surprised, therefore, if we do not make it our business to make it easy for you to find pretexts for applying this 'pleasant' law."

As the sun is reflected in a little drop of water, so the entire political system of Russia was reflected in the incident of August 31. A Bonapartist government; capital punishment; a penal law; the sugar-coating of these things, "pleasant" for the provocateurs, with phrases strikingly similar to those peddled by Louis Napoleon about equality, fraternity, liberty, the honour and dignity of the fatherland, the traditions of the great revolution, the suppression of anarchy.

The sugary, nauseatingly sweet petty-bourgeois Ministers and ex-Ministers who beat their breasts asserting that they have souls, that they lead their souls to perdition when they introduce and apply capital punishment against the masses, and weep about it—are a revised edition of that "pedagogue" of the 'sixties of the last century who, following in the footsteps of Pirogov, did his flogging not in the simple, usual way, not in the old-fashioned way, but shed humane tears over the little fellow subjected to a "lawful" and "just" thrashing.

The peasants, deceived by their petty-bourgeois leaders, continue to believe that out of the marriage between the S.-R.-Menshevik bloc and the bourgeoisie may be born the abolition of private property in land without compensation.

The workers . . . but about what the workers think we had better keep silence until the "humane" Tsereteli has abolished his new penal law.

Rabochy, No. 2, September 8, 1917.

ON THE STOCKHOLM CONFERENCE

AGAIN many are interested in the Stockholm Conference. Its significance is a problem extensively discussed in the papers. This problem is inseparably bound up with an appreciation of the very foundations of present-day Socialism as a whole, particularly in its relation to the imperialist war. This is why we ought to dwell in greater detail on the Stockholm Conference.

The revolutionary Social-Democrats, *i.e.*, the Bolsheviks, from the very beginning came out against participating in this conference. In doing so, they acted from reasons of principle. Every one knows that throughout the world, in every country, belligerent and neutral, the Socialists have split into two large, fundamental divisions differing in their attitude towards the war. Some joined the side of their governments, their bourgeoisie. Those we call "social-chauvinists," *i.e.*, Socialists in words, chauvinists in deeds. One who uses the term "defence of the fatherland" to cover up a defence of the predatory interests of "his" ruling classes is a chauvinist. In the present war, the bourgeoisie of both belligerent coalitions pursue predatory aims: the German bourgeoisie is fighting for the robbing of Belgium, Serbia, etc.; the English and French, to rob the German colonies, etc.; the Russians, to rob Austria (Lemberg), Turkey (Armenia, Constantinople).

This is why those Socialists who have taken the point of view of their bourgeoisie in the present war have ceased to be Socialists, have betrayed the working class, have in fact gone over into the camp of the bourgeoisie. They have become class enemies of the proletariat. And the history of European and American Socialism, particularly during the period of the Second International, *i.e.*, the period between 1889 and 1914, shows us that such cases of Socialists, particularly the majority of the leaders and parliamentarians, going over to the side of the bourgeoisie, are no accident. Indeed, it is precisely the opportunist wing of Socialism in all countries that has furnished the main body of the social-chauvinists. Social-chauvinism, viewed scientifically, *i.e.*, not picking out individuals, but taking the development of the entire international movement with all its social connections, is opportunism that has reached its logical end.

There is to be observed among the proletarian masses everywhere, in a more or less clear and sharp form, a consciousness of the betrayal of Socialism by the social-chauvinists, a hatred and contempt for the most prominent social-chauvinists, like Plekhanov in Russia, Scheidemann in Germany, Guesde, Renaudel and Co. in France, Hyndman, et al., in England, etc., etc.

Notwithstanding desperate persecution by the bourgeoisie, and notwithstanding the suppression of free speech and press, there has become outlined in every country during the war a trend of revolutionary internationalism. This trend has remained faithful to Socialism. It has not yielded to chauvinism; it has not allowed it to be covered up by lying phrases about defence of the fatherland; but, on the contrary, it has exposed all the falsehood of these phrases, the whole criminal nature of the present war which the bourgeoisie of both coalitions is waging with predatory aims in view. To this trend belong, for instance, MacLean in England, who was sentenced to a year and a half of hard labour for his struggle against the predatory English bourgeoisie, Karl Liebknecht in Germany, who was sentenced to hard labour by the German imperialist robbers for the "crime" of advocating a revolution in Germany and exposing the predatory character of the war on the German side. To this trend belong also the Bolsheviks in Russia, who are being persecuted by the agents of Russian republican and democratic imperialism for the same "crime" for which MacLean and Karl Liebknecht are being persecuted.

This trend is the only one that is true to Socialism. This trend alone has not betrayed the solemn statement of its convictions, the solemn pledge signed by the Socialists of all the world, of every country without exception, in November, 1912, in the Basle Manifesto. This manifesto speaks, not of war in general—for there are different kinds of wars—but of a war like that which was openly being prepared in 1912 and broke out in 1914, namely, a war for world domination between Germany and England with their allies. In face of this imminent war, the Basle Manifesto fails to mention in one single syllable either the duty or the right of Socialists to "defend their fatherland," (*i.e.*, to justify their participation in the war); on the contrary, it states most definitely that such a war must lead to the "proletarian revolution." The betrayal of Socialism by the social-chauvinists is particularly evident from the fact that like a thief avoiding the scene of his crime, they all cowardly evade that passage in the Basle Manifesto which speaks about the connection between the present war and the proletarian revolution.

It is easily understood what an impassable chasm exists between the Socialists who have remained true to the Basle Manifesto and "respond" to the war by preaching and preparing a proletarian revolution, and the social-chauvinists who respond to the war by supporting "their" national bourgeoisie. It is easily understood how helpless, naïve and hypocritical are the attempts to "reconcile" or "unite" the two trends.

Such attempts, poor as they may be, may be seen on the part of a third trend in world Socialism, the so-called "centre" or Kautskyism" (after the name of the most outstanding representative of the "centre," Karl Kautsky). During the whole three years of the war, this trend has revealed in every country its complete lack of ideas and its helplessness. In Germany, for instance, the course of events has forced the Kautskyists to split away from the German Plekhanovs and to form their own so-called "Independent Social-Democratic Party,"[54] and still that party is afraid to draw the necessary conclusions; it preaches "unity" with the social-chauvinists on an international scale; it continues to deceive the working masses with the hope of re-establishing such unity in Germany; it hampers the only correct proletarian tactics of revolutionary struggle with one's "own" government, a struggle that goes on even during the war, a struggle that can and must change its form but cannot be delayed or put aside.

Such is the state of affairs within international Socialism. Without clearly appraising this situation, without viewing all trends of international Socialism from the point of view of principle, it is not possible even to approach a question of a practical nature, as, for instance, the question of the Stockholm Conference. Still, an appraisal of *all* trends of international Socialism from the point of view of principle was made *only* by the party of the Bolsheviks in a detailed resolution adopted at a conference, May 7-12, 1917,* and confirmed by the Sixth Congress of our party in August. To forget this appraisal made from the point of view of principle, and to argue about the Stockholm Conference without considering it, means to abandon principles altogether.

As a sample of the abandonment of principles prevailing among

* See V. I. Lenin, *The Revolution of 1917, Collected Works*, Vol. XX, Book II, p. 405.—*Ed.*

all the petty-bourgeois democrats, the Socialist-Revolutionaries and Mensheviks, we may point out an article in the issue of the *Novaya Zhizn* for August 23. This article deserves attention just because it combines in one place, in a paper occupying the extreme Left Wing of the petty-bourgeois democrats, the most widespread errors, prejudices, and lack of ideas as regards Stockholm.

> One may, for one reason or another—says the leading article in the *Novaya Zhizn*—take a negative stand towards the Stockholm Conference; one may renounce in principle the attempts at reconciling the "defensist majorities." But why deny something that is perfectly apparent? After the well-known decision of the English workers, which caused a political crisis in the country and brought about the first deep cleft in the "national unity" of Great Britain, the conference acquired a significance that it had hitherto lacked.[55]

The lack of principles in this argument is exemplary. How, indeed, is it possible to conclude from the barren fact that the "national unity" has suffered a deep cleft on the question of the Stockholm Conference, that we are obliged to mend rather than to deepen that cleft? Looked at from the point of view of principle, the question is put in this way, and in this way only: either a break with the defensists (social-chauvinists) or an agreement with them. The Stockholm Conference was one of the many attempts to reach an agreement. It failed. Its failure was caused by the fact that the Anglo-French imperialists *at present* are unwilling to conduct peace negotiations, while the German imperialists are willing. The English workers have come to realise more clearly than before that they are being deceived by the English imperialist bourgeoisie.

The question is: how shall we utilise this situation? We revolutionary internationalists say: it must be utilised to deepen the split between the proletarian masses and the social-chauvinists, to bring this split to completion, to remove every possible obstacle to the development of the revolutionary struggle of the masses against their governments, against their bourgeoisie. In doing so we, and we alone, are deepening the cleavage and bringing matters to the breaking point.

But what about those who are going to Stockholm, or rather, who preach to the masses the necessity of going there at present, when life itself has "annulled" this undertaking—what do they really accomplish? The only thing they do is try and heal the breach, for the Stockholm Conference is known to have been called and to be supported by persons who support *their* governments, by the ministerialists, the Chernovs and Tseretelis, the Staunings, the Brantings, the Troelstras, not to speak of the Scheidemanns.

It is this that is "perfectly apparent." It is this that the opportunists of the *Novaya Zhizn* forget or slur over when they argue in an entirely unprincipled way, without appraising social-chauvinism in general as a trend. The Stockholm Conference is a conversation among Ministers, members of the imperialist governments. Try as it may, the *Novaya Zhizn* cannot evade this fact. To urge the workers to go to Stockholm, to urge them to wait for Stockholm, to urge them to place any hopes whatever in Stockholm, means to say to the masses: "You can, you must expect benefits from an agreement among the petty-bourgeois parties and Ministers who are members of imperialist cabinets and support imperialist governments."

It is this most unprincipled, harmful propaganda that the *Novaya Zhizn* is carrying on, without noticing what it is doing.

Due to the conflict between the Anglo-French social-chauvinists and their governments, it forgets that the Chernovs, the Skobelevs, the Tseretelis, the Avksentyevs, the Brantings, the Staunings and Scheidemanns are no less social-chauvinists, that they too support their governments. Isn't this unprincipled?

Instead of saying to the workers: "Look, the Anglo-French imperialists have not allowed even their social-chauvinists to go and converse with the German social-chauvinists; this means that the war is a predatory one *also* on the part of England and France, consequently, there is no salvation except through a break with *all* the governments, with *all* the social-chauvinists, without any reservations"—instead of saying this, the *Novaya Zhizn* consoles the workers with illusions:

> In Stockholm—it says—preparations are being made to reach a peace agreement and collectively to work out a general plan of **struggle**: refusal to vote for war credits, a break with "national unity," recall of Ministers from the cabinets, etc.

All it can do to substantiate this absolutely false phrase is to set up the word "struggle" in bold-face type. Fine proof, indeed!

After three years of war, they still feed the workers with the most empty promises: "Preparations are being made at Stockholm" to break with national unity. . . .

Who makes these preparations? The Scheidemanns, the Chernovs, the Skobelevs, the Avksentyevs, the Tseretelis, the Staunings, the Brantings, *i.e.*, the very persons (and parties) who for months and years have been carrying out the policy of national unity. No matter how sincere the faith of the *Novaya Zhizn* in such a miracle may be, no matter how honestly it may cherish the conviction that this is possible, we still must say that the *Novaya Zhizn* is spreading the greatest deception among the workers.

The *Novaya Zhizn* deceives the workers when it imbues them with confidence in the social-chauvinists. What it says amounts, in fact, to asserting that, although hitherto the social-chauvinists have been members of cabinets, and have been carrying out a policy of national unity, still, when they come to Stockholm in the near future, they will reach an understanding, an agreement, a compact, and will cease acting this way. They will begin a struggle for peace. They will refuse to vote credits, and so on, and so forth. . . .

All this is one great deception. All this means pacifying and bullying the workers in a reactionary way, imbuing them with confidence in the social-chauvinists. But the truth is that the Socialists who "fight for peace" not in words, not to deceive themselves, not to deceive the workers, have long since started such a struggle, without waiting for international conferences; they have started such a struggle by breaking up national unity in the very same way as it was done by MacLean in England, by Karl Liebknecht in Germany, by the Bolsheviks in Russia.

> We understand perfectly well—says the *Novaya Zhizn*—the legitimate and sound skepticism of the Bolsheviks as regards Renaudel and Scheidemann, but the publicists from the *Rabochy i Soldat*, in their doctrinaire fashion, do not wish to see the woods for the trees; they do not take into account the change in the mood of the masses on which Renaudel and Scheidemann rely.

No, gentlemen, this is not skepticism; we are not like you, whose prevailing mood is an intellectuals' skepticism that covers up and expresses absence of principle. We are not skeptics as far as Renaudel and Scheidemann are concerned; we are their enemies. This makes a vast difference. We have broken with them and we appeal to the masses to break with them. It is we, and we alone, who "took into account" both the change in the mood of the masses and something very much more important and more profound than a mood and its change, namely, the fundamental interests of the masses, the impossibility of reconciling these interests with the policy of social-chauvinism as represented by the Renaudels and Scheidemanns. In Stockholm, the fine gentlemen from the *Novaya Zhizn,* together with the Ministers of the Russian imperialist government, will meet nobody but the Scheidemanns and Renaudels (for Stauning and Troelstra, not to speak of Avksentyev and Skobelev, differ in nothing substantial from the Renaudels). We, on the other hand, turn away from the comedy enacted in Stockholm by the social-chauvinists and among the social-chauvinists, in order to open the eyes of the *masses,* in order to express their interests, to call them to revolution, to utilise the change in their mood not for an unprincipled adaptation to a given mood, but for a struggle on the basis of principles and for a complete break with social-chauvinism.

The Bolsheviks—says the *Novaya Zhizn*—love to flaunt in the eyes of the internationalists who are going to Stockholm, their agreements with the Scheidemanns and Hendersons; they do not notice, however, that, as far as the conference is concerned, they—of course, for entirely different reasons—go hand in hand with the Plekhanovs, Guesdes and Hyndmans.

It is not true that, as far as the conference is concerned, we go hand in hand with the Plekhanovs! This is an obvious absurdity. It happens that our unwillingness to go to a half-hearted conference with part of the social-chauvinists coincides with Plekhanov's stand. But our *attitude* towards the conference is entirely different from that of the Plekhanovs, both in principle and in practice. You, on the other hand, who call yourselves internationalists, you actually go to the conference together with the Scheidemanns, the Staunings, the Brantings; you really make agreements with them. This is a fact. You call "the great cause of uniting the international proletariat" that petty and miserable cause of *uniting the social-chauvinists,* which, to a large extent, is a child of intrigues and depends upon the imperialists of one of the coalitions. This is a fact.

You would-be internationalists cannot preach to the masses participation at Stockholm (it is quite probable that the matter will not progress beyond preaching, for the conference will not take place; still, the ideological significance of the preaching will remain), you cannot preach to the masses participation in the Stockholm Conference without heaping up untruths, without spreading illusions, without painting the social-chauvinists better than they are, without imbuing the masses with hopes to the effect that the Staunings and Brantings, the Skobelevs and Avksentyevs are capable of seriously breaking with "national unity."

We Bolsheviks, on the other hand, in our propaganda against

Stockholm, tell the masses the whole truth; we continue to expose the social-chauvinists and the policy of agreements with them; we lead the masses towards a complete break with them. If affairs have taken such a turn that German imperialism considers the present moment opportune for participating at Stockholm, and is sending there its agents, the Scheidemanns, while English imperialism considers the moment inopportune, and does not even wish to talk peace, we expose English imperialism and we utilise the conflict between it and the English proletarian masses to deepen their class consciousness, to intensify the propaganda of internationalism, to make clear to them the necessity of a complete break with social-chauvinism.

The would-be internationalists of the *Novaya Zhizn* act like intellectual impressionists, *i.e.*, persons who feebly yield to the mood of the moment, forgetting the fundamental principles of internationalism. The people of the *Novaya Zhizn* argue that if English imperialism is *against* the Stockholm Conference, then they must be *for* it, then the conference must have acquired a significance that it has hitherto lacked.

To argue in this way means, in fact, to sink to an unprincipled attitude, for German imperialism is now *in favour* of the Stockholm Conference, since it serves its selfish and predatory imperialist interests. But what value has the "internationalism" of such "internationalists," who are afraid directly to recognise this undisputed and self-evident fact and are forced to hide from it? Where are your guarantees, gentlemen, that when you participate at Stockholm together with the Scheidemanns, Staunings, and Co., you will not actually turn out to be a plaything, an instrument in the hands of the secret diplomats of German imperialism? You cannot have such guarantees. There are none. The Stockholm Conference, even if it takes place, which is very unlikely, will be an attempt on the part of the German imperialists to sound out the ground as to the feasibility of a certain exchange of annexations. This is what the actual, real meaning of the eloquent speeches of the Scheidemanns, Skobelevs, and Co. will be. Should the conference fail to take place, your preaching to the masses will have real significance, imbuing them with false hopes in the social-chauvinists, with the idea that they will, possibly and probably, soon "go straight."

In either case you, wishing to be internationalists, in reality prove to be accomplices of the social-chauvinists of one or both coalitions.

We, on the other hand, taking into account all the vicissitudes and the details of politics, remain consistent internationalists, preaching a brotherly union of all the workers, a break with the social-chauvinists, and work for the proletarian revolution.

N. K—ov.

Rabochy, No. 2, September 8, 1917.

PEASANTS AND WORKERS

On September 1, No. 88 of the *Izvestiya* of the All-Russian Soviet of Peasant Deputies [56] published an exceedingly interesting article. This article should become one of the basic documents in the hands of every party propagandist and agitator working among the peasantry, in the hands of every class-conscious worker on the way to or in contact with the village.

This article consists of "Sample instructions comprising 242 instructions presented by local delegates before the All-Russian Congress of Peasant Deputies in Petrograd in the year 1917."

It would be extremely desirable for the Soviet of Peasant Deputies to publish the data concerning all these instructions in as detailed a form as possible (if it is absolutely impossible to publish them in full, which, of course, would be best of all). What is particularly indispensable, for instance, is a complete list of the provinces, districts, counties involved, information as to how many instructions came from each locality, the dates on which these instructions were prepared and presented, an analysis of at least the basic demands, so that we should be able to see wherein one district differs from another in the various points taken up. Let us say whether they are districts of individual or communal ownership of land, populated by Great Russians or other nationalities, in the centre of the country or in the outlying sections, districts that have known serfdom or not; do they vary, and how, in their formulation of the question concerning the abolition of private ownership of all *peasant* land, concerning periodic redistribution of land, concerning the inadmissibility of hired labour, concerning confiscation of the landlords' stocks and cattle, etc., etc.? Without such detailed data a scientific study of the unusually valuable material contained in the peasant instructions is impossible. And we Marxists must take great pains to study scientifically all the facts upon which our policy is based.

For the lack of better material, the *Summary of Instructions* (our name for the "Sample"), unless it be proved incorrect as to facts, remains the only material of its kind, and, we repeat, must be in the possession of every member of our party.

The first part of the *Summary* is devoted to general political statements, to demands for political democracy; the second, to the land question. (Let us hope that the All-Russian Soviet of Peasant Deputies, or some one else, will make a summary of the peasant instructions and resolutions on the war question.) We shall not dwell for the present on the details of the first part, and shall mention only two points. In § 6 the election of all officials is demanded; in § 11, the abolition, upon the conclusion of the war, of the standing army.[57] These points bring the political programme of the peasants very close to the programme of the Bolshevik Party. Stressing these points, we must point out and demonstrate in all our propaganda and agitation that the leaders of the Socialist-Revolutionaries and the Mensheviks are traitors not only to Socialism, but also to democracy. In Cronstadt, for instance, contrary to the will of the people, contrary to the principles of democracy, they insisted, to the great satisfaction of the capitalists, that a commissar's position required government *confirmation*, *i.e.*, that it was not purely elective. In the Borough Councils of Petrograd, as well as in other institutions of local self-government, the leaders of the S.-R.'s and Mensheviks, contrary to democratic principles, are fighting against the Bolshevik demands for the immediate organisation of a workers' militia which should subsequently change into a national militia.

The agrarian demands of the peasantry, according to the *Summary*, consist first of all in the demand for the abolition, without compensation, of all kinds of private ownership of land, peasant ownership included; for the transfer of all scientifically cultivated estates to the state or to the communes; for the confiscation of all livestock and implements on the lands confiscated (poor peasants' goods are excluded) and their transfer to the state or to the communes; for the prohibition of hired labour; for the equal distribution of land among the toiling masses, with periodic redistributions, etc. As measures calculated to meet the exigencies of the transition period before the convocation of the Constituent Assembly, the peasants demand the *immediate* issuance of decrees prohibiting the purchase and sale of land, abrogating the laws dealing with withdrawals from communes, with small holdings, etc.; decrees concerning the conservation of forests, fisheries and other resources; decrees providing for the annulment of long-term leaseholds, the revision of short-term ones, etc.

Even a perfunctory examination of the above demands shows the utter impossibility of realising them in alliance with the capitalists.

There must be a complete break with them, a most resolute and pitiless struggle with the capitalist class, a final destruction of their power.

The self-deception of the Socialist-Revolutionaries and their deception of the peasantry consist in that they accept and spread the idea that these changes, that such changes are feasible without the abolition of capitalist domination, without the passing of power into the hands of the proletariat, without the poorest peasants supporting the most sweeping revolutionary measures of the proletarian state against the capitalists. It is this that makes the crystallising Left Wing of the "Socialist-Revolutionaries" so significant. It proves that there is a growing awareness of this self-deception within that party itself.

Indeed, the confiscation of all privately owned lands means the confiscation of hundreds of millions of capital belonging to banks where these lands are for the most part mortgaged. Is such a thing conceivable, unless the revolutionary class breaks the resistance of the capitalists by revolutionary means? We must bear in mind that we are dealing here with the most centralised form of capital, bank capital, which is tied up by billions of threads with all the most important centres of the capitalist economy of a huge country and which can be vanquished only by the not less centralised power of the city proletariat.

Further, the taking over by the government of the scientifically cultivated estates. Is it not obvious that the "state" which would be capable of taking over and really managing such lands for the benefit of the workers, and not for the benefit of officials and the capitalists, must needs be a proletarian revolutionary state?

The confiscation of stud farms, etc., and of all livestock and implements, is not merely a tremendous blow to private ownership of the means of production—it is a step towards Socialism. For the transfer of the *stock* into "exclusive use by the state or the commune" implies the necessity of large-scale Socialist agriculture, or, at least, Socialist control of combined small estates, Socialist regulation of their economy.

And the "prohibition" of hired labour? This is an empty phrase, an impotent, unconsciously naïve yearning of down-trodden petty proprietors, who do not realise that all capitalist industry would come to a standstill if there were not in the village a reserve army of hired labour, that it is impossible to "prohibit" hired labour in the country, and allow it in the city, that, as a matter of fact, the "prohibition" of hired labour is nothing other than a step towards Socialism.

Here we approach the basic question in the relation of the workers to the peasants.

Since the great strikes of 1896, it is more than twenty years that Russian labour *en masse* has joined the movement for Social-Democracy. Through this large interval of time, through two great revolutions, through the entire political history of Russia, runs the crimson thread of the following question: will the working class lead the peasant forward, towards Socialism, or will the liberal bourgeoisie drag him backward, to a reconciliation with capitalism?

The opportunist wing of the Social-Democracy reasons along the following very wise formula: *since* the Socialist-Revolutionaries are petty bourgeois, "we" therefore cast aside their philistine-utopian conception of Socialism *in the name* of a bourgeois negation of Socialism. Marxism is safely replaced by Struvism, while Menshevism tumbles down to the rôle of a lackey to the Cadets, trying to "reconcile" the peasant to bourgeois domination. Tsereteli and Skobelev, arm in arm with Chernov and Avksentyev, are busy signing reactionary decrees of Cadet landowners in the name of "revolutionary democracy"—this is the final and most obvious illustration of their rôle.

The revolutionary Social-Democracy, never abandoning its criticism of the petty-bourgeois illusions of the S.-R.'s, *never combining* with them unless it be *against* the Cadets, always strives to *tear away* the peasants from under Cadet influence, and opposes to the philistine-utopian conception of Socialism not a liberal reconciliation with capital, but a revolutionary-proletarian road to Socialism.

Now that the war has tremendously accelerated the pace of evolution, has sharpened to the utmost the crisis of capitalism, has forced the peoples to choose without delay either ruin, or immediate and determined steps towards Socialism—now the abyss separating semi-liberal Menshevism from revolutionary-proletarian Bolshevism strikes the eye as a practical question determining the action of tens of millions of peasants.

Accommodate yourselves to the reign of capitalism, *because* for Socialism "we" are not yet ripe—this is the piffle handed out to the peasants. Thus, by the way, do the Mensheviks substitute an abstract question of "Socialism" in general for the very concrete problem whether the wounds caused by the war can be healed without resolute strides towards Socialism.

Come to an agreement with capitalism, *because* the Socialist-Revolutionaries are petty-bourgeois Utopians—this is what the Mensheviks tell the peasants, hastening meanwhile to the support of the Cadet Government. . . .

And the S.-R.'s, beating their breasts, assure the peasants that they are opposed to any kind of peace with the capitalists, that they have never regarded the Russian Revolution as bourgeois; *that that is precisely why* they are entering a bloc with the opportunist Social-Democrats, and are going to support precisely the bourgeois government. . . . The S.-R.'s sign all kinds, even the most revolutionary programmes of the peasantry—only not to carry them out, only to file them away, to deceive the peasants with empty promises, and in fact busying themselves for months with agreements with the Cadets in the coalition cabinet.

This crying, practical, direct, and tangible betrayal of peasant interests by the S.-R.'s greatly changes the situation. We must take account of this change. We must not simply agitate in the old way against the S.-R.'s, just as we did in the years 1902-1903 and 1905-1907. We must not confine ourselves merely to theoretical confutations of petty-bourgeois illusions such as "the socialisation of land," "equalisation in the use of land," "prohibition of hired labour," etc.

We were then on the eve of a bourgeois revolution, or an incomplete bourgeois revolution, and our immediate task was to bring about the downfall of the monarchy.

The monarchy is now overthrown. The bourgeois revolution has reached its culmination in that Russia is now a democratic republic, with a government made up of Cadets, Mensheviks, and Socialist-Revolutionaries. But the war has in three years dragged us thirty years ahead, has established in Europe universal conscription of labour and forced trustification of enterprises, has reduced the most advanced countries to hunger and unprecedented ruin, and forced them to take steps towards Socialism.

Only the proletariat and the peasantry could overthrow the monarchy—that, in accordance with the times, was the fundamental statement of our class policy. And this position was correct. February and March, 1917, proved this again.

Only the proletariat, leading the poorest peasantry (semi-proletarians, as our programme calls them), can end the war with a democratic peace, can heal its wounds, can begin to make the absolutely necessary and *urgent* steps towards Socialism—this is the present statement of our class policy.

From this follows: the centre of gravity in our propaganda and agitation against the S.-R.'s must rest on the fact that the latter have betrayed the peasants. They represent not the indigent peasant masses, but a minority of opulent property owners. They lead the peasantry not to an alliance with the workers, but to an alliance with the capitalists, *i.e.*, to subjection. They have sold the interests of the toiling and exploited masses for berths in the Cabinet, for coalition with the Mensheviks and the Cadets.

History, accelerated by the war, has made such a stride forward that old formulas have become filled with a new content. "Prohibition of hired labour" was formerly *only* an empty phrase of the petty-bourgeois intellectual. Now, in life, it means something entirely different: in 242 instructions millions of poor peasants declare that they demand the abolition of hired labour, but do not know how to accomplish this. We do know how. We know that this can be achieved only in alliance with the workers, under their leadership, against the capitalists, but not by "conciliation" with the capitalists.

This is how we must change the basic line of our propaganda and agitation against the S.-R.'s, the basic line of our speeches to the peasants.

Comrade peasants, the Socialist-Revolutionary Party has betrayed you. It has betrayed the cottages and sides with the palaces; if not the palaces of the monarch, then the palaces where the Cadets—the worst enemies of the revolution, particularly the peasant revolution—preside in the same government with the Chernovs, the Peshekhonovs, the Avksentyevs.

Only the revolutionary proletariat, only its unifying vanguard, the Bolshevik Party, can *really* carry out the programme advanced by the poor peasants in their 242 instructions. For the revolutionary proletariat is *actually* advancing towards the abolition of hired labour along the only correct road—the overthrow of capitalism, and not by forbidding the hiring of a labourer, not by prohibiting hired labour. The revolutionary proletariat is actually marching towards the confiscation of lands, of stock, of technical agricultural enterprises, towards everything that the peasants want, and that the S.-R.'s *cannot* give them.

This is how we must change the line of the speeches of workers to peasants. We workers can and will give you what the poorest peasants want and seek, not always knowing where and how to seek it. We workers defend our own interests, as well as the interests of the overwhelming majority of the peasantry, *against the capitalists*, while the S.-R.'s, allied with the capitalists, betray those interests.

Let us remind the reader what Engels said with regard to the peasant question, shortly before his death. Engels emphasised that the Socialists do not even dream of expropriating the small peasants, that only *by force of example* will the peasants be made to realise the advantage of socialistic mechanisation of agriculture.[58]

The war has now put before Russia a practical question precisely of this kind. There is little stock. It must be confiscated, but the highly cultivated estates must be kept intact, they must not be "divided."

The peasants have begun to understand this. Need forced them to understand. The war forced them to, for stock is nowhere to be gotten. What we have must be saved. Large-scale economy means the saving of labour on stock, as well as on many other items.

The peasants want to retain their small holdings, to keep them within certain norms, periodically to equalise them. . . . Let them. No intelligent Socialist would quarrel with them on this point. If the land is confiscated, it *means* that the rule of the banks will be undermined; if the stock is confiscated, it *means* that the rule of capital is undermined, and *under the rule of the proletariat in the centre* and with the transfer of political power to the proletariat, the rest will get along *by itself*, will come as a result of the "force of example," will be prompted by experience itself.

The transfer of political power to the proletariat—that is the crux of the matter. After that, everything essential, basic, and important in the 242 instructions *will be possible of realisation*. Life will show what modifications will be necessary. This is the last thing to worry about. We are not doctrinaires. Our philosophy is not a dogma, but a guide to action.

We do not claim that Marx or the Marxists know the road to Socialism in all its completeness. That is nonsense. We know the direction of this road, we know what class forces lead along it, but concretely and practically it will be learned from the *experience of the millions* when they take up the task.

Trust the workers, comrade peasants, break the alliance with the capitalists! Only in close unity with the workers can you begin to realise the programme of the 242 instructions. In alliance with the capitalists, under the direction of the S.-R.'s, you will never see even one determined irretrievable step in the spirit of this programme.

But when in union with the city workers, in a merciless struggle against capital, you *begin* to realise the programme of the 242 instructions, then the whole world will come to your aid and ours; then the success of this programme—not as it is now formulated, but in its real essence—will be assured. Then will come an end to the domination of capital and to wage slavery. Then will begin the reign of Socialism, the reign of peace, the reign of the toilers.

N. LENIN.

Rabochy, No. 6, September 11, 1917.

ON SLANDERERS

In the *Ryech* for September 2, and also in the *Russkaya Volya*, a paper founded with notoriously shady money and which recommends to the voters, if they are "socialistically inclined," to vote for the *Yedinstvo* and for the People's Socialists, there have again been published slanderous declarations against me.[59]

This information was furnished, according to both papers, "by the War Ministry," the *Ryech even asserting* that it was based on "documentary evidence and numerous depositions of individual persons."

The law on libel in the press has practically been suspended in Russia. The slanderers, especially in the bourgeois press, have obtained complete freedom: they can come out in the press anonymously, they can lie and slander to their heart's content, they can hide behind alleged official information not signed by any official person—they can get away with anything! The filthy slanderers, headed by Messrs. Milyukovs, enjoy the privilege of immunity.

The slanderers assert that I had certain connections with the Union for the Liberation of the Ukraine. Milyukov's paper writes: "The German government instructed Lenin to agitate for peace." "In Berlin," it says, "there were two gatherings of Socialists in which Lenin and Yoltukhovsky participated." The *Russkaya Volya* adds to the latter phrase: "Lenin stopped at Yoltukhovsky's."

Since Mr. Milyukov and similar scoundrels, knights of filthy slander, have been granted immunity, only one thing remains for me: to repeat once more that this is slander, once more to confront the blackmailing heroes who talk about witnesses' depositions, with at least one witness known to the masses.

One of those active in the Union for the Liberation of the Ukraine, a man by the name of Basok, has been known to me since 1906 when, as a Menshevik, he participated together with me in the Stockholm Congress. In the autumn of 1914, or early in 1915, when I was living in Berne, I was visited at my home by the well-known Caucasian Menshevik, Tria, who had come from Constantinople. Tria told me of Basok's participation in the Union for the Liberation of the Ukraine, and of the connection between this Union and the German government. Tria also handed me a letter from Basok in which he expressed sympathy with me and a hope that our views would become closer. I was so indignant that immediately, in the presence of Tria, I wrote an answer to Basok * and gave that letter to Tria to give to him, since Tria was about to go back to Constantinople.

In the letter to Basok I declared that since he was entering into relations with one of the imperialists, our roads parted decisively and we had nothing in common.

These are all the "relations" I have ever had with the Union for the Liberation of the Ukraine.

N. LENIN.

Rabochy, No. 8, September 12, 1917.

* See V. I. Lenin, *The Imperialist War, Collected Works*, Vol. XVIII, p. 111.—*Ed.*

TO THE CENTRAL COMMITTEE OF THE RUSSIAN SOCIAL-DEMOCRATIC LABOUR PARTY [60]

It is possible that these lines will come too late, for events are developing with a rapidity that is sometimes absolutely giddy. I am writing this on Wednesday, September 12, and the recipients will read it not earlier than Friday, September 15. But in any case, on a chance, I consider it my duty to write the following:

Kornilov's revolt is an extremely unexpected (unexpected at such a moment and in such a form) and a downright unbelievably sharp turn in the course of events.[61]

Like every sharp turn, it calls for a revision and change of tactics. And, as is the case with every revision, one must be extremely cautious lest one lose sight of principles.

It is my conviction that those who (like Volodarsky) roll down to defensism or (like other Bolsheviks) to a *bloc* with the S.-R.'s, to *supporting* the Provisional Government, are unprincipled. This is absolutely incorrect, this is unprincipled. We shall become defensists *only after* the passing of power to the proletariat, *after* peace has been offered, *after* the secret treaties and connections with banks have been severed, but *only after*. Neither the fall of Riga, *nor the fall of Petrograd* will make us defensists (I would like very much to have this read by Volodarsky). Until then we stand for a proletarian revolution, we are against the war, we are *not* defensists.

And *even now* we must not support Kerensky's government. This is unprincipled. One may ask: must we not fight against Kornilov? Of course we must! But this is not the same thing; there is a dividing line here; it is being stepped over by some Bolsheviks who fall into "conciliation," who allow themselves to be *carried away* by the flow of events.

We will fight, we are fighting against Kornilov, even *as Kerensky's troops do*, but we do not support Kerensky. *On the contrary*, we expose his weakness. There is the difference. It is rather a subtle difference, but it is highly essential and one must not forget it.

Wherein, then, consists the change of our tactics after Kornilov's revolt?

In that we are changing the *form* of our struggle against Kerensky. Without in the least relaxing our hostility towards him, without taking back a single word said against him, without renouncing the task of overthrowing Kerensky, we say: we must *take into account* the present moment; we shall not overthrow Kerensky right now; we shall approach the task of struggling against him *in a different way*, namely, we shall point out to the people (which struggles against Kornilov) the *weakness* and *vacillation* of Kerensky. That has been done even before. Now, however, it has become the main thing. Therein lies the change.

The change, further, consists in this, that the main thing is now to intensify our propaganda in favour of some kind of "partial demands" to be presented to Kerensky, demands saying: arrest Milyukov; arm the Petrograd workers; summon the Cronstadt, Vyborg and Helsingfors troops to Petrograd; disperse the State Duma; [62] arrest Rodzyanko; legalise the transfer of the landowners' lands to the peasants; introduce workers' control over bread and factories, etc., etc. With these demands we must address ourselves not only to Kerensky, *not so much* to Kerensky, as to the workers, soldiers and peasants who have been *carried away* by the course of the struggle against Kornilov. Keep up their enthusiasm; encourage them to beat up the generals and officers who express themselves in favour of Kornilov; urge *them* to demand the immediate transfer of the land to the peasants; give *them* the idea of the necessity of arresting Rodzyanko and Milyukov, dispersing the State Duma, shutting down the *Ryech* and other bourgeois papers, and instituting investigations against them. The "Left" S.-R.'s must be especially pushed on in this direction.

It would be erroneous to think that we have moved *away* from the task of the proletariat conquering power. No. We have come tremendously nearer to it, though not directly, but from one side. *This very minute* we must conduct propaganda not so much directly against Kerensky, as *indirectly* against the same man, that is, by demanding an active and most energetic, really revolutionary war against Kornilov. The developments of this war alone can lead *us* to power, and we must *speak* of this as little as possible in our propaganda (remembering very well that even tomorrow events may put power into our hands, and then we shall not relinquish it). It seems to me that this should have been transmitted to the propagandists in a letter (not in the press); it should have been transmitted to propagandist groups, to the members of the party in general. As to phrases about the defence of the country, about a united front of revolutionary democracy, about supporting the Provisional Government, etc., we must fight against them mercilessly, since they are *phrases*. What we must say is that now is the time for *action;* you, Messrs. S.-R.'s and Mensheviks, have long since worn these phrases threadbare. Now is the time for *action;* the war against Kornilov must be conducted in a revolutionary way by drawing in the masses, by arousing them, by inflaming them (as to Kerensky, he is *afraid* of the masses, he is *afraid* of the people). In the war against the Germans *action* is required right now; *immediate and unconditional peace must be offered on definite terms.* If we do this we *can* attain either a speedy peace or a transformation of the war into a revolutionary one; otherwise all the Mensheviks and Socialist-Revolutionaries remain lackeys of imperialism.

P. S. Having read six copies of the *Rabochy after* this was written, I must say that there is perfect harmony in our views. I greet with all my heart the splendid editorials, press reviews and articles by V. M——n and Vol——y. As to Volodarsky's speech, I have read his letter to the editors, which "liquidates" my reproaches as well. Once more, best greetings and wishes!

LENIN.

Written September 12, 1917.
First published in *Pravda*, No. 250, November 7, 1920.

FROM A PUBLICIST'S DIARY

1. The Root of the Evil

EVERYBODY will probably agree that the writer N. Sukhanov of the *Novaya Zhizn* is not the worst but one of the best representatives of the petty-bourgeois democracy. He has a sincere leaning towards internationalism, which he proved in the most difficult times when tsarist reaction and chauvinism held sway. He has knowledge and a desire to find his way independently in serious problems, which he has proven by his long evolution from Socialist-Revolutionism towards revolutionary Marxism.

The more characteristic it is that even such persons, speaking about the fundamental questions of the revolution, speaking in the most responsible moments of the revolution, can treat their readers to such flimsy arguments as the following:

> . . . No matter how many revolutionary gains we have lost in the last weeks, one, and perhaps the most important of all, remains in full force: the government and its policies can be maintained only with the will of the Soviet majority. All the influence of revolutionary democracy has been given up by it voluntarily; the democratic organs can still restore it very easily; with the proper understanding of the demands of the moment, they could still, without difficulty, direct the policies of the Provisional Government into the proper channel. (*Novaya Zhizn*, No. 106, September 2.) [63]

In these words we find a most flippant, most monstrous untruth concerning the most important question of the revolution, an untruth which was most often spread in the various countries in the petty-bourgeois democracy and which has, more than anything else, ruined revolutions.

When you examine closely the sum total of petty-bourgeois illusions contained in the above reasoning, you are compelled to think almost against your will that it is not an accident that the citizens of the *Novaya Zhizn* sit at the "unity" congress [64] together with the Ministers, with the ministerial Socialists, with the Tseretelis and Skobelevs, with the members of the cabinet who are the comrades of Kerensky, Kornilov and Co. Not an accident at all. They have in reality one common ideological foundation: a foolish trustfulness taken over from the inert petty-bourgeois environment, a philistine belief in good intentions. Such confidence permeates all of Sukhanov's reasoning as well as the activities of those defensist Mensheviks who act sincerely. This petty-bourgeois trustfulness is the root of the evil in our revolution.

Sukhanov no doubt would unhesitatingly subscribe to what Marxism demands of serious politics, namely, that it be based, that it be built on *facts* capable of exact objective testing. From the viewpoint of this demand let us examine Sukhanov's assertion contained in the above quotation.

What facts lie at the basis of this assertion? How could Sukhanov prove that the government "can be maintained only with the will" of the Soviets, that the latter could "very easily" "restore their influence," that they could "without difficulty" change the policies of the Provisional Government?

Sukhanov could refer, first, to his general impression, to the "obvious" strength of the Soviets, to Kerensky's appearing before the Soviets, to the friendly words of one or the other Minister, etc. This would certainly be poor proof—rather an admission of the absolute absence of proof, of objective facts.

Sukhanov could refer, secondly, to the objective fact that an enormous majority of the resolutions of workers, soldiers and peasants determinedly express themselves for the Soviets and in favour of supporting them. These resolutions, he might say, prove the will of the majority of the people.

This kind of reasoning is as common in philistine circles as the first kind. It is, however, entirely untenable.

In all revolutions, the will of the majority of the workers and peasants, *i.e.*, undoubtedly the will of the majority of the population, has been for democracy. Nevertheless, the large majority of revolutions ended with the defeat of democracy.

Proceeding from the experience of the majority of revolutions, particularly that of 1848 (which resembles our present revolution most), Marx mercilessly ridiculed the petty-bourgeois democrats who wished to gain victories through resolutions and references to the will of the majority of the people.

Our own experience proves this still more clearly. In the spring of 1906, most of the resolutions of the workers and peasants were undoubtedly in favour of the First Duma. A majority of the people undoubtedly were for it. However, the Tsar succeeded in dispersing it because the rise of the revolutionary classes (workers' strikes and peasant revolts in the spring of 1906) proved too weak for a new revolution.

Think of the experience of the present revolution. Both in March-April and in July-August, 1917, the majority of the resolutions were for the Soviets, the majority of the people were for the Soviets. Still, everybody sees, knows and feels that in March-April the revolution was moving forward, whereas in July-August it is moving backwards. Consequently, reference to the majority of the people decides nothing, as far as the concrete questions of a revolution are concerned.

This reference to resolutions as proof is in itself an example of petty-bourgeois illusions; it shows unwillingness to admit that, in a revolution, the enemy classes must be *vanquished*, the state power that defends them must be *overthrown*, and that the "will of the majority of the people" is not sufficient to bring this about. What is needed is the *strength* of the revolutionary classes that can and will fight, strength which, at the decisive moment and place, will *crush* the enemy's strength.

How often has it happened during revolutions that the small but well-organised army and the centralised strength of the ruling classes, the landowners and the bourgeoisie, piecemeal have suppressed the strength of the "majority of the people" which was badly organised, badly armed and scattered.

To refer "generally" to the "will of the people" instead of the class struggle at a moment when the struggle has been particularly sharpened by the revolution, is worthy only of the most stupid petty bourgeois.

Thirdly, Sukhanov advances in the above reasoning another "argument" also very common in philistine circles. He refers to the fact that "all the influence of revolutionary democracy has been given up by it voluntarily." Hence he seems to conclude that what was given up "voluntarily" can be easily taken back.

Bad reasoning, indeed. First of all, the return of what was voluntarily ceded presupposes the "voluntary consent" of the beneficiary of the concession. It follows that such voluntary agreement is at hand. Who has received the *"concession"?* Who has utilised the "influence" given up by "revolutionary democracy"?

It is highly characteristic that this question, fundamental to all but a headless politician, was entirely evaded by Sukhanov. . . . Still, this is the core, this is the essence of the question: in whose hands is, *in practice*, that which "revolutionary" (excuse me for the expression) "democracy" has "voluntarily given up"?

Sukhanov evades this substance of the question, as do all the Mensheviks and Socialist-Revolutionaries, all the petty-bourgeois democrats in general.

Further. It may be that, in the nursery, a "voluntary concession" indicates the easiness of taking the thing back: if Katya has voluntarily let Masha have her ball, it is conceivably "perfectly easy" to "take it back." But not many outside of Russian intellectuals would venture to apply such conceptions to politics, to the class struggle.

In politics a voluntary cession of "influence" proves such impotence in the ceding element, such flabbiness, such lack of character, such meekness, that, generally speaking, only one thing can be "concluded": he who gives up something voluntarily is "worthy" of being deprived not only of his influence but also of his right to exist. In other words, the fact of voluntarily giving up influence "proves" *per se* only this, that the beneficiary of this voluntarily ceded influence will inevitably deprive the owner even of his rights.

If "revolutionary democracy" has voluntarily given up its influence, this means that it was not a revolutionary but a vile, philistine, cowardly democracy not above servility, that after such cession its enemies can either disperse it or simply reduce it to nothing, allowing it to die just as "voluntarily" as it "voluntarily" gave up its influence.

To regard the action of political parties as a *caprice* means to renounce every *study* of politics. Such action as the "voluntary giving up of influence" by two large parties which, according to all information, reports, and objective election data, represent the majority of the people, such action must be *explained*. It cannot be accidental. It must be connected with the present economic situation of some large class of the people. It must be linked up with the history of the development of those parties.

Sukhanov's reasoning is remarkably typical of thousands upon thousands of similar petty-bourgeois arguments because, in substance, it is based on the conception of good will ("voluntarily"), ignoring the *history* of the parties under consideration. Sukhanov has simply eliminated history from his consideration, forgetting that voluntary cession of power began in fact after March 13 when the Soviet expressed confidence in Kerensky and approved of the "argument" with the Provisional Government. May 19 was again a direct cession of influence on a gigantic scale. Taken as a whole, we have before us clear and obvious phenomenon: the S.-R. and Menshevik Parties from the very beginning placed themselves on an inclined plane and began to roll down with ever greater velocity. After July 16-18, they sank into the pit completely.

To say at present that the influence was given up voluntarily, that it is "very easy" to make great political parties about-face, that it is possible "without difficulty" to induce them to take a direction opposite to that followed by them for many years (and for many months during the revolution), to crawl out of the pit "very easily" and to reach the top over the inclined plane—is this not the height of folly?

Fourthly and lastly, Sukhanov could in defence of his opinion refer to the fact that the workers and soldiers who express confidence in the Soviet are armed and therefore could "very easily" take back their influence. It is on this most important point, however, that the philistine reasonings reproduced by the writer of the *Novaya Zhizn* are most faulty.

To be as concrete as possible, let us compare May 3-4 with July 16-18.

On May 3 the indignation of the masses against the government bursts forth. An armed regiment goes into the streets of Petrograd, intending to arrest the government. No arrest takes place. The government, however, sees clearly that it has nobody to rely on. The army is not for it. *Such* a government is "very easily" overthrown, to be sure, so the government confronts the Soviet with an ultimatum: either you support me, or I leave.

On July 17, a similar outburst of mass indignation, an outburst which all the parties tried to restrain, but which broke out in spite of *all* restraining influence. As on May 3, we have an armed antigovernment demonstration. There is, however, an enormous difference, namely, the S.-R. and Menshevik leaders, confused and detached from the people, *as early as July 16* agree with the bourgeoisie to call to Petrograd Kaledin's troops. This is the crux of the issue!

With a soldier's frankness, Kaledin stated this at the Moscow Conference: "You, Socialist Ministers," he said, "called us to aid you on July 16. . . ." Nobody dared refute Kaledin at the Moscow Conference, because he spoke the truth. Kaledin mocked the

Mensheviks and S.-R.'s, who were compelled to keep silent. The Cossack general spat in their faces, and they wiped themselves off, saying: "Divine dew!" [65]

The bourgeois papers reported these words of Kaledin, whereas the Menshevik *Rabochaya Gazeta* and the S.-R. *Dyelo Naroda* suppressed this highly important political declaration made at the Moscow Conference.

It came about that for the first time the government had expressly resorted to Kaledin's troops, whereas the determined, really revolutionary troops and the workers were disarmed. Here is the fundamental fact which Sukhanov has "very easily" evaded and forgotten, but which remains a fact. It is a decisive fact characterising this phase of the revolution, the *first* revolution.

Power at a decisive place at the front, then in the army, has passed into the hands of the *Kaledins*. This is a fact. The most active of the troops hostile to them have been disarmed. That the Kaledins do not utilise their power immediately to establish full dictatorship, does not at all disprove that the power is theirs. Was not the Tsar in possession of power after December, 1905? And did not circumstances compel him to use his power so cautiously that he called two Dumas before he took possession of *full power,* i.e., before he made a *coup d'état?*

Power is to be judged not by words, but by deeds. The deeds of the government since July 18 prove that power is in the hands of the Kaledins who slowly but *relentlessly* move ahead, receiving every day "concessions" large and small. Today, immunity for the Cadets who raid the *Pravda,* who kill the Pravdists, who make arbitrary arrests; tomorrow, a law on suppressing newspapers and a law dispersing gatherings and conferences, exiling citizens abroad without trial; a law imposing jail sentences for insulting "friendly ambassadors"; a law punishing attempts against the government, with hard labour; a law introducing capital punishment at the front, and so on *and so forth.*

The Kaledins are no fools. Why necessarily go full speed, lumber ahead with all might, risking defeat, when they receive bit by bit, every day, the things they need? While this is going on, the foolish Skobelevs and Tseretelis, Chernovs and Avksentyevs, Dans and Libers shout: "Triumph of democracy! Victory!" At every forward step of the Kaledins they discern "victory" in the fact that the Kaledins, Kornilovs and Kerenskys do not swallow them at once.

The root of the evil is that the petty-bourgeois mass, by virtue of its very economic situation, is prepared for astonishing gullibility and lack of enlightenment, that it is still half-asleep, and in its sleep it mumbles, "It is 'very easy' to take back the things given up voluntarily!" Try and get the Kaledins and Kornilovs to give back things voluntarily!

The root of the evil is that "democratic" journalism supports this somnolent, petty-bourgeois, stupid, slavish illusion, instead of fighting against it.

If we look at things the way an historian of politics in general and a Marxist in particular ought to look at them, *i.e.*, examining events in this connection, it becomes perfectly clear that a decisive turn is at present not only not "easy," but, on the contrary, absolutely impossible *without a new revolution.*

I do not touch here upon the question of whether such a revolution is desirable; I do not dwell on the question of whether it can take place peacefully and lawfully (generally speaking, there have been examples of peaceful and lawful revolutions in history); I only state here the historic impossibility of a decisive turn without a new revolution. For power is *already* in other hands; it is already not in the hands of "revolutionary democracy"; power has *already* been seized and consolidated. As to the conduct of the S.-R. and Menshevik Parties, it is not accidental; it is a product of the economic situation of the petty bourgeoisie and the result of a long chain of political events from March 13 to May 19, from May 19 to June 22, from June 22 to July 1 and 2 (offensive), etc. A change is needed in the allocation of power, in its whole composition, in all the conditions of activity of the major parties, in the "sentiment" of the class which sustains them. Such changes are historically unthinkable *without a new revolution.*

Instead of explaining to the people all the main historic conditions of the new revolution, its economic and political postulates, its political aims, the interrelation of classes that corresponds to it, etc., Sukhanov and a host of petty-bourgeois democrats *put the people to sleep* by playing gewgaws, by talking about resigning, by asserting that "we shall get back everything without difficulty," "very easily," that the "most important" revolutionary conquests "remain in force" and similar shallow, ignorant, downright criminal nonsense.

Signs of a deep-going social change are apparent. They clearly indicate the direction of work to be done. The influence of the S.-R.'s and Mensheviks is obviously waning among the proletariat, the influence of the Bolsheviks is obviously growing. Among others, even the elections of September 2, compared with the July elections, showed an *increase* in the Bolshevik representation to the Borough Councils of Petrograd; this notwithstanding the bringing of "Kaledin troops to Petrograd!" [66]

Among the petty-bourgeois democracy, which cannot help vacillating between the bourgeoisie and the proletariat, the change is objectively indicated by the strengthening, consolidation and development of revolutionary internationalist tendencies: Martov and others among the Mensheviks, Spiridonova, Kamkov and others among the S.-R.'s. Needless to say, the approaching famine, economic ruin, military defeat, are capable of extraordinarily hastening this turn towards the transition of power to the proletariat supported by the poorest peasantry.

2. Serfdom and Socialism

The most irate opponents of Socialism sometimes do it a service by the unreasonable zeal of their "revelations." They assail the very things that deserve sympathy and emulation. They open the eyes of the people to the meanness of the bourgeoisie by the very nature of their attacks.

Just this happened in the case of one of the meanest bourgeois papers, the *Russkaya Volya*, which, in its issue of September 2, published a correspondence from Ekaterinburg under the title, "Serfdom." This is what we read in that correspondence:

... The Soviet of Workers' and Soldiers' Deputies has introduced in our city, for the citizens who own horses, a service in kind, consisting in every one's placing his horses in turn at the disposal of the Soviet members traveling on official business.

A special schedule of service has been elaborated and every "horse-owning citizen" receives accurate written instructions as to when and where and at what precise hour he must appear with his horse to do duty.

To make it more impressive, the "order" adds: "In case of non-fulfilment of this demand, the Soviet will hire cabmen at your expense to the amount of 25 rubles. ..."

The defender of the capitalists is, of course, indignant. The capitalists look on with perfect equanimity when an overwhelming majority of the people pine away in want all their lives, not only "in serfdom," but right in the prison of factory, mine and other wage labour, often without work and starving. This the capitalists look upon quite calmly.

But here the workers and soldiers have introduced one little social duty for the capitalists, and the exploiters raise a howl, "serfdom"!!

Ask any worker, any peasant, whether it would be bad if the Soviets of Workers' and Soldiers' Deputies were the only power in the state and introduced everywhere social duty for the rich, for instance, compulsory duty with horses, automobiles, bicycles, compulsory daily clerical work to keep a record of products, of the needy people, etc., etc.

Every worker and every peasant, except perhaps the kulak,* will say that it would be good.

And this is true. It is not Socialism as yet, it is only one of the first steps towards Socialism, but it is just the thing urgently and immediately necessary for the poor people. Without such measures, the people cannot be saved from hunger and ruin.

Why, then, does the Ekaterinburg Soviet remain a rare exception? Why have similar measures not been adopted all over Russia long since? Why is not a whole system of measures of this kind developed?

Why, after the establishment of social duty for the rich in the matter of making horses available, is a similar social duty for the rich not introduced to make available full accounts of their financial operations, especially as to their contracts with the government, under a similar control of the Soviets, with similar "accurate written instructions" as to when and where the accounts should be presented, when and where and what amount of taxes should be paid?

Because at the head of an overwhelming majority of the Soviets are S.-R. ("Socialist-Revolutionary") and Menshevik leaders who have really gone over to the side of the bourgeoisie, have entered the bourgeois cabinet, have promised to support it, thus betraying not only Socialism but democracy. Those leaders are practicing "understandings" with the bourgeoisie which not only hinder, in Petrograd, for instance, the imposition of social duty on the rich, but for months have been holding up much more moderate reforms.

* From the word *fist*—rich peasant, village shark and exploiter of poor peasants.—*Ed.*

Those leaders deceive their own conscience and deceive the people by saying that "Russia is not ripe yet for the introduction of Socialism."

Why should such assertions be recognised as deceptions?

Because through such assertions the situation is falsely depicted in such a light as if it were a question of extremely complicated and difficult transformations which must break up the normal life of millions of people. The situation is falsely pictured as if somebody wished to "introduce" Socialism in Russia by one ukase, with no attention either to the existing technical level, or to the abundance of small enterprises, or to the habits and the wishes of the majority of the population.

All this is a fabric of lies. Nobody ever proposed anything of the kind. No party, no single individual was about to "introduce Socialism" by ukase. What we have been and are concerned with, are measures which, like the social duty established for the rich in Ekaterinburg, meet with the full approval of the mass of the poor, *i.e.*, of the majority of the population, measures that have perfectly matured, both technically and culturally, that give immediate relief to the poor and permit the mitigation of the burdens of the war and their more equitable distribution.

Almost half a year of revolution has passed, and the S.-R. and Menshevik leaders still obstruct all such measures, thus betraying the interests of the people in the interests of "understandings" with the bourgeoisie.

Until the workers and the peasants realise that those leaders are traitors, that they must be driven out, removed from their posts, the toilers will inevitably remain enslaved by the bourgeoisie.

N. LENIN.

Rabochy, No. 10, September 14, 1917.

ON THE ZIMMERWALD QUESTION [67]

It is now particularly clear that it was a mistake *not* to leave it.

Everybody is being deceived by hope in Stockholm. In the meantime, the Stockholm Conference is being "postponed" month after month.

And Zimmerwald is *"waiting"* for Stockholm! The Kautskyists, the Italians, *i.e.*, the Zimmerwald majority, are "waiting" for Stockholm.

And we are participating in this comedy, bearing the *responsibility* for it before the workers.

This is a shame.

We must leave Zimmerwald *immediately*.

In remaining there for information only, we lose nothing, and are *not responsible* for the comedy of "waiting" for Stockholm.

When we leave rotten Zimmerwald, we must decide immediately, at the plenary session of September 16, 1917, *to call a conference of the Lefts*, the Stockholm representatives to be entrusted with the task.

For what happened is this, that having committed a folly, having remained in Zimmerwald, our party, the only party of internationalists in the world having as many as seventeen papers, etc., *plays the game of conciliation* with the German and Italian Martovs and Tseretelis, just as Martov conciliates Tsereteli, just as Tsereteli conciliates the Socialist-Revolutionaries, and just as the Socialist-Revolutionaries conciliate the bourgeoisie. . . .

And this is called "being in favour" of the Third International!!!

Written in the first half of September, 1917.
First published in the *Lenin Collection*, VII, 1928.

ON VIOLATION OF DEMOCRACY IN MASS ORGANIZATIONS

It is necessary to pass a resolution which brands as a fraud * worthy of Nicholas II, such practices as those of the Soviet of *Soldiers'* Deputies (one representative to 500 soldiers, while the workers have one representative to 1,000) or the Bureau of the trade unions (where the small unions have one representative to *a* members, whereas the large ones have one representative to *a-b* members).

If we tolerate such a fraud, what kind of *democrats* are we?

What is wrong then with Nicholas II, who also gave *unequal* representation to the peasants and the landowners??

If we tolerate such things we are prostituting democracy.

A resolution must be passed demanding *equal* suffrage (both in the Soviets and in the congresses of the trade unions), branding the *least* deviation from equality as a *fraud*, in just these words, as *a method of Nicholas II,* and this resolution of the plenum of the Central Committee, written in popular language, must be spread in leaflet form among the working masses.

You cannot tolerate a *fraud* in democracy if you call yourselves "democrats." We are not democrats, we are unprincipled people if we tolerate this!!

Written in the first half of September, 1917.
First published in the *Lenin Collection*, VII, 1928.

* "One representative, always and everywhere, to an *equal* number of electors" is the A B C of democracy. Anything else is a *fraud*.

ON COMPROMISES

Compromise in politics consists in a ceding of some demands, a renouncing of a part of one's demands in consequence of an agreement with another party.

The usual idea the man in the street has about the Bolsheviks, an idea supported by the press calumniating the Bolsheviks, is that the Bolsheviks will not agree to a compromise with any one, at any time.

Such an idea is flattering to us as a party of the revolutionary proletariat, for it proves that even enemies are compelled to recognise our loyalty to the fundamental principles of Socialism and revolution; still, we have to tell the truth: such an idea does not correspond to the facts. Engels was right when in his Critique of the Manifesto of the Blanquists-Communists (1873) he ridiculed their declaration, "No compromises!" [68] This, he said, was a mere phrase, for compromises are often unavoidably forced by circumstances upon a fighting party, and it is absurd once and for all to refuse to "take payments of a debt in instalments." The task of a truly revolutionary party is not to declare the impossible renunciation of all compromises, but to be able *through all compromises*, as far as they are unavoidable, to remain true to its principles, to its class, to its revolutionary task, to its cause of preparing the revolution and educating the masses of the people for victory in the revolution.

For instance, to agree to participate in the Third and Fourth Duma was a compromise, a temporary renunciation of revolutionary demands. But this was a compromise absolutely forced upon us, for the interrelation of forces excluded for us, for a given time, mass revolutionary struggle, and in order to prepare it during a long stretch of time one *had* to be able to work even inside such a "pigsty." That this formulation of the question by the Bolsheviks as a party turned out absolutely correct, is proven by history.

The question now is not of forced, but voluntary compromise.

Our party, like every other political party, strives after political domination *for itself*. Our task is the dictatorship of the revolutionary proletariat. Half a year of revolution has proven, with unusual vividness, force and persuasiveness, the correctness and inevitability of such a demand in the interests of *this particular* revolution, for otherwise the people can obtain neither a democratic peace, nor land for the peasantry, nor full freedom (an absolutely democratic republic). The course of events during half a year of our revolution, the struggle of the classes and parties, the development of the crises of May 3-4, June 22-23, July 1-2, July 16-18, and September 9-13, have manifested and proven this.

There has now arrived such a sharp and original turn in the Russian Revolution that we, as a party, can offer a voluntary compromise—true, not to the bourgeoisie, our direct and main class enemy, but to our nearest adversaries, the "ruling" petty-bourgeois democratic parties, the Socialist-Revolutionaries and Mensheviks.

Only as an exception, only by virtue of a special situation, which obviously will last only a very short time, can we offer a compromise to these parties, and, it seems to me, we must do so.

The compromise on our part is our return to the pre-July demand of all power to the Soviets, a government of S.-R.'s and Mensheviks responsible to the Soviets.

Now, and only now, perhaps *only for a few days* or for a week or two, such a government could be created and established in a perfectly peaceful way. In all probability it could secure a peaceful *forward* march of the whole Russian Revolution, and unusually good chances for big strides forward by the world movement towards peace and towards the victory of Socialism.

Only for the sake of this peaceful development of the revolution— a possibility that is *extremely* rare in history and *extremely* valuable, a possibility to be found only in exceptional cases—can and must the Bolsheviks, partisans of a world revolution, partisans of revolutionary methods, agree to such a compromise, in my opinion.

The compromise would consist in this: that the Bolsheviks, without claiming participation in the government (which is impossible for an internationalist without an actual realisation of the conditions of a dictatorship of the proletariat and the poorest peasantry), would refrain from immediately advancing the demand for the passing of power to the proletariat and the poorest peasants, from revolutionary methods of struggle for the realisation of this demand. The condition which is self-evident and not new to the S.-R.'s and Mensheviks would be full freedom of propaganda and the convocation of the Constitutent Assembly without any new procrastination or perhaps even convocation at an earlier date.

The Mensheviks and S.-R.'s, as the governmental bloc, would then agree (assuming that the compromise has been reached) to form a government solely and exclusively responsible to the Soviets, under the condition of giving over all power to the Soviets also locally. This would constitute the "new" condition. No other condition would, I think, be advanced by the Bolsheviks, who would be confident that really full freedom of propaganda and the immediate realisation of a new democracy in the composition of the Soviets (new elections to them) and in their functioning would in themselves secure a peaceful forward movement of the revolution, a *peaceful outcome* of the party strife within the Soviets.

Perhaps this is *already* impossible? Perhaps. But if there is even one chance in a hundred, the attempt at realising such a possibility would still be worth while.

What would both "contracting" parties gain by this "compromise," *i.e.*, the Bolsheviks on the one hand, and the bloc of S.-R.'s and Mensheviks on the other? If *both* sides gain nothing, then the compromise must be recognised as impossible, and there is nothing to say about it. No matter how difficult that compromise may be at present (after July and August, two months equal to two decades of "peaceful," somnolent times), it seems to me there is a small chance of its being realised, and this chance has been created by the decision of the S.-R.'s and Mensheviks not to participate in a government jointly with the Cadets.

The Bolsheviks would gain the possibility of freely propagating their views and of trying to gain influence in the Soviets under conditions of really full democracy. In words, "everybody" now recognises this freedom for the Bolsheviks. In reality it is *impossible* under a bourgeois government or under a government in which the bourgeoisie participates, under any government other than that of the Soviets. Under a Soviet government such freedom would be *possible* (we do not say it would really be secured, still it would be possible). For the sake of such a possibility at such a difficult time, it would be worth while to enter into a compromise with the Soviet majority of today. *We* have nothing to fear under a real democracy, for the realities of life are with us, and even the course of development of currents within the S.-R. and Menshevik Parties that are hostile to us, confirms the correctness of our stand.

The Mensheviks and S.-R.'s would gain in that they would at once obtain full possibility of realising the programme of *their* bloc, while basing themselves on the admitted overwhelming majority of the people and having secured for themselves the "peaceful" use of their majority in the Soviets.

Of course, from this bloc, which is heterogeneous both because it is a bloc and because petty-bourgeois democracy is *always* less homogeneous than the bourgeoisie and the proletariat, two voices would probably make themselves heard.

One voice would say: "We cannot travel along the same road with the Bolsheviks, with the revolutionary proletariat. It will make excessive demands anyway and it will entice the poor peasantry by demagogy. It will demand peace and a rupture with the Allies. This is impossible. We feel closer to and more secure with the bourgeoisie; we have not parted ways with it, we have only *quarreled* for a short time and only over the Kornilov incident. We have quarreled, we shall make peace. On the other hand, the Bolsheviks do not 'cede' us anything anyway, for their attempts at an uprising are as doomed to defeat under all circumstances, as was the Commune of 1871."

The other voice would say: "The allusion to the Commune is very superficial and even foolish. For in the first place, the Bolsheviks have learnt something since 1871; they would not fail to seize the bank, they would not even refuse to advance on Versailles; and under such conditions even the Commune might have been victorious. Besides, the Commune could not offer the people at once what the Bolsheviks will be able to offer when they become the power, namely, land to the peasants, an immediate offer of peace, a real control over production, an honest peace with the Ukrainians, Finns, etc. The Bolsheviks, to use a slang expression, have ten times more 'trumps' in their hands than the Commune had. In the second place, the Commune, whatever you may say about it, means a grave civil war, a retarding of peaceful, cultural development for a long time afterwards, an opportunity for freer operations and machinations on the part of all sorts of MacMahons and Kornilovs, which operations are a menace to our whole bourgeois society. Is it reasonable to run the risk of a Commune?

"But a Commune is unavoidable in Russia if we do not take power into our hands, if things remain in as grave a situation as they were between May 19 and September 13. Every revolutionary worker and soldier will inevitably think about the Commune and believe in it; he will inevitably make an attempt to realise it, for he will think in the following way: 'The people are perishing; war, famine, ruin, are going on and on. Only the Commune will save us. Let us then perish, let us die, all of us, but let us make the Commune a reality.' Such thoughts are inevitable among the workers, and it will not be so easy to crush the Commune now as it was in 1871. The Russian Commune will have allies throughout the world that are a hundred times stronger than the Commune had in 1871. . . . Is it reasonable to run the risk of a Commune? Neither can I agree that, strictly speaking, the Bolsheviks do not cede us anything by their compromise. In all cultured countries, cultured Ministers value highly every agreement with the proletariat in wartime, however slight. They value it very, very highly. And those are men of affairs, real Ministers. Now, the Bolsheviks are fast becoming stronger, notwithstanding repressions, notwithstanding the weakness of their press. . . . Is it reasonable for us to run the risk of a Commune?

"We have a safe majority; the awakening of the poor peasantry is still far off; what we have will suffice for a lifetime. I do not believe that the majority would follow the extremists in a peasant country. And against a recognised majority, no revolt is possible in a really democratic republic." This is what the second voice would say.

A third voice also may perhaps be heard, from among such elements as the adherents of Martov or Spiridonova, which would say: "I am indignant, 'Comrades,' that both of you, speaking about the Commune and its possibilities, unhesitatingly join the side of its opponents. Both of you, one in one form, the other in another, are on the side of those who suppressed the Commune. I will not undertake to make propaganda in favour of the Commune; I cannot promise beforehand to fight in its ranks as every Bolshevik will do; still I must say that *if* the Commune did flare up *in spite of* my efforts, I would rather help its defenders than its opponents. . . ."

The medley of voices in the "bloc" is great and unavoidable, for in every petty-bourgeois democracy a host of shadings is represented—from a quite ministerial bourgeois down to a semi-pauper who is as yet not capable to grasp the position of a proletarian. What will be the result of this discord of voices at any given moment, nobody knows.

The above lines were written Friday, September 14, but due to accidental causes (under Kerensky, history will say, not all the Bolsheviks were free to choose their dwelling places) they did not reach the editorial office on the very same day. After reading Saturday's and Sunday's papers, I say to myself: Perhaps the offer of a compromise is already too late. Perhaps those few days during which a peaceful development was *still* possible, have *already* passed. Yes, to all appearances, they have already passed. Kerensky will, in one way or another, move away both from among the ranks of the S.-R. Party and from the S.-R.'s themselves and will consolidate his position by means of the bourgeoisie *without* the S.-R.'s, thanks to their sluggishness. . . . Yes, to all appearances the days when the road of peaceful development accidentally became possible, have *already* passed. What remains is to send these notes to the editor with the request to have them entitled: "Belated Thoughts." Perhaps belated thoughts are sometimes not devoid of interest.

N. Lenin.

Written September 14-16, 1917.
Published in *Rabochy Put [Workers' Road]*,[69] No. 3, September 19, 1917.

DRAFT RESOLUTION ON THE POLITICAL SITUATION [70]

ON the basis of the resolution on the political situation adopted by the Sixth Congress of the R. S.-D. L. P. (Bolsheviks), and adapting this resolution to the present moment, the Central Committee of the R. S.-D. L. P. at its plenary session declares:

1. In the two months from July 16 to September 16, the course of the class struggle and the development of political events, as a result of the unparalleled speed of the revolution, have carried the whole country so far forward that it would have taken the country a long period of years to advance to this point in time of peace, without revolution and war.

2. It becomes more and more apparent that the events of July 16-18 were the turning point of the whole revolution. Without a correct analysis of those events it is impossible to have a correct analysis either of the tasks of the proletariat, or of the speed of the development of revolutionary events, which does not depend upon our will.

3. The slander against the Bolsheviks, disseminated by the bourgeoisie with incredible zeal and widely scattered among the masses of the people with the aid of the millions invested in capitalist papers and publishing houses, is being exposed ever faster and to more and more people. First the working masses in the capital and in the large cities, and then the peasantry begin to realise more and more that the slander against the Bolsheviks is one of the main weapons of the landowners and capitalists in the struggle against the defenders of the interests of the workers and poorest peasants, *i.e.*, the Bolsheviks.

4. An attempt was made to camouflage the revolt of Kornilov, *i.e.*, of generals and officers, in back of whom are the landowners and the capitalists headed by the Cadet Party (the "People's Freedom" Party), by bringing up again the old slanders against the Bolsheviks, and this helped finally to open the eyes of the broad masses of the people to the real significance of the bourgeois slanders against the Bolshevik workers' party, the party of the real defenders of the poor.

5. Had our party refused to support the July 16-17 movement, which burst out spontaneously despite our attempts to restrain it, it

would have been a direct and complete betrayal of the proletariat, since the masses came into motion because of their well-founded and just indignation against the continuation of the imperialist war (*i.e.*, a war of seizure and plunder, conducted in the interests of the capitalists), and against the inactivity of the government and the Soviets in regard to the bourgeoisie which intensifies and aggravates the economic ruin and famine.

6. In spite of all the efforts of the bourgeoisie and the government, in spite of the arrest of hundreds of Bolsheviks, and seizure of their papers and documents, the search of their editorial rooms, etc., nobody has succeeded, and nobody will ever succeed in proving the calumny that the aim of our party in the July 16-17 movement was any other than a "peaceful and organised" demonstration with the slogan of transfer of all power in the state to the Soviets of Workers', Soldiers', and Peasants' Deputies.

7. It would have been an error if the Bolsheviks had made it their task to seize power on July 16-17, since the majority not only of the people but even of the workers at that time had not yet actually experienced the counter-revolutionary policies of the generals in the army, of the landowners in the village, of the capitalists in the city—policies revealed to the masses after July 18, and the outcome of a conciliatory policy of the Socialist-Revolutionaries and the Mensheviks with the bourgeoisie. Not one organisation of our party, either central or local, came out either in writing or by word of mouth with the slogan of seizing power on July 16-17; none of them even had this question under discussion.

8. The real error of our party on July 16-17, as now revealed by events, was only that the party considered the national situation *less* revolutionary than it proved to be, that the party *still* considered possible a peaceful development of political transformations through a change in the policies of the Soviets, whereas in reality the Mensheviks and S.-R.'s had already so much entangled and bound themselves by agreements with the bourgeoisie, and the bourgeoisie had become so counter-revolutionary, that there could no longer be any idea of peaceful development. But this erroneous view, sustained only by the hope that events would not develop too fast, could not have been gotten rid of by our party in any other way than by participating in the popular movement of July 16-17 with the slogan, "All Power to the Soviets," with the aim of giving the movement a peaceful and organised character.

9. The historic significance of the Kornilov revolt is that it opened the eyes of the masses of the people with extraordinary force to the truth that had been and is still hidden under the conciliationist phrases of the S.-R.'s and Mensheviks, namely, that the landowners and the bourgeoisie, headed by the Cadet Party and the generals and officers who are on their side, have organised themselves, that they are now ready to commit, and are committing, the most outlandish crimes, such as giving up Riga (and afterwards Petrograd) to the Germans, laying the war front open, putting the Bolshevik regiments under fire, starting a mutiny, leading troops against the capital with the "Wild Division" * at their head, etc.— all in order to seize all power and put it in the hands of the bourgeoisie, to consolidate the power of the landowners in the villages, to drench the country in the blood of workers and peasants.

The Kornilov revolt has proven for Russia what has been proven throughout history for all countries, namely, that the bourgeoisie will betray the fatherland and resort to every crime in order to hold on to its power over the people, and its profits.

10. The workers and peasants of Russia have no other way out, absolutely none, outside of the most determined struggle against, and a victory over, the landowners and the bourgeoisie, the Cadet Party and the generals and officers who sympathise with it. Into such a struggle and to such victory the people, *i.e.*, all the toilers, can be led only by the working class of the cities, if all state power passes into its hands and if it is supported by the poorest peasants.

11. Events in the Russian Revolution, particularly after May 19, and still more so after July 16, have been developing with such incredible, storm- and hurricane-like velocity, that it can by no means be the task of the party to hasten them; on the contrary, all efforts must be directed towards not lagging behind events, towards keeping up with our work of explaining to the workers and to the toilers in general, as far as it is in our power, the changes in the situation and in the course of the class struggle. This is the main task of our party at present: to explain to the masses that the situation is terribly critical; that every action may end in an explosion; that therefore a premature uprising may cause the greatest harm. At the same time, the critical situation inevitably leads the working class—perhaps even with catastrophic speed—to a situation where, due to a change in events independent of its will, it will find itself

* A division of Caucasian mountaineer troops.—*Ed.*

compelled to enter into a decisive battle with the counter-revolutionary bourgeoisie and to conquer power.

12. The Kornilov revolt fully disclosed the fact that the army, the entire army, *hates General Headquarters.* Even the Mensheviks and S.-R.'s, who by months of effort have proven their hatred for the Bolsheviks and their defence of the policies of a conciliation between the workers and peasants on the one hand and the landowners and the bourgeoisie on the other, were compelled to admit this. The hatred of the army for General Headquarters will not diminish; rather will it become stronger now that Kerensky's government has done nothing but substitute Alexeyev for Kornilov, leaving Klembovsky and other Kornilovist generals, doing absolutely nothing substantial to democratise the army and to remove the counter-revolutionary commanding staff. The Soviets, which tolerate and support this weak, vacillating, unprincipled policy of Kerensky; the Soviets which again failed to utilise a moment when they could have taken all the power peaceably, while the Kornilov revolt was being liquidated, these Soviets have become guilty not only of conciliation but even of criminal conciliation.

The army, which hates General Headquarters and does not want to fight a war to whose annexationist character its eyes have been opened, is inevitably doomed to new catastrophes.

13. The working class, when it conquers power, will alone be able to pursue a policy of peace, not in words, like the Mensheviks and S.-R.'s, who in practice support the bourgeoisie and its secret treaties, but in deeds. It will immediately and under any military situation whatever, even should the Kornilovist generals, after giving up Riga, give up Petrograd too, offer to *all* peoples open, precise, clear, *just* conditions of peace. The working class can do this in the name of the whole people, since an overwhelming majority of the workers and peasants of Russia has expressed itself against the present annexationist war and for a peace on just conditions, without annexations or indemnities.

The S.-R.'s and Mensheviks are deceiving themselves and deceiving the people, talking for months about such a peace. The working class, having conquered power, will propose it to all without losing a single day.

The capitalists of all countries have so much difficulty in restraining the workers' revolution against war, which is growing everywhere, that, should the Russian Revolution pass from impotent and pitiful yearning for peace to a direct peace proposal coupled with an agreement to scrap secret treaties, etc., there are ninety-nine chances in a hundred that peace would come soon, that the capitalists would not be able to stand in the way of peace.

And if the least probable case should happen, namely, if the capitalists reject the peace conditions of the Russian workers' government, in spite of the will of their peoples, then a revolution in Europe would come a hundred times nearer, and the army of our workers and peasants would select for itself not hated but respected commanders and military leaders; it would become convinced of the justice of the war once peace has been offered, the secret treaties scrapped, the alliance with the landowners and the bourgeoisie severed, the land all given to the peasants. Only then would the war on the part of Russia become a just war; only such a war would the workers and peasants wage, not under the club but voluntarily, and such a war would bring still nearer the inevitable workers' revolution in the advanced countries.

14. The working class, when it has conquered power, will alone be able to guarantee the immediate transfer of all the landowners' land to the peasants without compensation. This should not be delayed. The Constituent Assembly will legalise it, but it is not the peasants' fault that the Constituent Assembly is being delayed. The peasants become more convinced every day that it is impossible to get the land by agreements with the landowners and the capitalists. The land can be gotten only through a most intimate, brotherly alliance between the poorest peasants and the workers.

Chernov's resignation from the government after he had for months tried to defend the interests of the peasants by means of little and big concessions to the Cadet landowners, and after all these attempts had failed, demonstrates with particular clearness the hopelessness of a policy of conciliation.[71] As to the peasants locally, they see and know, they feel and sense that after July 18 the landowners became arrogant in the villages and that it is necessary to bridle them and render them harmless.

15. The working class, when it has conquered power, will alone be able to put an end to economic ruin and threatening famine. Since May 19 the government has kept on promising control, but has been unable to do anything because the capitalists and the landowners obstruct all the work. Unemployment is growing; famine is looming; currency is becoming depreciated; Peshe-

khonov's resignation after the fixed prices had doubled will aggravate the crisis; and this again shows all the feebleness and impotence of the government. Only workers' control over production and distribution can save the situation. Only a workers' government will curb the capitalists, call forth among all the toilers heroic support of the efforts of the *state power*, establish order and a fair exchange of bread for manufactured goods.

16. The confidence of the poor peasantry in the urban working class, temporarily undermined by the slander of the bourgeoisie and by hopes placed in the policy of conciliation, has been returning, particularly after the arrests in the villages and the various kinds of persecution of the toilers after July 18, later also the Kornilov revolt, opened the eyes of the people. One of the signs that the people are losing faith in conciliation with the capitalists is the fact that among the S.-R.'s and Mensheviks, the two main parties which conducted this policy of conciliation and brought it to a culmination, there has grown, especially after July 18, a dissatisfaction within the parties, a struggle against the policy of conciliation, an opposition which at the last "Council" of the Socialist-Revolutionary Party [72] and at the congress of the Menshevik Party had reached about two-fifths (40%).

17. The whole course of events, all economic and political conditions, all occurrences in the army, are preparing faster and faster the success of the conquest of power by the working class, which will give peace, bread, freedom, and which will hasten the victory of the revolution of the proletariat in other countries.

Written September 16, 1917.
First published in the *Lenin Collection*, IV, 1926.

ONE OF THE FUNDAMENTAL QUESTIONS OF THE REVOLUTION

The main question of every revolution is, undoubtedly, the question of state power. In the hands of which class power is—this decides everything. And when the paper of the chief government party in Russia, the *Dyelo Naroda*, recently complained (in No. 147) that owing to the controversies over power, both the question of the Constituent Assembly and the question of bread are being forgotten, one should have answered these Socialist-Revolutionaries, "Blame yourselves." [73] For it is the vacillations and the indecision of *your* party that are mostly to blame both for the rapid changes of the Cabinet, and for the interminable postponements of the Constituent Assembly, as well as for the capitalists undermining the planned and adopted measures of a grain monopoly and of securing food for the country.

The question of power can be neither evaded nor brushed aside; for this is the fundamental question which determines *everything* in the development of a revolution, in its foreign and domestic policies. That our revolution has "squandered" half a year in vacillations as to the composition of power, is an undisputed fact, a fact determined by the vacillating policy of the S.-R.'s and Mensheviks. And the policy of these parties was determined, in the long run, by the class position of the petty bourgeoisie, by its lack of economic stability in the struggle between capital and labour.

The whole question at present is whether the petty-bourgeois democracy has learned anything during this great half year, so unusually rich in content. If not, then the revolution is lost, and only a victorious uprising of the proletariat will be able to save it. If it has, then we must begin with the immediate creation of a stable, not vacillating, power. To be stable during a popular revolution, *i.e.*, such as has aroused to life the masses, the majority of workers and peasants, is possible only for a power that is based, consciously and unconditionally, *on a majority* of the population. Up to the present time state power has actually remained in Russia in the hands of the *bourgeoisie*, which is only compelled to make frequent concessions (only to begin withdrawing them the following day), to hand out promises (only to fail to carry them out), to search for all sorts of shields to screen its domination (only to fool the people by an ostensibly "honest coalition") etc., etc. In words, a popular, democratic, revolutionary government; in deeds, an anti-popular, anti-democratic, counter-revolutionary, bourgeois government—this is the contradiction which has hitherto existed and has been the source of the complete instability and the vacillations of power, and of all that "ministerial leap-frog" which Messrs. S.-R.'s and Mensheviks have been engaged in with such lamentable (for the people) ardour.

Either disruption of the Soviets and their ignominious death, or all power to the Soviets, I said before the All-Russian Congress of Soviets early in June, 1917, and the history of July and August thoroughly and convincingly confirmed the correctness of these words.* Only the power of the Soviets can be stable, being based on a clear majority of the people, no matter what the lackeys of the bourgeoisie may say—those Potresovs, Plekhanovs and others who designate as a "widening of the basis" of power its virtual transfer to an insignificant minority of the people, to the bourgeoisie, the exploiters.

Only the Soviet power could be stable; only this power could not be overthrown even in the stormiest moments of the stormiest revolution; only such a power could assure the continuous and broad development of the revolution and the peaceful struggle of parties within the Soviets. So long as such a power has not been created, we inevitably must have indecision, instability, vacillations, endless "crises of power," a continual comedy of ministerial leap-frog, outbursts from the Right and from the Left.

But the slogan, "Power to the Soviets," is very often, if not most of the time, understood quite incorrectly as meaning a "Cabinet composed of the parties of the Soviet majority," and on this profoundly erroneous idea we should like to dwell with more detail.

A "Cabinet composed of the parties of the Soviet majority" means a personal change in the composition of the Ministers while the old apparatus of governmental power remains intact—an apparatus thoroughly bureaucratic, thoroughly undemocratic, incapable of carrying out serious reforms, such as are contained even in the programme of the S.-R.'s and Mensheviks.

* See V. I. Lenin, *The Revolution of 1917, Collected Works*, Vol. XX, Book II, p. 195*ff.—Ed.*

"Power to the Soviets" means a radical change in the entire old state apparatus, in that bureaucratic apparatus which hampers everything democratic; it means removing this apparatus and substituting for it a new popular one, *i.e.*, a truly democratic apparatus of Soviets, the organised and armed majority of the people, the workers, the soldiers, the peasants; it means allowing the majority of the people initiative and independence not only in the selection of deputies, but also in the management of the state, in the realisation of reforms and social changes.

To make this difference more clear and comprehensible, we shall recall a valuable admission made some time ago by the paper of the governmental party of the S.-R.'s, the *Dyelo Naroda*. This paper wrote that even in those Cabinets which had been put in the hands of Socialist Ministers (this was written during the famous coalition with the Cadets, when some Mensheviks and S.-R.'s were Ministers)—*even* in those Cabinets the entire apparatus had remained as of old and was hampering the work.

This is easily understood. The entire history of the bourgeois-parliamentary, and to a considerable extent also of the bourgeois-constitutional countries, shows that a change of Ministers means very little, for the real work of administration is in the hands of an enormous army of officials. This army, however, is saturated through and through with an anti-democratic spirit, it is connected by thousands and millions of threads with the landowners and the bourgeoisie and it depends upon them in every way. This army is surrounded by an atmosphere of bourgeois relations; it breathes only this atmosphere; it is inert, petrified, fossilised; it has not the power to extricate itself from this atmosphere; it cannot think, feel, or act otherwise than in the old way. This army is bound by the relations of rank worship, by certain privileges of "state" service, while the upper ranks of this army are, through the medium of stocks and banks, entirely enslaved by finance capital, being to some degree its agent, the vehicle of its interests and influence.

To attempt, by means of *this* state apparatus, to carry out such reforms as the abolition of landowners' property in land without compensation, the grain monopoly, etc., is the greatest illusion, the greatest self-deception and a deception of the people. This apparatus *can* serve a republican bourgeoisie, creating a republic in the shape of a "monarchy without a monarch," like the **Third Republic** in France, but of carrying out reforms seriously undermining or limiting the rights of capital, the rights of "sacred private property," not to speak of abolishing them—such a state apparatus is absolutely incapable. This is why we have, under all sorts of "coalition" Cabinets with the participation of "Socialists," the phenomenon that these Socialists, even where individual persons among them are absolutely sincere, in reality prove to be either a useless ornament or a screen for the bourgeois government, a lightning rod to divert the people's indignation from that government, an instrument for that government to deceive the masses. This was the case with Louis Blanc in 1848; this was the case dozens of times in England and France when the Socialists participated in the Cabinets; this was the case with the Chernovs and Tseretelis in 1917; so it has been and so it will be as long as the bourgeois system persists and as long as the old bourgeois, bureaucratic state apparatus remains intact.

The Soviets of Workers', Soldiers' and Peasants' Deputies are particularly valuable because they represent a new *type* of state apparatus, which is immeasurably higher, incomparably more democratic. The S.-R.'s and Mensheviks have done everything, possible and impossible, to turn the Soviets (particularly the Petrograd Soviet and the All-Russian Soviet, *i.e.*, the Central Executive Committee) into useless talking shops which, under the guise of "control," busy themselves with passing useless resolutions and wishes which the government shelves with the most polite and kindly smile. But the "fresh breeze" of the Kornilov affair, which promised a real storm, was sufficient to dispel for a time all that was musty in the Soviet, and the initiative of the revolutionary masses began to assert itself as something majestic, powerful, invincible.

Let all people of little faith learn from this historic example. Let those who say: "We have no apparatus to replace the old one, which inevitably gravitates towards the defence of the bourgeoisie," be ashamed of themselves. For this apparatus *exists*. It is the Soviets. Do not be afraid of the initiative and independence of the masses; entrust yourselves to revolutionary organisations of the masses—and you will see in *all* realms of state life the same strength, majesty, invincibility of the workers and peasants as they displayed in their unity and ardour against the Kornilov affair.

Lack of faith in the masses, fear of their initiative, fear of their independence, trepidation before their revolutionary energy instead of thorough and unstinted support of it—this is where the S.-R.'s and Menshevik leaders have sinned most. This is where we find the deepest roots of their indecision, their vacillations, their endless and utterly fruitless attempts to pour new wine into the old bottles of the old bureaucratic state apparatus.

Take the history of the democratisation of the army in the Russian Revolution of 1917, the history of Chernov's ministry, the history of Palchinsky's "reign," the history of Peshekhonov's resignation—and at every step you will see the most striking confirmation of what we have just said. Without full confidence in the elected soldiers' organisations, without absolutely carrying out the principle of superiors being elected by the soldiers, the Kornilovs, Kaledins and counter-revolutionary officers came to be at the head of the army. This is a fact. And whoever does not wish deliberately to close his eyes cannot fail to see that *after* the Kornilov affair Kerensky's government is *leaving everything as of old,* that *in reality it is bringing back Kornilov plotting.* The appointment of Alexeyev, the "peace" with the Klembovskys, Gagarins, Bagrations and other Kornilovists, leniency in the treatment of Kornilov and Kaledin themselves—all this proves most clearly that Kerensky is in reality bringing back Kornilov plotting.

There is no middle road. Experience has shown that there is no middle road. Either all power to the Soviets and a full democratisation of the army, or a Kornilov affair.

And what about the history of Chernov's ministry? Did it not prove that every more or less earnest step towards actually satisfying the needs of the peasants, every step manifesting confidence in them, in their own mass organisations and actions, called forth the greatest enthusiasm of all the peasantry? It fell to Chernov's lot to keep "haggling" for almost four months with the Cadets and bureaucrats, who by endless delays and intrigues forced him finally to resign without having accomplished anything. For these four months and *during* these four months the landowners and capitalists "won the game": they saved the landowners' property in land, they delayed the convocation of the Constituent Assembly, they started a series of repressions against the land committees.

There is no middle road. Experience has shown that there is no middle road. Either all power to the Soviets both centrally and locally; either all land to the peasants *immediately,* pending the decision of the Constituent Assembly, or the landowners and the capitalists will obstruct every step, restore the landowners' power, drive the peasants into a rage and bring matters to an exceedingly violent peasant uprising.

The very same story repeated itself when the capitalists (with the aid of Palchinsky) crushed every more or less serious attempt to control production; when the merchants brought to naught the grain monopoly and the beginning of a regulated democratic distribution of grain and other supplies initiated by Peshekhonov.

What is necessary now in Russia is not to invent "new reforms," not to engage in "plans" of some "all-embracing" changes. Nothing of the kind. This is how the situation is depicted—knowingly depicted in a false light—by the capitalists, the Potresovs, the Plekhanovs, who fume against "introducing Socialism," against the "dictatorship of the proletariat." In reality the situation in Russia is such that the unprecedented burdens and miseries of the war, the unparalleled and most formidable danger of economic ruin and famine have by themselves suggested the way out, have by themselves pointed out, and not only pointed out, but advanced as absolutely necessary reforms and changes: grain monopoly, control over production and distribution, limiting of the issuance of paper money, equitable exchange of foodstuffs for manufactured goods, etc.

Measures of this kind are recognised by all as unavoidable; they have been begun in many localities and from many angles. *They have already been begun,* but they are being sabotaged everywhere and have been sabotaged by the resistance of the landowners and the capitalists, effected both through the Kerensky government (a government *in reality* bourgeois and Bonapartist), through the bureaucratic apparatus of the old state and through the direct and indirect pressure of the Russian and "allied" finance.

Not so long ago I. Prilezhayev, lamenting the resignation of Peshekhonov and the collapse of the fixed prices, the collapse of the grain monopoly, wrote the following in the *Dyelo Naroda* (No. 147):

> Courage and decisiveness are what our governments of all compositions have lacked. . . . Revolutionary democracy must not wait; it must itself manifest initiative and intervene in economic chaos in a planned way. . . . If ever, it is here that a firm course and a strong authority are necessary.[74]

What is true is true. Golden words. The author only failed to consider that the question of a firm course of courage and decisiveness is not a personal matter, but a question of the *class* which is capable of manifesting courage and decisiveness. The only class of this kind is the proletariat. Courage, decisiveness of authority, and a firm course are nothing but the dictatorship of the proletariat and the poorest peasants. I. Prilezhayev unknowingly longs for *this dictatorship*.

For what would such a dictatorship signify in practice? Nothing but the fact that the resistance of the Kornilovists would be broken and the democratisation of the army restored and completed. Ninety-nine hundredths of the army would be enthusiastic supporters of such a dictatorship two hours after its establishment. This dictatorship would give the land to the peasants and full power to the peasant committees locally; how then can any one who is not out of his mind doubt that the peasants would accept this dictatorship? What Peshekhonov only *promises* ("the resistance of the capitalists has been broken" were the literal words of Peshekhonov in his famous speech before the Soviet Congress), this dictatorship would introduce in life, would turn into a reality while in no way discarding the democratic organisations of supply, control, etc., that have already begun to form, but, on the contrary, supporting and developing them and removing all obstacles in the way of their work.

Only the dictatorship of the proletarians and the poorest peasants is capable of crushing the resistance of the capitalists, of manifesting a real grandiose courage and decisiveness of authority, of securing for itself the enthusiastic, devoted, really heroic support of the masses both in the army and in the peasantry.

Power to the Soviets—this is the only thing that can secure further progress, gradual, peaceful and smooth, keeping perfect pace with the consciousness and the resolve of the majority of the masses of the people, with their own experience. Power to the Soviets—this means the complete transfer of the administration of the country and control over economic life into the hands of the workers and the peasants, to whom *nobody* would dare offer resistance and who would *soon learn* in practice, through their own experience, how to distribute equitably the land, produce and bread.

N. Lenin.

Rabochy Put, No. 10, September 27, 1917.

HOW IS THE SUCCESS OF THE ELECTIONS TO THE CONSTITUENT ASSEMBLY TO BE ASSURED?

ON THE FREEDOM OF THE PRESS

EARLY in April, expounding the attitude of the Bolsheviks to the question whether the Constituent Assembly ought to be convened, I wrote:

> Yes, and as soon as possible. Yet, to make it successful and to have it convoked, one condition is necessary: increase the number and strengthen the *power* of the Soviets of Workers', Soldiers', and Peasants', etc., Deputies; organise and arm the masses. This is the only guarantee.*

Five months have passed since then and the correctness of these words has been proved by a series of delays, by dragging out the convocation through the fault of the Cadets; it has finally been excellently confirmed by the Kornilov affair.

Now, in connection with the calling of the Democratic Conference [75] for September 25, I should like to dwell on another aspect of the matter.

Both the Menshevik *Rabochaya Gazeta* and the *Dyelo Naroda* express regret over the fact that little is being done among the peasants by way of propaganda in order to enlighten this real *mass* of the Russian people, its real majority. All admit and recognise that the success of the Constituent Assembly depends upon the enlightenment of the peasants, but ridiculously little is being done about this. The peasants are being deceived, fooled, and frightened by the thoroughly deceitful and counter-revolutionary bourgeois and "yellow" press, in comparison with which the press of the Mensheviks and Socialist-Revolutionaries (not to speak of the Bolsheviks) is very, very weak.

Why is this so?

Just because the ruling parties, the S.-R.'s and Mensheviks, are weak, undecided, inactive, because, not agreeing that full power should be taken over by the Soviets, they leave the peasantry in

---

* See V. I. Lenin, *The Revolution of 1917, Collected Works*, Vol. XX, Book I, p. 161.—*Ed.*

ignorance and despair, a prey to the capitalists, *their* press and *their* propaganda.

While boastfully calling our revolution great, while shouting to the right and left loud, bombastic phrases about "revolutionary democracy," the Mensheviks and S.-R.'s *in reality* leave Russia in a condition of most ordinary, most petty-bourgeois revolution which, having overthrown the Tsar, leaves everything else as before and undertakes nothing, absolutely nothing earnest, for the political enlightenment of the peasants, to overcome the peasants' ignorance —this *last* (and strongest) bulwark, the *bulwark* of the exploiters and oppressors of the people.

Just at this time it is timely to recall this. Just at present, with the Democratic Conference before us, two months before the "appointed" (till a new delay) convocation of the Constituent Assembly, is a good time to show how easily matters could have been mended, how much could have been done for the political enlightenment of the peasants if only—if only!—our "revolutionary democracy" in quotation marks were really revolutionary, *i.e.*, capable of acting in a revolutionary way, and really democratic, *i.e.*, taking into account the will and the interests of the majority of the people and not the capitalist minority which continues to hold power (the Kerensky government) and with which, indirectly if not directly, in a new if not in an old form, the S.-R.'s and Mensheviks are still anxious to have "agreements."

The capitalists (and after them, either from ignorance or inertia, many S.-R.'s and Mensheviks) call it "freedom of the press" when censorship has been abolished and all parties freely publish all kinds of papers.

In reality this is not freedom of the press, but freedom for the rich, for the bourgeoisie to deceive the oppressed and exploited masses of the people.

Take, for instance, the Petrograd and Moscow papers. You will see at once that by far the largest circulation prevails among bourgeois newspapers, the *Ryech*, the *Birzhevka*, the *Novoye Vremya*, the *Russkoye Slovo* [*Russian Word*] [76] and so on, and so forth (for there are a great many such papers). What is this prevalence based upon? Not at all upon the will of the majority, for the elections have shown that in both capitals the majority (a gigantic majority at that) is on the side of democracy, *i.e.*, the S.-R.'s, Mensheviks and Bolsheviks. The number of votes secured by these three parties is from three-quarters to four-fifths of the total, whereas the circulation of the papers they publish is certainly less than a quarter or even less than one-fifth that of the whole bourgeois press (which, as we know and see now, directly and indirectly supported the Kornilov affair).

Why is this so?

Everybody knows perfectly well why. Because the publication of a paper is a big and profitable capitalist enterprise, in which the rich invest millions upon millions of rubles. The "freedom of the press" of bourgeois society consists in freedom for the *rich*, systematically, consistently, daily, in millions of copies, to deceive, corrupt, fool the exploited and oppressed masses of the people, the poor.

This is that simple, commonly known, obvious truth which everybody sees, everybody knows, and "almost everybody" "bashfully" passes over in silence, timorously evades.

The question is: is it possible to fight against this crying evil, and how?

First of all there is a very simple, very good and perfectly legal means which I long since pointed out in the *Pravda*, which it is particularly timely to recall now before September 25 and which workers ought always to have in mind, for they will hardly manage without it after they have conquered political power.*

This means is a state monopoly of private advertisements in the papers.

Look at the *Russkoye Slovo*, the *Novoye Vremya*, the *Birzhevka*, the *Ryech*, etc.—you will see a mass of private advertisements which yield a tremendous income, even the principal income, for the capitalists who publish those papers. This is how bourgeois papers, the world over, manage their affairs, this is how they get rich, *this is how they buy and sell poison for the people.*

There are papers in Europe which have a circulation of, say, one-third of the number of inhabitants of a city (for instance, 12,000 copies in a city with a population of 40,000), which deliver the paper *free to every house,* and at the same time yield their owners a goodly income. Such papers live by advertisements for which private people pay, while the free delivery of the paper into every house secures the best circulation of the advertisements.

* See V. I. Lenin, *The Revolution of 1917, Collected Works*, Vol. XX, Book II, p. 262.—*Ed.*

The question is why a democracy that calls itself revolutionary has not been able to realise such a measure as declaring private advertisements in the papers a state monopoly, or has not prohibited the publication of advertisements anywhere *outside* the papers that are published by the Soviets in the provincial towns and cities and by the *Central Soviet* in Petrograd for the whole of Russia? Why is "revolutionary" democracy obliged to tolerate such a thing as the enriching through private advertisements of rich men, adherents of Kornilov, disseminators of lies and calumnies against the Soviets?

Such a measure would be absolutely just. It would be of tremendous advantage both to those who publish private advertisements and to the whole people, particularly for the most oppressed and ignorant peasantry, which would be enabled to have, for a small fee or even free of charge, *Soviet* papers with supplements for the peasants.

Why not introduce it? Only because private property and hereditary rights (to profits from advertisements) are sacred to the capitalist gentlemen. And is it possible to recognise such rights as "sacred" while calling oneself a revolutionary democrat in the twentieth century, in the second Russian Revolution?!

One may say: this is interference with the freedom of the press.

Not at all. It would mean broadening and restoring the freedom of the press, for freedom of the press means that all opinions of *all* citizens may be freely promulgated.

And now? Now the rich *alone* have this monopoly and also the big parties. But if large *Soviet* papers were to be published with all the advertisements available, it would be perfectly possible to assure the expression of opinion to a much larger number of citizens, say, for every group which has collected a certain number of signatures. Freedom of the press would *in practice* become much more democratic, it would become incomparably more complete after such a change.

But one may say: where shall we get printing presses and paper?

That's just it! It is not a matter of "freedom of the press," but it is the sacred property of the exploiters in the printing presses and the stocks of paper they have seized!

In the name of what must we workers and peasants recognise this sacred right? Wherein is this "right" to publish false information better than the "right" to own serfs?

Why is it that during a war all sorts of requisitions of houses, apartments, vehicles, horses, grain and metals are allowed and practiced everywhere, while the requisition of printing presses and paper is not allowed?

No, the workers and peasants may be temporarily deceived, if such measures are represented as unjust or difficult to realise, but the truth will conquer after all.

State power in the shape of Soviets takes *all* printing presses and *all* paper and distributes them *justly:* in the first place, the state— in the interests of the majority of the people, the majority of the poor, particularly the majority of the peasants who for centuries have been tortured, crushed and benumbed by the landowners and capitalists.

In the second place, the large parties, say, such as have polled in both capitals one or two hundred thousand votes.

In the third place, the smaller parties, and then every group of citizens which has a certain number of members or has gathered a certain number of signatures.

Such distribution of paper and printing presses would be just, and, with power in the hands of the Soviets, it would be realised without any difficulty.

Then, two months before the Constituent Assembly, we could really help the peasants, we could secure the delivery into *every* village of half a dozen pamphlets (or issues of a newspaper, or special supplements) in *millions* of copies from *every* large party.

This would be a "revolutionary-democratic" preparation for the elections to the Constituent Assembly; this would be aid to the village on the part of the advanced workers and soldiers; this would be state aid to education and not a stultification and deception of the people; this would be real freedom of the press for *all*, and not for the rich; this would be a break with that accursed slavish past which compels us to suffer the usurpation by the rich of the great work of informing and teaching the peasantry.

N. LENIN.

Rabochy Put, No. 11, September 28, 1917.

THE THREATENING CATASTROPHE AND HOW TO FIGHT IT

THE THREATENING CATASTROPHE AND HOW TO FIGHT IT

FAMINE IS APPROACHING

RUSSIA is threatened with an inevitable catastrophe. Railroad transportation is unbelievably disorganised and is being disorganised more and more. The railroads will stop running. The delivery of raw materials and coal to the factories will cease. The delivery of grain will cease. The capitalists are deliberately and consistently sabotaging (damaging, stopping, wrecking, hampering) production, hoping that a terrible catastrophe may mean the collapse of the republic and democracy, of the Soviets and the proletarian and peasants' unions, thus facilitating the return of a monarchy and the restoration of the full power of the bourgeoisie and landowners.

A catastrophe of extraordinary dimensions, and a famine, are unavoidably threatening. This has been stated innumerable times in all the papers. An immense number of resolutions has been adopted both by the parties and by the Soviets of Workers', Soldiers', and Peasants' Deputies, resolutions which admit that the catastrophe is inevitable, that it is looming close at hand, that a desperate fight against it is necessary, that "heroic efforts" on the part of the people are necessary to avert the calamity, and so forth.

Everybody says that. Everybody recognises that. Everybody has agreed to that.

And nothing is being done.

Half a year of revolution has passed. The catastrophe has come still closer. Things have come to a state of mass unemployment. Think of it: the country is suffering from a lack of commodities; the country is perishing from lack of products, from lack of working hands at a time when there is a sufficient quantity of food and raw materials—and still, in a country like this, at a critical moment like this, mass unemployment has developed! What other proof is necessary for the fact that during half a year of revolution (which some call great, but which so far it would be more correct to call rotten), under a democratic republic with an abundance of unions, organs, institutions that proudly call themselves "revolutionary-democratic," in reality nothing, absolutely *nothing* serious has been done against the catastrophe, against the famine! We are approaching nearer and nearer to a crash, for the war does not wait and the disorganisation of all realms of people's life resulting from it is becoming ever greater.

And yet, a very small amount of attention and reflection is sufficient to convince one that there are means of fighting the catastrophe and the famine, that the means of struggle are perfectly clear and simple, perfectly realisable, perfectly within reach of the people's forces, and that those measures are *not* being undertaken *only and solely* because their realisation would infringe upon the immense profits of a handful of landowners and capitalists.

Indeed, you can wager that you won't find a single speech, a single article in a paper of any political tendency, a single resolution of any gathering or institution where there would not be recognised with perfect clarity and precision the fundamental means of fighting, the means of preventing catastrophe and famine. This means is control, supervision, accounting, state regulation, the establishment of a correct distribution of labour forces in the production and distribution of products, husbanding the resources of the people, elimination of any waste of forces, the utmost economy. Control, supervision, accounting—this is the first word in the fight against catastrophe and famine. This is what arouses no objection and is universally admitted. And it is just this which is *not being done*, out of fear of encroaching upon the omnipotence of the landowners and capitalists, upon their enormous, unheard-of, scandalous profits which are being made through the high cost of living, through deliveries of military supplies (it is well known that every one is "working" for the war, directly or indirectly), profits which every one knows about, every one observes, every one laments and bemoans.

And it is just for a more or less serious control, accounting and supervision on the part of the state that nothing whatever is being done.

Complete Inactivity of the Government

Everywhere a systematic, methodical sabotage of all control, supervision and accounting, of every attempt on the part of the state to organise them, is going on. An unbelievable naïveté is required not to understand, a deep hypocrisy is required to pretend not to understand, whence this sabotage comes and by what means it is being carried on. For this sabotage on the part of the bankers and capitalists, their *disruption* of all control, supervision and accounting, adapts itself to the state forms of a democratic republic, it adapts itself to the existence of "revolutionary-democratic" institutions. The capitalist gentlemen have wonderfully assimilated the truth which, in words, is recognised by all adherents of scientific Socialism, but which the Mensheviks and the Socialist-Revolutionaries tried to forget immediately after their friends had secured the berths of Ministers, Assistant Ministers, etc. This truth is that the economic essence of capitalist exploitation is not in the least interfered with by the substitution of republican-democratic forms of government for the monarchist form, and that, consequently, the reverse is also true, namely, that it is necessary to change only the *form* of struggle for the inviolability and sanctity of capitalist profits to defend it under a democratic republic just as successfully as it was defended under an absolute monarchy.

The present-day, modern republican-democratic sabotage of every control, accounting and supervision, consists in that the capitalists in words "warmly" recognise the "principle" of control and its necessity (as do all the Mensheviks and S.-R.'s, of course), but that they only insist on the introduction of this control being "gradual," planned and "regulated by the state." In reality these innocent little words are used to cover up the *disruption* of control, its transformation into nothing, into a fiction, into a mere game; they are used to delay all business-like and serious practical steps; to create unusually complicated, bulky and bureaucratically lifeless institutions of control entirely dependent upon the capitalists and doing, and able to do, absolutely nothing.

In order to substantiate our statements, we shall refer to witnesses from among the Mensheviks and S.-R.'s, *i.e.*, those very people who had a majority in the Soviets during the first half year of the Revolution, who participated in the "coalition government" and who are therefore politically responsible before the Russian workers and peasants for their being lenient to the capitalists, for the latter's disruption of all control.

In the official organ of the highest of the so-called "plenipotentiary" (no joking!) organs of the revolutionary democracy, namely, in the *Izvestiya* of the C.E.C. (*i.e.*, the Central Executive

Committee of the All-Russian Congress of the Soviets of Workers', Soldiers', and Peasants' Deputies), in No. 164, September 20, 1917, there has been published a *decision* of a special institution for dealing with control questions, created by the same Mensheviks and S.-R.'s and entirely in their hands. This special institution is the Economic Section of the Central Executive Committee. In this decision there is officially recognised, as a fact, *"the absolute lack of activity on the part of the central organs created to work with the government for the regulation of economic life."* [77]

Can one imagine a more eloquent testimonial to the collapse of the Menshevik and S.-R. policy than this, signed by the Mensheviks and S.-R.'s themselves?

Even under tsarism the necessity of regulating economic life was recognised, and some institutions were created for this purpose. But under tsarism economic ruin was growing and growing, reaching monstrous proportions. It was immediately recognised as the task of a republican, revolutionary government to take earnest, decisive measures for doing away with economic ruin. When the "coalition" government, with the participation of the Mensheviks and S.-R.'s, was being organised, a promise was made in the government's solemn public declaration of May 19, and an obligation was undertaken, to establish state control and regulation. The Tseretelis and Chernovs, as well as all the Menshevik and S.-R. leaders, swore emphatically that they were not only responsible for the government but that the "plenipotentiary organs of revolutionary democracy" in their hands actually did follow up the work of the government and examine it.

Four months have passed since May 19, four long months, during which Russia has sacrificed hundreds of thousands of soldiers in an absurd imperialist "advance"; during which economic ruin and catastrophe have been approaching with seven league boots, during which the summer time opened exceptional possibilities for doing a great deal with regard to water transportation, agriculture and prospecting in the realm of mining, etc., etc.; and now after four months, the Mensheviks and S.-R.'s are compelled officially to recognise the "absolute lack of activity" on the part of the control institutions created to work with the government!!

And those very same Mensheviks and S.-R.'s prattle now with the earnest mien of statesmen (we are writing these lines on the very eve of the Democratic Conference of September 25) that matters can be remedied by changing the coalition with the Cadets into a coalition with the commercial and industrial Kit Kityches,* Ryabushinskys, Bublikovs, Tereshchenkos and Co.

The question is: how can this amazing blindness of the Mensheviks and S.-R.'s be explained? Shall we consider them infant statesmen who, because of extreme stupidity and naïveté, are unconscious of what they are doing and are erring in good faith? Or has the abundance of posts for Ministers, Assistant Ministers, governor-generals, commissars and similar berths the property of generating specific "political" blindness?

Universally Known and Easy Measures of Control

The question may arise as to whether the methods and measures of control represent something extraordinarily complicated, difficult, never tried out, even unknown. Is not the delay to be explained by the fact that the statesmen of the Cadet Party, of the commercial and industrial class, of the S.-R. and Menshevik Parties, have already been labouring in the sweat of their brow for half a year searching out, studying, discovering measures and methods of control, but that the problem is proving tremendously difficult and is still unsolved?

Alas! There is an attempt here to "bamboozle" the unenlightened, illiterate and downtrodden peasants and "man in the street," who believe everything and do not probe into anything—an attempt to present the case in this way. In reality even tsarism, even the "old régime," by creating War Industries Committees, *was familiar* with the fundamental measures, with the main method and way of control: uniting the population in groups according to profession, purpose of work, branch of labour, etc. Tsarism, however, *was afraid* of uniting the population; it therefore limited in every possible way, cramped artificially, this universally known, very easy, perfectly applicable method and way of control.

All the belligerent states, experiencing extreme burdens and miseries of war, experiencing in one degree or another economic ruin and famine, have long since mapped out, determined, adopted, tested *a whole series* of control measures which almost always

* Kit Kitych, a character in a play by the classic Russian playwright, Ostrovsky. It personifies a rich, wilful and ignorant man who rules despotically over his family and his subordinates.—*Ed.*

reduce themselves to uniting the population, to creating or encouraging all sorts of unions with the participation of representatives of the state, with supervision on the part of the state, etc. All these measures of control are universally known; much has been spoken and written about them; the laws promulgated by the advanced belligerent powers relative to control have been translated into Russian or reported in detail in the Russian press.

If our state really *wished* to realise control in a business-like, serious manner, if its institutions had not doomed themselves, through their servility before the capitalists, to "absolute inactivity," the government would only have to draw liberally from the very rich source of control measures that are already known and have already been adopted. The only obstacle to this step—an obstacle which the Cadets, S.-R.'s and Mensheviks screen from the eyes of the people—has been and is this: that control would disclose the enormous profits of the capitalists and would undermine these profits.

In order to elucidate more graphically this highly important question (which in substance is tantamount to the question of a programme for *every* really revolutionary government which would undertake to save Russia from war and famine), let us enumerate those principal measures of control, and let us examine each of them.

We shall see that, for a government which calls itself revolutionary-democratic not in a mocking sense only, it would have been sufficient to decree (to decide, to order) in the very first week of its existence the introduction of the principal measures of control; to fix serious, heavy penalties for capitalists who fraudulently evade control; and to appeal to the population itself to watch the capitalists, to see to their scrupulous observance of the decisions concerning control. Had this been done, control would long since have been put into effect in Russia.

Here are those principal measures:

1. Unification of all banks into one; state control over its operations, or nationalisation of the banks.

2. Nationalisation of the syndicates, *i.e.*, the largest monopoly associations of the capitalists (the sugar, naphtha, coal, metallurgical syndicates, etc.).

3. Abolition of commercial secrets.

4. Compulsory syndication (*i.e.*, compulsory unification into as-

sociations) of industrialists, merchants and employers in general.

5. Compulsory organisation of the population into consumers' associations; or encouragement of such unification and the control over them.

Let us examine the significance each of those measures would have, provided they were realised in a revolutionary-democratic way.

NATIONALISATION OF THE BANKS

Banks are known to represent centres of modern economic life; they are the main nerve centres of the entire capitalist system of national economy. To speak of "regulation of economic life" while evading the question of nationalisation of the banks means either to exhibit utter ignorance or to deceive the "plain people" by fine words and high-sounding promises with the premeditated intention of not carrying these promises out.

To control and regulate the delivery of foodstuffs and the production and distribution of products generally without controlling or regulating bank operations is an absurdity. It is like hunting after kopecks that cross your way accidentally, while closing your eyes to millions of rubles. Modern banks have become so intimately and indissolubly connected with trade (in grain and everything else) and industry that, without "laying hands" on the banks, it is absolutely impossible to do anything serious, anything "revolutionary-democratic."

But, perhaps, this operation of the state "laying hands" on the banks is some sort of very difficult and complicated matter? There is usually an attempt to frighten the philistines by such a picture—the efforts are made, of course, by the capitalists and their defenders because it is to their advantage.

In reality, nationalisation of the banks, without taking away from any "owner" a single kopeck, presents absolutely no difficulties, either technical or cultural, and is being thwarted *exclusively* by the interests of filthy greed on the part of an insignificant handful of the rich. If nationalisation of the banks is so often confused with confiscation of private property, the dissemination of this confusion of terms is to be blamed on the bourgeois press, to whose interest it is to deceive the public.

Ownership of the capital which is manipulated by the banks, and which is concentrated in the banks, is attested by printed and written certificates, called stocks, bonds, notes, promissory notes, etc. None of these certificates is lost or changed when the banks are nationalised, *i.e.*, when all the banks are fused into one state bank. Whoever had 15 rubles in a savings bank account remains the owner of the 15 rubles after the nationalisation of the banks, and whoever had 15 millions will still have 15 millions in the form of stocks, bonds, promissory notes, commercial paper, and the like, even after the nationalisation of the banks.

Then what is the significance of the nationalisation of the banks?

The significance is that no real control is possible over individual banks and their operations (even after abolition of the commercial secret, etc.), for it is impossible to trace all those most complicated, most involved and subtle methods used in drawing up the balance-sheets, in organising bogus enterprises and branch banks, in using fictitious persons, and so on and so forth. Only the merging of all the banks into one, while in itself not signifying the least change in property relations, while, we repeat, not depriving a single owner of a single kopeck, offers the *possibility* of real control—of course, provided all the other measures indicated above are applied. Only when the banks are nationalised, is it possible to reach a stage where the state knows whither and how, from where and at what time millions and billions are flowing. And only control over the banks, over the centre, over the backbone and main mechanism of capitalist circulation, would allow, not in words but in deeds, the organisation of control over the whole economic life, over the production and distribution of the most essential products, the organisation of that "regulation of economic life" which otherwise is inevitably doomed to remain a ministerial phrase to fool the plain people. Only control over bank operations, provided they are merged into one state bank, will allow, simultaneously with other measures which can easily be put into effect, the actual levying of an income tax without concealment of property and income, while at present the income tax is to a very large degree a fiction.

It would be sufficient just to decree the nationalisation of the banks—the measure would then be carried out by the directors and employees themselves. No special apparatus, no special preparatory steps on the part of the state are here required; this measure can be actually realised by one decree, "at one blow." For the economic possibility of such a measure has been created by capitalism itself, once it has developed to the stage of promissory notes, stocks, bonds, etc. What remains to be done here is only the *unification of bookkeeping*, and if the revolutionary-democratic state decreed that in each city meetings should be called immediately, by telegraph, and in each region and throughout the country congresses of directors and employees should be called for the merging, without delay, of all banks into one state bank, this reform would be carried out within a few weeks. It is obvious that the directors and the higher officials would be the ones to offer resistance, to try and deceive the state, to delay the matter, etc., for these gentlemen would lose their particularly lucrative berths, would lose the opportunity of particularly profitable fraudulent operations—*and this is where the crux of the matter is*. But as to technical difficulties in the way of merging the banks, there are none whatever, and if the state power were revolutionary not only in words (*i.e.*, if it were not afraid to break with inertia and routine), if it were democratic not only in words (*i.e.*, if it acted in the interests of the majority of the people and not of a handful of rich persons), it would be sufficient to decree the confiscation of property and prison as punishment for the directors, board members and large shareholders for the least delay and for attempting to conceal documents and accounts; it would, for instance, be sufficient to unite the poor employees *separately* and to give them premiums for uncovering frauds and delays on the part of the rich— and the nationalisation of the banks would be accomplished most smoothly, most swiftly.

The advantages from the nationalisation of the banks for the whole people, and *not* especially for the workers (for the workers have little to do with banks) but for the mass of peasants and small industrialists, would be enormous. The saving of labour, as a result, would be gigantic, and assuming that the state would retain the former number of bank employees, the nationalisation would signify a highly important step in the direction of making the use of the banks universal, in the direction of increasing the number of their branches, the accessibility of their operations, etc., etc. The accessibility and the easy terms of credit, particularly for *small* owners, for the peasantry, would increase immensely. As for the state, it would for the first time be in a position to *survey* all the main monetary operations without concealing them, then to *control* them, then to *regulate* economic life, and finally to *obtain* millions and billions for large state operations, without paying the capitalist gentlemen sky-high "commissions" for their "services." This is the reason—the only reason—why all the capitalists, all the bourgeois professors, all the bourgeoisie, all the Plekhanovs, Potresovs, and Co. serving the bourgeoisie are foaming at the mouth fighting against the nationalisation of the banks, inventing thousands of pleas against this greatest and most urgent measure, although *even* from the standpoint of "defending" the country, *i.e.*, from the military standpoint, this measure would be a gigantic plus, enhancing the "military prowess" of the country to an enormous degree.

One may perhaps object, asking why such advanced states as Germany and the United States of America are putting into practice a splendid "regulation of economic life," without even thinking of nationalising the banks.

The reason is, we answer, that these states, though one is a monarchy and the other a republic, are *both* not only capitalist but also imperialist. As such they carry out the necessary reforms in a reactionary-bureaucratic way, whereas we here speak of a revolutionary-democratic way.

This "little difference" has very substantial significance. In most cases "it is not proper" to think about it. The words "revolutionary democracy" have become with us (particularly with the S.-R.'s and Mensheviks) almost a conventional phrase, like the expression "Thank God" used also by people who are not so ignorant as to believe in God, or like the expression "worthy citizen" sometimes addressed even to a contributor of the *Dyen* or *Yedinstvo*, although every one surmises that these papers were founded and are maintained by the capitalists and in the interests of the capitalists, and that, therefore, the participation in them of quasi-Socialists is but very little "worthy."

If the words "revolutionary democracy" are to be used not as a stereotyped official phrase, not as a conventional nickname, but as something whose meaning has to be *thought* about, then to be a democrat means to take into account the interests of the majority and not of a minority of the people; to be a revolutionary in reality means to smash, in the most decisive, the most merciless manner, all that is injurious, all that is obsolete. Neither in America nor in Germany do the government or the ruling classes claim, as far as we know, the title "revolutionary democracy" which our S.-R.'s and Mensheviks claim (and which they prostitute).

There are only *four* very large private banks in Germany of general national importance; there are only *two* such banks in America. It is easier, more convenient, more profitable for the financial kings of these banks to unite privately, secretly, in a reactionary, not in a revolutionary way, in a bureaucratic, not in a democratic way, bribing state officials (which is a general rule both in America *and in Germany*), retaining the private character of the banks just for the purpose of retaining the secrecy of operations, just for the purpose of getting millions upon millions of "super-profits" from that same state, just for the purpose of safeguarding fraudulent financial tricks.

Both America and Germany "regulate economic life" in such a manner as to create a *military prison* for the workers (partly for the peasants) and a *paradise* for the bankers and capitalists. Their regulation consists in "tightening the screw" on the workers to the extent of near-famine, and securing for the capitalists (secretly, in a reactionary, bureaucratic way) *larger* profits than those they had before the war.

Such a way is quite possible also for republican-imperialist Russia; it is being realised not only by the Milyukovs and Shingarevs but also by the Kerenskys jointly with Tereshchenko, Nekrasov, Bernatsky, Prokopovich, and Co., who *also defend* in a reactionary, bureaucratic way the "inviolability" of the banks, their sacred rights to enormous profits. This being the case, let us speak the *truth*. The wish in republican Russia is to regulate the economic life in a reactionary, bureaucratic way; but one is often hampered in carrying it out by the existence of the Soviets, which Kornilov Number One has not succeeded in dispersing, but which a Kornilov Number Two will attempt to disperse....

This will be the truth. And this simple though bitter truth is more useful for the enlightenment of the people than the sugary lie about "our" "great" "revolutionary" democracy....

The nationalisation of the banks would greatly facilitate the simultaneous nationalisation of the insurance business, *i.e.*, the merging of all insurance companies into one, the centralisation of their activities, the control over them by the state. Congresses of employees of insurance companies would here, too, carry out this merging immediately and without any difficulty, if the revolutionary-democratic state decreed it and ordered the directors of the boards and the large shareholders to carry it out without the least delay, on the strict responsibility of every one. The insurance business has hundreds of millions invested in it by the capitalists, and all the work is done by employees. A merger in this business would lower the insurance premiums and would yield a great number of conveniences and advantages to the insured; it would make it possible to extend the field of insurance with the same expenditure of forces and means. No other circumstances besides inertia, routine, and greed on the part of a handful of holders of lucrative posts are in the way of this reform, which would, again, raise the "defensive capacity" of the country, too, by saving people's labour, by opening a number of most earnest possibilities for "regulating economic life" not in words but in deeds.

Nationalisation of the Syndicates

Capitalism differs from the old pre-capitalist systems of national economy in that it has created the most intimate connection and interdependence between its various branches. If it were not for that, no steps towards Socialism, we may say in passing, would be technically realisable. As to modern capitalism, with the domination of the banks over production, it has developed this interdependence of the various branches of national economy to the highest degree. Banks and the largest branches of industry and commerce have grown into one indissoluble whole. This means, on the one hand, that it is impossible to nationalise the banks without taking steps towards the creation of a state monopoly of commercial and industrial syndicates (the sugar, coal, iron, oil and other syndicates), without nationalising those syndicates; on the other hand, it means that the regulation of economic life, if it is to be realised in earnest, demands a simultaneous nationalisation of both banks and syndicates.

Let us take the sugar syndicate as an example. It was created under tsarism and it then led to uniting in a large-scale capitalist way splendidly equipped plants, this uniting, of course, having been permeated through and through by a most reactionary and bureaucratic spirit, securing scandalously high profits for the capitalists and placing the employees and the workers in the position of humiliated, degraded slaves without any rights. The state then controlled and regulated production in favour of the wealthy magnates.

What remains here is *only* to turn the reactionary-bureaucratic regulation into a revolutionary-democratic one by a simple decree ordering the convocation of a congress of employees, engineers, directors and shareholders, the introduction of a uniform accounting system, control by the trade unions, etc. This is the simplest thing—and it remains undone!! *In reality,* there remains under a democratic republic the reactionary-bureaucratic regulation of the sugar industry; everything remains as of old: the plunder of the people's labour, routine and inertia, enrichment of the Bobrinskys and Tereshchenkos. To call on the democracy and not the bureaucracy, the workers and employees and not the "sugar kings," to show independent initiative—this could and should have been done in a few days, at one blow, if the S.-R.'s and Mensheviks had not befogged the consciousness of the people by plans of a "coalition" with these very same sugar kings, a coalition with the rich, which quite inevitably leads to "complete inactivity" of the government as far as the regulation of economic life is concerned.*

Take the oil industry. It was already "socialised" on a gigantic scale by the preceding development of capitalism. A couple of oil kings—those are the ones who manipulate millions and hundreds of millions, clipping coupons, gathering fabulous profits from a "business" which is *already* practically, technically, and socially organised on a national scale, which is *already* being managed by hundreds and thousands of employees, engineers, etc. The nationalisation of the oil industry is possible *at once,* and is obligatory for a revolutionary-democratic state, especially at a time when it is passing through a great crisis, when it is necessary at all costs to conserve people's labour and to increase the production of fuel. It is obvious that here bureaucratic control will yield nothing, will change nothing, for the "oil kings" will as easily be able to manage the Tereshchenkos, Kerenskys, Avksentyevs, and the Skobelevs, as they managed the Tsar's Ministers—resorting to procrastination, excuses, promises, even directly and indirectly bribing the bourgeois press (which is called "public opinion" and which the Kerenskys and the Avksentyevs "take into consideration"), bribing the officials

---

* These lines had already been written when I read in the newspapers that the Kerensky government was introducing a sugar monopoly, and, of course, introducing it in a reactionary-bureaucratic way, without meetings of the employees and workers, without publicity, and without curbing the capitalists!!

(who are being left by the Kerenskys and Avksentyevs in their old posts in the old, intact state apparatus).

In order to do something serious, one must pass, in a really revolutionary way, from bureaucracy to democracy, *i.e.*, declare a war against the oil kings and shareholders, decree the confiscation of their property, and jail sentences for delaying the nationalisation of the oil industry, for concealing incomes or accounts, for sabotaging production, for not taking steps towards increasing production. One must turn to the initiative of the workers and employees, to call *them* immediately into conferences and congresses, to give over to *them* a certain share of the profits on condition that a thorough control be organised and the production be increased. Had such revolutionary-democratic steps been taken immediately, promptly, in April, 1917, then Russia, one of the richest countries of the world in reserves of liquid fuel, could have done during the summer, with the aid of water transportation, a great deal in the way of furnishing the people with the necessary amount of fuel.

Neither the bourgeois nor the coalition government of S.-R.'s, Mensheviks and Cadets did anything; they confined themselves to playing at reforms in a bureaucratic way. Not a single revolutionary-democratic step did they dare to undertake. The same oil kings, the same inertia, the same hatred of the workers and employees towards the exploiters, the same state of dilapidation in this realm, the same plundering of people's labour—all as it was under tsarism, with a change only in the *titles* of the documents issued and received by the "republican" offices!

Concerning the coal industry, which is no less "ready," technically and culturally, for nationalisation, which is no less shamelessly managed by the coal kings, the robbers of the people, we have a number of very telling *facts* of direct sabotage, of direct *wrecking* and stopping of production by the industrialists. Even the ministerial Menshevik *Rabochaya Gazeta* has admitted these facts. And the result? Nothing, absolutely nothing has been done except old, reactionary-bureaucratic "half and half" conferences, with equal numbers of delegates from the workers and from the bandits of the coal syndicates!!

Not a single revolutionary-democratic step; not a shadow of an attempt to establish the only real control *from below*, through a union of employees, through the workers, by means of terror against the coal operators who are ruining the country and stopping production! How can it be otherwise when we "all" are in favour of a "coalition," if not with the Cadets, then with the commercial and industrial circles, and when coalition means leaving power with the capitalists, letting them go unpunished, letting them obstruct business, blame everything on the workers, increase economic ruin, and prepare *in this way* a new Kornilov affair.

Abolition of Commercial Secrets

Without abolishing commercial secrets, control over production and distribution either remains the most idle promise, necessary only for the Cadets to fool the S.-R.'s and Mensheviks and for the S.-R.'s and Mensheviks to fool the labouring classes, or it can be realised only by reactionary-bureaucratic methods and measures. Obvious as this may be for every unbiased person, insistent as was the *Pravda* * in demanding the abolition of commercial secrets (which was largely the reason why it was shut down by Kerensky, who is servile before capital), neither our republican government nor the "plenipotentiary organs of revolutionary democracy" as much as gave a thought to this *first word* of real control.

It is here that we have the key to all control. It is here that we have the most sensitive spot of capital which robs the people and sabotages production. It is for this reason that the S.-R.'s and Mensheviks are afraid to touch this point.

The usual argument of the capitalists, thoughtlessly repeated by the petty bourgeoisie, is that capitalist economy by no means allows the abolition of commercial secrets generally, for private property in the means of production and the dependence of individual enterprises upon the market necessitates, they say, the "sacred inviolability" of books and commercial, including banking, transactions.

Persons in one way or another repeating these and similar arguments, allow themselves to be fooled and in turn fool the people by closing their eyes to the two most fundamental, most important and generally known facts of modern economic life. First fact: large-scale capitalism, *i.e.*, the peculiar economy of banks, syndicates, large factories, etc. Second fact: war.

It is precisely modern large-scale capitalism, becoming everywhere monopoly capitalism, which removes every shadow of

* V. I. Lenin, *The Revolution of 1917, Collected Works*, Vol. XX, Book II, p. 141.—*Ed.*

reasonableness from the commercial secret, which makes it a hypocritical thing and an instrument solely for the concealment of financial swindles and the incredible profits of large-scale capital. Large-scale capitalist economy is, by its technical nature, socialised economy, *i.e.*, it both works for millions of people and unites by its operations, directly and indirectly, hundreds, thousands, and tens of thousands of families. This is not the same as the economy of the small artisan or middle peasant, who as a rule keep no books at all, and who are therefore in no way affected by the abolition of commercial secrets!

In large-scale economy the operations are known to hundreds and more persons, anyway. The law safeguarding commercial secrets serves here not the requirements of production or exchange but of speculation and enrichment in the crudest form; it aids direct swindle, which, as is well known, is particularly widespread in stock companies, and is most cleverly concealed by accounts and balance-sheets so contrived as to fool the public.

If the commercial secret is unavoidable in small commodity economy, *i.e.*, among small peasants and artisans where production itself is not socialised, where it is atomised and distributed among many, then in large-scale capitalist economy the safeguarding of this secret means safeguarding the privileges and profits of literally a handful of people *against* the entire people. This has already been recognised even by law, in so far as the publication of the accounts of stock companies has been introduced. But *this* control, already realised in all the advanced countries, as well as in Russia, is reactionary-bureaucratic control, which does not open the eyes of the people, which *does not allow* them to know *the whole truth* concerning the operations of stock companies.

In order to act in a revolutionary-democratic fashion, it would be necessary immediately to put in force a law abolishing commercial secrets, demanding of large-scale establishments and of rich people the completest accounts, granting any group of citizens comprising a substantial democratic number (say 1,000 or 10,000 voters) the right to examine *all* the documents of any large-scale enterprise. Such a measure can be easily and completely realised by a simple decree; and it is such a measure *alone* that would allow the *people's* initiative of control to unfold itself through the unions of employees, through the unions of workers, and through all the political parties; only such a measure would render control earnest and democratic.

Add to this the war. An immense majority of the commercial and industrial enterprises are now working not for the "open market," but *for the government*, for the war. I have already pointed out in the *Pravda* that those who argue against us by pleading the impossibility of introducing Socialism, are lying, they are thrice lying, for what we are here dealing with is not the introduction of Socialism immediately, for the present day, but the exposure *of treasury looting*.*

Capitalist economy working "for the war" (*i.e.*, economy directly or indirectly connected with war contracts) is systematic, legalised *treasury looting*. And the Cadet gentlemen, together with the Mensheviks and S.-R.'s who are against the abolition of commercial secrets, are nothing but *aiders and abettors* of treasury looters.

The war costs Russia fifty million rubles *daily*. Most of these fifty millions daily go to war contracts. Out of these fifty millions, at least five, and possibly ten and more *every day*, form the "legitimate profits" of the capitalists and the officials who are in collusion with them in one way or another. The particularly large firms and banks which loan money for war contract operations, reap unheard-of profits in this respect; they wax rich on treasury looting —for no other name can be found for this swindling and skinning of the people "on the occasion" of war disasters, "on the occasion" of the death of hundreds of thousands and millions of people.

"Everybody" knows of these scandalous profits made on contracts, of "promissory notes" issued by the banks, of fortunes made out of the mounting high prices; everybody speaks of it in "society" with a smirk. A good deal of exact information concerning this situation is to be found *even* in the bourgeois press, which, as a rule, evades "ticklish" questions. Everybody knows this, and everybody keeps quiet; everybody tolerates it, and everybody is at peace with the government, which talks grandiloquently about "control" and "regulation"!

Revolutionary democrats, if they were really revolutionists and democrats, would immediately promulgate a law abolishing commercial secrets, obliging contractors and merchants to render accounts, prohibiting them from relinquishing their field of activities

* V. I. Lenin, *The Revolution of 1917, Collected Works*, Vol. XX, Book II, p. 236.—*Ed.*

without permission of the authorities, introducing confiscation of property and the firing squad * for hiding anything and defrauding the people, organising examination of affairs and control *from below* in a democratic way, on the part of the people itself, on the part of unions, employees, workers, consumers, etc.

Our S.-R.'s and Mensheviks fully deserve the appellation "frightened democrats," for as far as this question is concerned, they repeat the things talked of by all frightened philistines, namely, that the capitalists would "run away" if the measures applied to them were "too severe," that without the capitalists "we" could not manage, that perhaps even the Anglo-French millionaires who "support" us may "be offended," and so forth. One would think that the Bolsheviks are proposing something unprecedented in the history of mankind, something never tested, something "Utopian"; whereas, as early as one hundred and twenty-five years ago, in France, men who were real "revolutionary democrats," who were really convinced of the just defensive character of the war on their part, who really based themselves on the masses of the people, sincerely convinced of the same things—those men knew how to establish a *revolutionary* control over the rich, and how to achieve results that commanded the admiration of the whole world. During the last century and a quarter the development of capitalism, having created banks, syndicates, railroads, etc., etc., has rendered measures of a really democratic control on the part of the workers and peasants over the exploiters, the landowners, and capitalists, a hundred times easier and more simple.

Strictly speaking, the entire question of control reduces itself to the point of who controls whom, *i.e.*, which class is the controlling and which is the controlled one. Up to now, in our republican Russia, with the connivance of the "plenipotentiary organs" of quasi-revolutionary democracy, the landowners and the capitalists are recognised and retained as controllers. As a result, capitalist looting is inevitable, with the accompanying indignation of the people, and with the economic ruin which is artificially fostered by the capitalists. What is necessary is to pass over, decisively, un-

---

* I have already had occasion to point out in the Bolshevik press that an argument against capital punishment must be recognised as correct only when it is against applying it *to the masses* of the toilers on the part of the exploiters, in the interests of safeguarding exploitation. It is doubtful whether any revolutionary government will be able to get along without capital punishment applied to the exploiters (*i.e.*, landowners and capitalists).

hesitatingly, not being afraid of breaking with the old, not being afraid of courageously building the new, to control *over* the landowners and capitalists by the workers and peasants. And it is precisely this which the S.-R.'s and Mensheviks are afraid of more than fire.

Compulsory Organisation Into Unions

Compulsory syndication, *i.e.*, compulsory organisation into unions, *e.g.*, the unions of industrialists, has already been put into practice in Germany. There is nothing new in this either. Here, too, it is the fault of the S.-R.'s and Mensheviks that we see complete stagnation in republican Russia, which these none-too-esteemed parties entertain with a quadrille which they dance with the Cadets, with the Bublikovs, or with Tereshchenko and Kerensky.

Compulsory syndication signifies on the one hand a certain acceleration of capitalist development brought about by the state. This development leads always and everywhere to the organisation of the class struggle, to the growth of the number, variety, and importance of unions. On the other hand, this compulsory "unionisation" is the necessary prerequisite for any sort of earnest control and any saving of the people's labour. The German law, for instance, makes it compulsory for the leather manufacturers of a given locality, or of a whole state, to unite into an association, with a representative of the state participating in the board for the purpose of control. Such a law does not directly, in itself, infringe upon the relations of private property in any degree; it does not take away a single kopeck from any owner, and it does not presage whether the control would be conducted in reactionary-bureaucratic or in revolutionary-democratic forms, trends or spirit.

Such laws could and should be put into force in our country immediately, losing not one week of the precious time, and leaving it to the *social circumstances themselves* to determine the more concrete forms of realising the law, the means of supervising its realisation, etc. The state needs here neither a special apparatus nor special research, nor any preparatory investigations for putting such a law into effect; what is needed is only the determination to break with some private interests of the capitalists who are "not used" to such interference, who are not willing to lose the super-profits which are assured as long as the old business method of no control prevails.

Neither an apparatus nor "statistics" (which Chernov wished to substitute for the revolutionary initiative of the peasantry) are necessary for the promulgation of such a law. Its realisation must be charged to the manufacturers or industrialists themselves, to the *existing* social forces; it must be carried out also under the control of existing social (*i.e.*, non-governmental, non-bureaucratic) forces, but necessarily under the control of those hailing from the so-called "lower estates," *i.e.*, from the oppressed, exploited classes which, throughout history, have always proved to be immeasurably *higher* than the exploiters, as far as capacity for heroism, for self-sacrifice, for comradely discipline is concerned.

Let us assume that we have a really revolutionary-democratic government and that it decrees that all manufacturers and industrialists in every branch of production, in cases where they employ, say, no less than two workers, are obliged immediately to unite into county and province associations. Responsibility for the scrupulous carrying out of this law is put primarily on the manufacturers, the directors, the members of the boards, the large shareholders (for these are the real leaders of modern industry, its real masters). For evading the work of immediately carrying the law into practice, these people are looked upon as deserters from military service, and are punished as such by being responsible, all for one and one for all, with their property subject to confiscation. In the second place, responsibility is placed on all the office employees, who are also obliged to form *one* union, as well as on the workers with their trade unions. The aim of "unionisation" is the establishment of the most complete, the most drastic and detailed accounting, and, above all, the *unification of operations* in the purchase of raw materials, in the selling of manufactured goods, in the conservation of national resources. When scattered individual enterprises are united into one syndicate, this conservation of national resources is tremendous; this is proved by economic science and the example of syndicates, cartels, and trusts. It must be repeated once more that, in itself, organisation into a syndicate does not change one iota the relations of private property and does not deprive a single owner of a single kopeck. This circumstance must be particularly stressed, for the bourgeois press continually "frightens" the small and middle-sized owners, telling them that the Socialists in general, the Bolsheviks in particular, wish to "expropriate" them—a notoriously false assertion, for *even after the complete Socialist revolu-*

tion the Socialists do not intend, cannot, and will not expropriate the small peasants. And we talk the whole time *only* of those immediate and urgent measures which have already been introduced in Western Europe, and which every more or less consistent democracy should have immediately introduced in our country for the struggle against the impending and unavoidable catastrophe.

The unification into associations of the small and very small enterprises would meet with serious difficulties, both technical and cultural, due to the extremely small size of the enterprises, their technical primitiveness, the illiterate or uneducated state of the owners. But such enterprises could be excluded from the law (as pointed out above in our hypothetical example) and their non-unification or their belated unification could not create serious difficulties, for the rôle of the overwhelming majority of small enterprises in the sum total of production, as far as their importance for the national economy in general is concerned, is *negligible*, and besides, they are often, in one way or another, dependent upon the large-scale enterprises.

Decisive importance is attached only to the large-scale enterprises where technical and cultural means as well as forces for "unionisation" *are in existence;* what is lacking to put these forces and means into operation is only a firm, decisive initiative of *revolutionary* power, mercilessly severe with the exploiters.

The poorer a country is in technically educated and intelligent forces in general, the more *urgent* it is as quickly and as decisively as possible to decree compulsory unification and to begin introducing it with the large and very large enterprises. For it is such a unification that will *conserve* intelligent forces, that will allow full utilisation and correct distribution of them. If even the Russian peasantry in its remote villages, working under the tsarist government, against a thousand odds created by it, was able, after 1905, to make a gigantic stride forward in the work of creating all sorts of associations, then it is obvious that the unification of large-scale and medium-sized industry and commerce could be introduced in a few months, if not sooner, provided this were urged by a really revolutionary-democratic government, based on the aid, participation, interestedness, and advantages of the "lower estates," the democracy, the office and factory workers, and appealing to them to exercise control.

Regulation of Consumption

The war has compelled all the belligerent and many of the neutral countries to introduce the regulation of consumption. The bread card made its appearance, became a customary phenomenon, and was followed by other cards. Russia did not remain untouched, but also introduced bread cards.

But it seems that just by this example we can furnish the best comparison between the reactionary-bureaucratic methods of fighting the catastrophe, methods striving to confine themselves to a minimum of reforms, and the revolutionary-democratic methods, which to deserve their name must make it their immediate task to break forcibly with the obsolete old and to accelerate as far as possible the movement forward.

The bread card, this typical sample of regulated consumption in the modern capitalist states, has as its aim and (at best) realises one thing: it distributes the existing food reserve in a manner to make it suffice for all. A minimum consumption is introduced not for all, but for the "staple" products. And this is all. Nothing more is cared for. The existing food reserves are bureaucratically taken stock of, divided by the number of persons; then a norm is established and introduced, and this is all. Articles of luxury are not touched because they are scarce "anyway," and they are "anyway" so expensive that they are inaccessible to the "people." This is why in *all* the belligerent countries without exception, even in Germany, which without risking contradiction may be considered an example of the most exact, most pedantic, most rigid regulation of consumption, even in Germany we observe how the rich constantly *evade* "norms" of consumption. This is also known to "everybody"; everybody speaks of this with a smirk, and in the German Socialist press and sometimes even in the bourgeois press, one can always find, notwithstanding the fierceness of the rigorous German censorship, notes and comment on the "menu" of the rich, on how they get white bread in unlimited quantities in some watering place or other (frequented by all who have the money to do so under the pretext of being sick), on the substitution by the rich of exquisite and rare articles of luxury for products used by the common people.

The reactionary capitalist state which is *afraid* of undermining the foundations of capitalism, the foundations of wage slavery, the foundations of the economic mastery of the rich, is *afraid* of developing the initiative of the workers and the toilers in general; it is *afraid* to "incite" them to demand more and more; *such* a state needs nothing but bread cards. Such a state does not lose sight for a moment, not at a single step, of the reactionary aim of strengthening capitalism, of not allowing it to be undermined, of limiting the "regulation of economic life" in general, the regulation of consumption in particular, to such measures as are absolutely necessary in order to be able to feed the people, without in the least degree *attempting* actually to regulate consumption in the sense of *control over the rich*, in the sense of imposing on those people who are better situated, privileged, sated, and over-fed in peace time, *greater* burdens in time of war.

The reactionary-bureaucratic solution of the problem put before the people by the war, is limited to the bread card, to equal distribution of the "common" products absolutely necessary for feeding the people, without deviating one iota from bureaucracy and reactionary policy, that is, from the aim: self-reliant activity on the part of the poor, the proletariat, the masses of the people (the *demos*), of not allowing any loopholes for the rich to gorge themselves with articles of luxury. And in *all* countries, we repeat, even in Germany—not to speak of Russia—a large number of loopholes are left, for the "common people" are starving while the rich frequent watering places, supplementing the meagre governmental ration by all sorts of "additional products" on the side and *not* allowing *themselves* to be controlled.

In Russia, which has just brought about a revolution against tsarism in the name of freedom and equality; in Russia, which has become at once a democratic republic as far as its actual political institutions are concerned, the ease with which the "bread cards" are evaded by the rich in a manner obvious to *all*, particularly strikes the eye of the people, particularly arouses discontent, irritation, anger, and indignation on the part of the masses. And this ease is particularly great. In a "clandestine" way, and for particularly high prices, especially when you have *"connections"* (which only the rich have), everything can be gotten in large quantities. The people are starving. Regulation of consumption is confined to very narrow bureaucratic reactionary limits. Not a shadow of consideration, not a shadow of care on the part of the government to place this regulation on a really revolutionary-democratic basis.

The queues are an evil from which "everybody" suffers, but ...

the rich send their servants to stand in line, and they even hire special help for this purpose! Here is democracy for you!

During the extraordinary sufferings the country is going through, and in order to fight the impending catastrophe, a revolutionary-democratic policy would not confine itself to bread cards, but would add, first, compulsory organisation of the population into consumers' societies, for without such an organisation it is impossible fully to introduce control over consumption; secondly, it would introduce the labour duty for the rich with the proviso that they must provide these consumers' societies with secretarial and other labour free of charge; thirdly, it would introduce among the population equal distribution of all articles of consumption without exception, so that the burdens of the war may really be equally distributed; fourthly, it would introduce such organisation of control that the consumption of the rich would be controlled by the poor classes of the population.

The introduction of real democracy in this realm, the manifestation of the real revolutionary spirit in the organisation of control on the part of the neediest classes of the people, would serve as a great stimulus towards straining every available intelligent force, towards developing the really revolutionary energy of the whole people. At present the Ministers of republican and revolutionary-democratic Russia, exactly like their brethren in all the other imperialist countries, use fine phrases about "labour for the benefit of the people," about "straining all efforts," but the people themselves sense, see, and feel the hypocrisy of these words.

The result is marking time, while economic deterioration spreads unchecked, and a catastrophe is approaching. For on the one hand, our government cannot introduce military prison labour for the workers, after the pattern of Kornilov, Hindenburg, and the imperialists, due to the fact that the traditions, memories, traces, habits, and institutions of the *revolution* are still too fresh in the mind of the people; on the other hand, it cannot take really earnest steps on the revolutionary-democratic road, for it is soaked through with, and entangled from top to bottom in, the relations of dependence upon the bourgeoisie, of a "coalition" with it, and with the fear of infringing upon its real privileges.

The Destruction of the Work of Democratic Organisations by the Government

We have reviewed the various means and methods of fighting the catastrophe and the famine. We have seen everywhere the irreconcilable contradictions existing between democracy, on the one hand, and the government, as well as the bloc of S.-R.'s and Mensheviks who support it, on the other. To prove that these contradictions exist in reality, and not only in our exposition, and that the impossibility of harmonising them is *actually* proven by conflicts of nation-wide importance, it suffices to recall two particularly typical "results" and lessons of the half year's history of our revolution.

The history of Palchinsky's "reign" is one lesson. The history of Peshekhonov's "reign" and fall is another lesson.*

The measures described above of fighting the catastrophe and the famine reduce themselves in reality to thorough encouragement (up to compulsion) of "unionising" the population, and in the first place the democracy, *i.e.*, the majority of the population; that is, in the first place, the oppressed classes, the workers and peasants, especially the poorest peasants. This path was spontaneously taken by the population itself, for the purpose of fighting the extraordinary difficulties, burdens, and miseries of the war.

Tsarism thwarted the independent and free "unionisation" of the population in every possible way. After the fall of the tsarist monarchy, democratic organisations began to spring up and grow rapidly all over Russia. The struggle against the catastrophe began to be waged by independently arising democratic organisations—committees of supplies of all sorts, food committees, fuel conferences, and so on and so forth.

Now the most remarkable thing in the half year's history of our revolution, as far as the question under consideration is concerned, is the fact that the *government* which calls itself republican and revolutionary, the government *supported* by the Mensheviks and S.-R.'s in the name of the "plenipotentiary organs of revolutionary democracy," *has fought against* the democratic organisations and has *suppressed them!!!*

By this struggle, Palchinsky acquired a sad notoriety which is widespread throughout Russia. He acted behind the back of the

---

* Former Ministers of Commerce and Industry, and Supplies, respectively.—*Ed.*

government without openly appearing before the people (in the very same way as the Cadets generally preferred to act when they willingly put forward Tsereteli "for the people's sake," while they themselves manipulated all the important affairs on the quiet). Palchinsky thwarted and destroyed every serious measure on the part of the spontaneous democratic organisations. For not a single serious measure could go through without a "dent" in the immense profits and the self-willed rule of the Kit Kityches. And Palchinsky was a devoted defender and servant of the Kit Kityches. It went so far—and the fact was published in the papers—that Palchinsky directly cancelled the orders of the spontaneous democratic organisations!

The whole history of Palchinsky's "reign"—he "reigned" for many months, just at the time when Tsereteli, Skobelev, and Chernov were "Ministers"—is one continuous, hideous scandal; it is a violation of the will of the people, of the decisions of democracy, in favour of the capitalists, for the sake of their filthy greed. Only an insignificant fraction of Palchinsky's "exploits" could naturally appear in the papers; a full investigation of how he *hindered* the struggle against famine only a truly democratic government of the proletariat will succeed in carrying out when it will have conquered power and brought Palchinsky and his ilk before the people's court, without concealing the matter.

One may perhaps argue that Palchinsky after all was an exception and was removed. The trouble is that Palchinsky is not an exception but the *rule;* that with the removal of Palchinsky the situation has not improved one whit; that his place has been taken by similar Palchinskys bearing other names; that all the *"influence"* of the capitalists, all the policies of *hindering the struggle against famine to please the capitalists,* have remained intact. For Kerensky and Co. are nothing but a screen to shield the interests of the capitalists. The most striking proof of this is the resignation from the cabinet of Peshekhonov, the Minister of Supplies. It is well known that Peshekhonov is a very, very moderate Narodnik.* Still he wished to work conscientiously in organising supplies, he wished to work in conjunction with the democratic organisations, and basing himself on them. The *experience* of Peshekhonov's work and his *resignation* are the more interesting, since this most moderate Narodnik, a member of the "People's Socialist" Party, a man ready to enter

* Populist.—*Ed.*

into any kind of compromises with the bourgeoisie, was finally compelled to leave! For Kerensky's government, to please the capitalist landowners and kulaks, actually *raised* the fixed prices on grain!

This is how Mr. Smith describes this "step" and its meaning in the paper *Svobodnaya Zhizn*, September 15, No. 1.

A few days before the government adopted the measure of raising the fixed prices, this is what happened in the national supply committee. Rolovich, a representative of the Right, a stubborn defender of the interests of private trade and an uncompromising enemy of the grain monopoly and state interference in economic life, stated with a self-satisfied smile that according to his information the fixed prices on grain would soon be raised.

On the other hand, the representative of the Soviet of Workers' and Soldiers' Deputies, in reply, declared that he knew nothing of the kind, that as long as the revolution existed in Russia such a thing would not take place, that at any rate, the government could not take such a step without conferring with the plenipotentiary organs of democracy, the Economic Council and the National Supply Committee. This declaration was seconded by the representative of the Soviet of Peasant Deputies.

Alas, reality has furnished a cruel amendment to this controversy. Not the representatives of democracy but the representative of the propertied elements proved to be right. The latter proved excellently informed concerning the contemplated attempt on the rights of democracy, although its representatives indignantly denied the very possibility of such an attempt.[78]

Thus the representative of the workers and the representative of the peasantry both definitely make known their opinion in the name of a gigantic majority of the people—and still Kerensky's government acts the other way, in the interests of the capitalists!

Rolovich, a representative of the capitalists, proved excellently informed behind the back of democracy. This is in keeping with what we have always observed and observe now—that the bourgeois papers, the *Ryech* and the *Birzhevka*, are best informed about what is going on in Kerensky's cabinet.

What does this remarkable possession of information indicate? Clearly it indicates that the capitalists have their own "avenues" and that they *actually* hold power in their hands. Kerensky is a figure-head which they put forward wherever and whenever it suits them. The interests of tens of millions of workers and peasants prove to be sacrificed to the profits of a handful of the rich.

What do our S.-R.'s and Mensheviks say to this revolting mockery of the people? Would they perhaps address the workers and the peasants with an appeal saying that after this the only place for Kerensky and his colleagues is in jail?

God forbid. The S.-R.'s and Mensheviks, acting through the

"Economic Section" which belongs to them, confined themselves to a stern resolution, which we have already mentioned! In this resolution they declared that the raising of the grain prices by Kerensky's government was a *"pernicious* measure which aimed the *greatest blow* both at the work of supply and at the whole economic life of the country," and that those pernicious measures were adopted in direct *"violation"* of the law!

Such are the results of a policy of compromise, a policy of flirting with Kerensky and of wishing to "spare" him!

The government violates the law to please the rich, the landowners, and capitalists, adopting a measure which *ruins* all the work of control, of furnishing supplies and of salvaging the extremely shaky finances, while the S.-R.'s and Mensheviks continue to talk about an understanding with the commercial and industrial circles, while they continue to attend conferences with Tereshchenko, to spare Kerensky and to confine themselves to paper resolutions of protest which the government very calmly pigeon-holes!

This is where the truth of the fact that the S.-R.'s and Mensheviks have betrayed the cause of the people and the revolution, and that the Bolsheviks have become the real leaders of the masses, *even of* the S.-R. and Menshevik masses, is revealed in the most striking manner.

For it is the conquest of power by the proletariat, with the party of the Bolsheviks at its head, that alone would be capable of putting an end to the mischief done by Kerensky and Co., and of restoring the work of the democratic organisations of supply, etc., which Kerensky and his government are *ruining*.

The Bolsheviks come forward—as may be seen with absolute clarity in the above example—as the representatives of the interests of the *whole* people, the interests of securing the work of supply, the interests of satisfying the most urgent needs of the workers *and the peasants*, despite the vacillating, undecided, truly traitorous policy of the S.-R.'s and Mensheviks, a policy that has brought the country to shame, such as this rise in the price of grain!

Financial Collapse and Measures Against It

The question of the rise in the fixed price of grain has yet another side to it. This rise means a new chaotic increase in the issue of paper money, a new step forward in the process of increasing the high cost of living, increasing the financial disorganisation, and bringing nearer a financial collapse. Everybody recognises that the issue of paper money is the worst kind of a compulsory loan, that it worsens the conditions principally of the workers, of the poorest section of the population, that it is the chief evil in the financial confusion.

And it is this measure that Kerensky's government, supported by the S.-R.'s and Mensheviks, resorts to!

There is no other way of earnestly fighting the financial disorganisation and the inevitable financial collapse than a revolutionary rupture with the interests of capital and organisation of really democratic control, *i.e.*, control "from below," control of the workers and the poorest peasants *over* the capitalists—that way which all our preceding analysis deals with.

The unlimited issue of paper money encourages speculation, allows the capitalists to make millions, and places tremendous obstacles in the path of the much-needed expansion of production; for the dearth of materials, machines, etc., grows and progresses by leaps and bounds. How can matters be improved when the riches acquired by the rich through speculation are being concealed?

An income tax with progressive and very high rates for large and extra-large incomes, may be introduced. Our government, following the other imperialist governments, has introduced this tax. But to a considerable extent it remains a fiction, a dead letter, for, in the first place, the value of money is sinking faster and faster; secondly, the concealment of incomes is the more general the more their source is speculation and the more the preservation of commercial secrets is safeguarded.

To make the tax real and not fictitious, real control and not one on paper is required. Control over the capitalists, however, is impossible if it remains bureaucratic, for the bureaucracy itself is connected and intertwined with the bourgeoisie by thousands of threads. This is why in the Western European imperialist states, whether monarchies or republics, financial stability is achieved only at the price of introducing "labour duty" which creates for the workers *military penal labour* or *military slavery.*

Reactionary bureaucratic control—this is the only means known to the imperialist states, the democratic republics of France and America not excluded; this is how they shift the burdens of the war onto the proletariat and the labouring masses in general.

The fundamental contradiction of our governmental policy is that in order not to quarrel with the bourgeoisie, not to destroy the "coalition" with it, it is compelled to introduce reactionary-bureaucratic control, calling it "revolutionary-democratic," deceiving the people at every step, irritating and embittering the masses who have just overthrown tsarism.

Still, it is precisely revolutionary-democratic measures, in combining into unions the oppressed classes, the workers and peasants, the masses in general, that would make it possible to establish most effective control *over the rich*, and to fight most successfully against the concealment of incomes.

The circulation of checks is being encouraged to combat the excessive issue of paper money. To the poor this measure is of no consequence, since the poor population lives from hand to mouth anyway, completing its "business turnover" within one week, and thus returning to the capitalists the meagre pittance which it manages to earn. As far as the rich are concerned, the circulation of checks would be of enormous importance, for it would allow the state, especially in connection with such measures as the reorganisation of the banks and the abolition of commercial secrets, *really* to control the incomes of the capitalists, really to tax them, really to "democratise" (and at the same time to stabilise) the financial system.

But here the fear of touching upon the privileges of the bourgeoisie, of breaking the "coalition" with it, is an obstacle. For without really revolutionary measures, without the most grave compulsion, the capitalists will not submit to any control, they will not make known their budgets, nor will they put their reserves of paper money "in the care" of the democratic state.

In nationalising the banks, in making the circulation of checks compulsory by law for all the rich, in abolishing commercial secrets, in introducing the confiscation of property for concealing incomes, etc., the workers and peasants, organised in unions, could most easily render control both effective and universal, *i.e.*, control over the rich, control which would *return to the treasury* the paper money issued by it, by taking it away *from those* who have it, *from those* who conceal it.

For this purpose a revolutionary dictatorship of the democracy headed by the revolutionary proletariat is necessary, *i.e.*, for this purpose democracy must become revolutionary *in deeds*.

This is the whole crux of the matter. This is what our S.-R.'s and Mensheviks do not wish to have when they deceive the people by the flag of revolutionary democracy, and when they in reality support the reactionary-bureaucratic policy of the bourgeoisie, which is guided, now as ever, by the principle of *après nous le déluge*—after us, the deluge.

Ordinarily we do not even notice how deeply ingrained in us are the anti-democratic habits and prejudices concerning the "sacredness" of bourgeois property. When an engineer or a banker publishes information concerning the income and expenditures of a worker, when he publishes data concerning his earnings and the productivity of labour, this is considered perfectly legitimate and just. Nobody undertakes to discover here an attempt on the "private life" of the workers, "spying" or "informing" on the part of the engineer. Labour and the earnings of the hired workers are looked upon as an open book which every bourgeois may look into, using it to expose the "extravagance" of the worker, his alleged "laziness," etc.

But what about the reverse? What if the unions of office workers, clerks and *domestic* servants were to be invited by the *democratic* state to go over the records of income and expenditure of the capitalists, to publish data concerning these items, to aid the government in fighting against the concealment of incomes?

What a savage howl the bourgeoisie would then raise against "snooping," against "informing"! When the "masters" control the domestics, when the capitalists control the workers, it is considered quite the ordinary thing; the private life of the toilers and exploited is *not* considered inviolate; the bourgeoisie has a right to call to account every "wage slave," to discuss his income and expenditures. But the attempt on the part of the oppressed to control the oppressor, to reveal *his* expenditures and incomes, to disclose *his* extravagances, even during the war when this extravagance is the direct cause of famine and of the destruction of armies at the front—oh, no, then the bourgeoisie will not allow any "snooping" or "informing"!

The question still reduces itself to this: the rule of the bourgeoisie is *incompatible* with true democracy that is truly revolutionary. It is impossible to be a revolutionary democrat in the twentieth century and in a capitalist country *if one is afraid* to march towards Socialism.

Is It Possible to Go Forward While Being Afraid of Socialism?

The reader impressed with the current opportunist ideas of the S.-R.'s and the Mensheviks may raise the following objection to the preceding argument: are not most of the measures here described in essence not democratic, but *definitely* Socialist measures?

This current argument, usually to be met in one or the other form in the bourgeois, S.-R. and Menshevik press, is a reactionary defence of backward capitalism, a Struve-like, masked defence. It amounts to saying that we are not yet ripe for Socialism, that it is early to "introduce" Socialism, that our revolution is a bourgeois one, that therefore we must be servants of the bourgeoisie (although the great bourgeois revolutionists of France made their revolution of one hundred and twenty-five years ago great by means of *terror* against all oppressors and against the landowners and capitalists!).

The mock-Marxists who are in the service of the bourgeoisie and who have been joined by the S.-R.'s, in arguing this way fail to understand (if we examine the theoretical foundations of their opinions) what imperialism is, what capitalist monopoly is, what the state is, and what revolutionary democracy is. For, once this is understood, it is impossible not to admit that no progress is possible without marching toward Socialism.

Everybody talks about imperialism. But imperialism is nothing but monopoly capitalism.

That in Russia, too, capitalism has become monopoly capitalism is eloquently confirmed by the coal trust, metal trust, sugar syndicate, etc. The same sugar syndicate shows clearly how monopoly capitalism develops into state monopoly capitalism.

And what is the state? It is the organisation of the ruling class; in Germany, for instance, the Junkers and capitalists. That is why the measure called "war Socialism" by the German Plekhanovs (Scheidemann, Lensch, and others) is in reality war-time state monopoly capitalism. Or to speak more plainly and clearly, it is military penal labour for the workers, military defence of the capitalists' profits.

But try and substitute for the Junker-capitalist, for the landowner-capitalist state, a *revolutionary democratic* state, i.e., such as would destroy *all* privileges in a revolutionary way without being afraid of introducing in a revolutionary way the fullest possible democracy

THE THREATENING CATASTROPHE 211

—and you shall see that, in a truly revolutionary-democratic state, state monopoly capitalism inevitably and unavoidably means progress towards Socialism.

For, once a large-scale capitalist enterprise becomes a monopoly, this means that it serves the entire people. Once it has become state monopoly, this means that the state (*i.e.*, the armed organisation of the population, primarily of the workers and the peasants, assuming there is a really *revolutionary* democracy) directs the entire enterprise—in whose interests?

Either in the interests of the landowners and capitalists; then we have not a revolutionary democratic but a reactionary bureaucratic state, an imperialist republic; or in the interests of revolutionary democracy; then *this is in reality a step towards Socialism.*

For Socialism is nothing but the next step forward from state capitalist monopoly. In other words, Socialism is nothing but state capitalist monopoly *made to benefit the whole people;* by this token it *ceases* to be capitalist monopoly.

There is no middle course here. The objective course of development is such that it is *impossible* to go ahead from monopolies (whose number, rôle and importance have been increased tenfold by the war) without moving towards Socialism.

Either you are a revolutionary-democrat in deeds—and then you do not have to be afraid of steps leading towards Socialism—or you are afraid of steps leading towards Socialism, you are denouncing them Plekhanov-fashion, by Dan arguments, by Chernov arguments, saying that our revolution is a bourgeois revolution, that it is impossible to "introduce" Socialism, etc.—then you must unavoidably sink to the level of Kerensky, Milyukov, Kornilov, *i.e.*, to the position of suppressing in a *reactionary-bureaucratic* manner the revolutionary-democratic tendencies of the workers and the peasant masses.

There is no middle course.

And therein lies the fundamental contradiction of our revolution.

It is impossible to stand still in history generally, in war time particularly. One must go either forward or backward. It is impossible to go forward in the Russia of the twentieth century, a Russia that has won a republic and a democracy in a revolutionary way, without *going* towards Socialism, without taking *steps* towards it (steps determined and circumscribed by the level of technique and culture, for large-scale machine economy cannot be "introduced" into peasant agriculture, and it cannot be abolished in the sugar industry). And if you are afraid to go forward, that means you are going backward, which is exactly what the Kerenskys are doing, to the delight of the Milyukovs and Plekhanovs and with the foolish aid of the Tseretelis and the Chernovs.

The dialectics of history are such that the war, having accelerated the transformation of monopoly capitalism into state monopoly capitalism, has *by the same token* brought humanity immeasurably closer to Socialism.

The imperialist war is the eve of the Socialist revolution. And this is so not only because the war with its horrors is generating a proletarian uprising—no uprising will create Socialism if it has not ripened economically—but because state monopoly capitalism is the fullest *material* preparation for Socialism, is its threshold, is that rung on the historic ladder between which rung and the one called Socialism *there are no intermediate rungs.*

Our S.-R.'s and Mensheviks approach the question of Socialism in a doctrinaire fashion; they approach it from the angle of a once memorised and badly digested doctrine. They regard Socialism as something far away, unknown, some hazy future.

In reality Socialism looks at us now through all the windows of present-day capitalism; the outline of Socialism appears before us *in practice;* it emerges from every large-scale measure forming a step forward on the basis of this modern capitalism.

What is universal labour duty?

It is a step forward on the basis of modern monopoly capitalism, a step towards regulating the economic life as a whole according to a certain general plan; it is a step towards saving the labour of the people, towards preventing its senseless waste by capitalism.

In Germany the Junkers (landowners) and capitalists are introducing universal labour duty, which inevitably becomes military penal labour for the workers.

Take, however, the same institution and analyse its meaning under the revolutionary democratic state. Universal labour duty, introduced, regulated, and directed by the Soviets of Workers', Soldiers', and Peasants' Deputies is *not yet* Socialism, but it is *no longer* capitalism. It is a tremendous *step* towards Socialism, a step from which, if complete democracy is retained, no backward step towards capitalism would be possible without the most atrocious violence perpetrated upon the masses.

The War and the Fight Against Economic Ruin

The question of measures to fight the approaching catastrophe makes it necessary to throw light on another most important question, namely, the question of the connection between internal and foreign politics, or, in other words, the interrelation between an imperialist war of conquest and a revolutionary, proletarian war, between a criminally predatory and a justly democratic war.

All the above measures of fighting the catastrophe would, as we have already pointed out, immeasurably strengthen the defensive power, or, in other words, the military strength of the country. This on the one hand. On the other hand, these measures cannot be introduced without transforming the predatory war into a just war, without transforming the war waged by the capitalists in the interests of the capitalists into a war waged by the proletariat in the interests of all the toilers and exploited.

The nationalisation of banks and syndicates, coupled with the abolition of commercial secrets and with the workers' control over the capitalists, would in fact mean not only a gigantic saving of the people's labour, a possibility of economising forces and resources, it would also mean an improvement in the situation of the labouring *masses* of the population, of its majority. It is well known that in modern wars economic organisation is of decisive importance. There is plenty of bread, coal, naphtha, iron in Russia. In this respect our situation is better than that of any of the belligerent European countries. In fighting against economic ruin by the means indicated above, by attracting to this struggle the initiative of the masses from below, by improving their conditions, by introducing the nationalisation of the banks and the syndicates, Russia would utilise its revolution and its democracy to raise the entire country to an immeasurably higher stage of economic organisation.

If the S.-R.'s and Mensheviks, instead of a "coalition" with the bourgeoisie which hampers all the measures of control and sabotages production, had brought about in April the passing of power to the Soviets, and if they had directed all their forces not to ministerial leap-frog, not to wearing out holes, side by side with the Cadets, in their Ministers' and Assistant Ministers' chairs, etc., etc., but to directing the workers and peasants in *their* control *over* the capitalists, in their *war against* the capitalists, Russia would now be a country fully reorganised economically, with the land in the hands of the peasants, with banks nationalised, that is, it would be *in this respect* (and these are the most important economic bases of modern life) *superior* to all the other capitalist countries.

When the banks are nationalised, the defensive strength, the military strength of a country is greater than when the banks remain in private hands. When the land is in the hands of peasant committees, the military strength of a peasant country is *greater* than that of a country where the land is in the hands of landowners.

The heroic patriotism and the marvels of military valour of the French in 1792-1793 are repeatedly cited. But the material, the economic conditions of that historic period, which alone made these marvels possible, are forgotten. Real revolutionary action against obsolete feudalism, the passing of all the country, with a swiftness, a decisiveness, a vigour, a determination that are truly revolutionary and democratic, to a higher method of production, to free peasant landownership—those were the material, the economic conditions that saved France with "marvellous" rapidity by *regenerating, rejuvenating* its economic basis.

The example of France tells us one thing and one only: to make Russia capable of defending herself, to achieve "marvels" of mass heroism here, all the old must be swept away with "Jacobin" ruthlessness. Russia must be rejuvenated, regenerated *economically*. And this cannot be done in the twentieth century by merely sweeping away tsarism (France did not confine itself to this one hundred and twenty-five years ago). This cannot be done even by merely abolishing landowners' property in land in a revolutionary way (we have not accomplished even that, for the S.-R.'s and Mensheviks have betrayed the peasantry), by merely giving over the land to the peasantry. For we are living in the twentieth century, and power over the land *without power over the banks* is not capable of regenerating, rejuvenating the life of the people.

The material, the economic regeneration of France by the end of the eighteenth century was combined with political and spiritual regeneration, with a dictatorship of the revolutionary democracy and revolutionary proletariat (from which democracy had not separated itself and which was as yet almost amalgamated with it), with a merciless war waged against everything reactionary. All the people, and particularly the masses, *i.e.*, the oppressed classes, were seized with a boundless revolutionary enthusiasm; *everybody* considered the war a just defensive war, and *it really was*. Revolutionary France defended itself against reactionary-monarchist Europe. Not in 1792-1793, but many years later, *after* the triumphant reaction within the country, the counter-revolutionary dictatorship of Napoleon transformed the wars waged by France from defensive wars to wars of conquest.

And in Russia? We are continuing to wage an imperialist war, in the interests of the capitalists, in alliance with the imperialists, in conformity with the secret treaties which the Tsar concluded with the capitalists of England, etc., and in which he promised the Russian capitalists to rob foreign countries, Constantinople, Lemberg, Armenia, and so forth.

The war remains an unjust, reactionary war, a war of conquest on the part of Russia as long as it has not offered a just peace and has not broken with imperialism. The social character of the war, its real meaning, is determined not by the location of the enemy troops (as the S.-R.'s and Mensheviks think, sinking to the vulgar conceptions of an unenlightened peasant). This character is determined by the policy which the war pursues ("war is a continuation of politics"), by the class that wages the war and the aims it pursues.

It is impossible to lead the masses into a robbers' war in accordance with secret treaties and still expect them to show enthusiasm. The foremost class of revolutionary Russia, the proletariat, realises ever more clearly the criminal character of the war, while the bourgeoisie not only has failed to shatter this conviction of the masses, but on the contrary, the consciousness of the criminal character of the war is growing. The proletariat of *both capitals* of Russia has become definitely internationalist. How can any one talk about mass enthusiasm here in favour of the war?

One thing is inseparably bound up with the other: internal politics with foreign politics. It is impossible to render the country capable of defending itself without the greatest heroism on the part of the people in courageously and decisively carrying out great economic transformations. And it is impossible to appeal to the heroism of the masses without breaking with imperialism, without offering to all the peoples a democratic peace, without thus transforming the war from a war of conquest, a predatory, criminal war, into a just, defensive, revolutionary war.

Only a decisively consistent break with the capitalists both in internal and foreign politics can save our revolution and our country, held in the iron grasp of imperialism.

Revolutionary Democracy and the Revolutionary Proletariat

To be really revolutionary, the democracy of present-day Russia must march in full unity with the proletariat, supporting its struggle as that of the only class that is thoroughly and consistently revolutionary.

This is the conclusion following from an analysis of the question as to the means of fighting the catastrophe which is as unavoidable as it is unprecedented in size.

But the war has brought about such an immense crisis, it has so strained the material and moral forces of the people, it has dealt such blows to the entire modern social organisation, that humanity is confronted with the alternative of either perishing or entrusting its fate to the most revolutionary class for the purpose of passing most speedily and in the most radical way to a higher method of production.

Due to a number of historic causes: the greater backwardness of Russia, the particular difficulties the country has encountered in the war, the great rottenness of tsarism, the extraordinarily vivid traditions of 1905, the revolution broke out in Russia sooner than in other countries. Due to the revolution, Russia, in its *political* structure, has caught up with the advanced countries in the course of a few months.

But this is not enough. War is implacable; it puts the question with merciless sharpness: either overtake the advanced countries and surpass them *also economically*, or perish.

It is possible to do this, for we have before us the experiences of a great number of advanced countries; we have available the results of their technique and culture. The growing protest against the war in Europe, the atmosphere of the rising world revolution of the workers, give us moral support. We are being forced, lashed into action by a revolutionary-democratic freedom that is unusually rare during an imperialist war.

Either full steam ahead, or perish. This is how history has put the question.

The attitude of the proletariat towards the peasantry at such a moment only confirms, while correspondingly modifying it, the old Bolshevik position that it is necessary to wrest the peasantry from the influence of the bourgeoisie. Here alone is the guarantee of saving the revolution.

But the peasantry is numerically the strongest representative of the whole petty-bourgeois mass.

Our S.-R.'s and Mensheviks have assumed a reactionary rôle: they wish to keep the peasantry under the influence of the bourgeoisie, to lead the peasantry to a coalition with the bourgeoisie and not with the proletariat.

The experience of the revolution teaches the masses rapidly. Accordingly, the reactionary policy of the S.-R.'s and the Mensheviks is suffering a collapse: they are beaten in the Soviets of both capitals.[79] The "Left" opposition is growing in both petty-bourgeois democratic parties. The city conference of the S.-R.'s in Petrograd yielded, September 23, 1917, a two-thirds majority to the *Left* S.-R.'s, who tend towards a union with the proletariat and reject a union (coalition) with the bourgeoisie.[80]

The S.-R.'s and Mensheviks keep repeating the bourgeoisie's favourite contradistinction: bourgeoisie and democracy. Such a contradistinction is just as senseless as comparing pounds with yards.

There is a democratic bourgeoisie, and there is a bourgeois democracy; only complete ignorance both of history and political economy can deny that.

The S.-R.'s and Mensheviks needed the incorrect contradistinction to *conceal* the undeniable fact that between the bourgeoisie and the proletariat stands the *petty bourgeoisie*. This petty bourgeoisie, in consequence of its economic class position, vacillates between the bourgeoisie and the proletariat.

The S.-R.'s and Mensheviks try to draw the petty bourgeoisie into a union with the bourgeoisie. This is the substance of all their "coalitions," of the whole coalition cabinet, of all the policies of Kerensky, that typical semi-Cadet. After a half year of revolution, this policy has suffered complete collapse.

The Cadets are full of malicious glee: the revolution, they say, has suffered collapse; the revolution has *not* been able to cope either with the war or with the economic ruin.

This is not true. It is the *Cadets*, the *S.-R.'s* and the *Mensheviks* who have suffered collapse, for it is this bloc that has ruled Russia for half a year, only to increase the economic ruin, to entangle and render more difficult the military situation.

The more complete the collapse of the *union* of the bourgeoisie with the *S.-R.'s and Mensheviks*, the sooner will the people *learn their lesson*, the easier will they find the *correct* way out: a union of the poorest peasantry, *i.e.*, the majority of the peasantry, with the proletariat.

Written September 23-27, 1917.
Published at the end of October, 1917, as a pamphlet, by the publishing firm "Soldiers' and Peasants' Library."

ON THE ROAD TO INSURRECTION

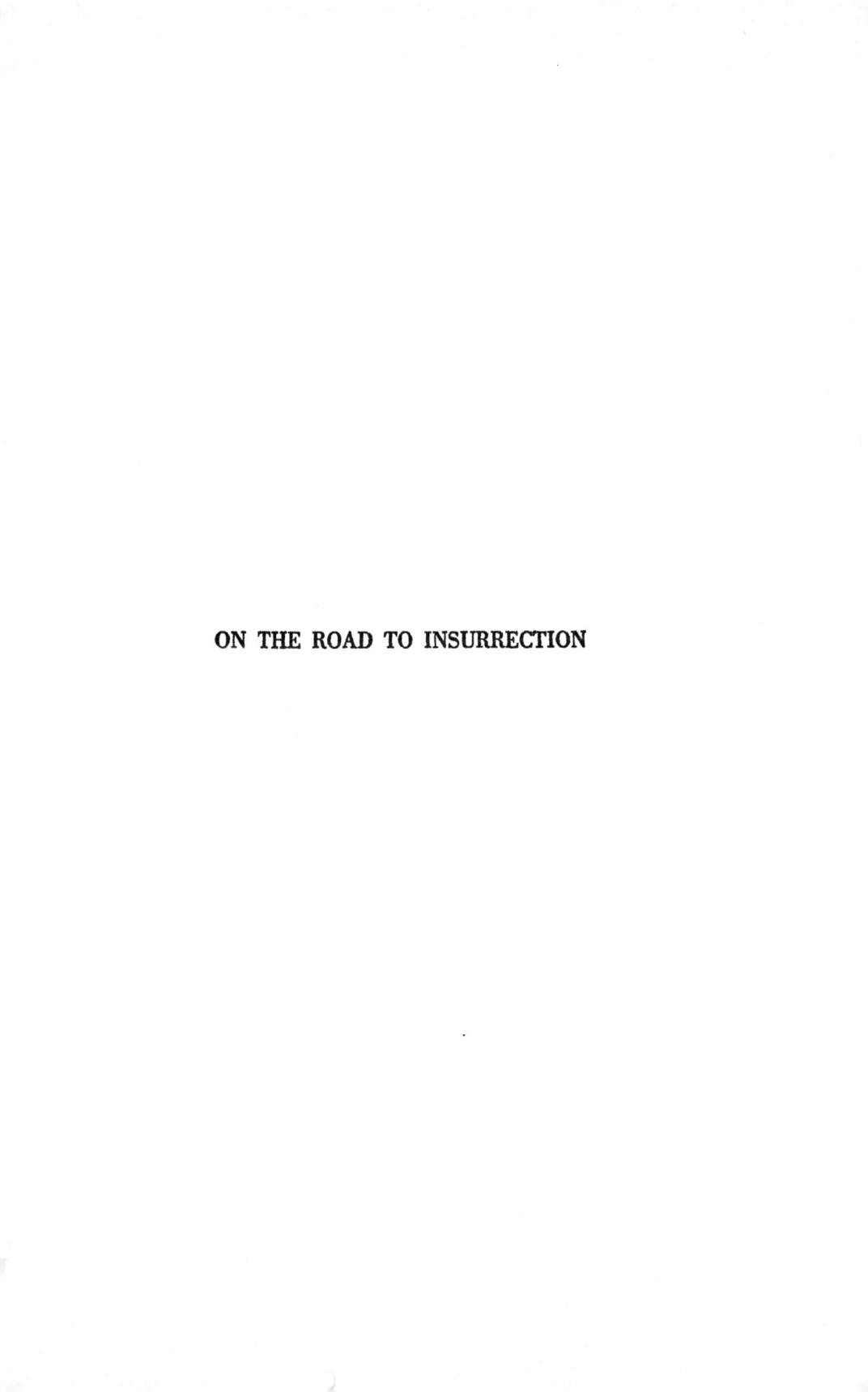

THE BOLSHEVIKS MUST ASSUME POWER [81]

LETTER TO THE CENTRAL COMMITTEE, THE PETROGRAD AND MOSCOW
COMMITTEES OF THE RUSSIAN SOCIAL-DEMOCRATIC LABOUR PARTY

HAVING obtained a majority in the Soviets of Workers' and Soldiers' Deputies of both capitals, the Bolsheviks can and must take power into their hands.

They can do so because the active majority of the revolutionary elements of the people of both capitals is sufficient to attract the masses, to overcome the resistance of the adversary, to vanquish him, to conquer power and to retain it. For, in offering immediately a democratic peace, in giving the land immediately to the peasants, in re-establishing the democratic institutions and liberties which have been mangled and crushed by Kerensky, the Bolsheviks will form a government which *nobody* will overthrow.

The majority of the people is *with* us. This has been proven by the long and difficult road from May 19 to August 12 and September 25: the majority in the Soviets of the capitals is the *result* of the people's progress *to our side*. The vacillation of the Socialist-Revolutionaries and Mensheviks, and the strengthening of internationalists among them, is proof of the same thing.

The Democratic Conference * does *not* represent the majority of the revolutionary people, but *only the conciliatory petty-bourgeois top layer*. One must not let himself be deceived by the election figures; elections are not everything: compare the elections to the city councils of Petrograd and Moscow with the elections to the Soviets. Compare the elections in Moscow with the strike of August 25. Here we have objective data as regards the majority of the revolutionary elements that lead the masses.

The Democratic Conference deceives the peasantry without giving it either peace or land.

The Bolshevik government *alone* will satisfy the peasantry.

---

* Called by the Kerensky government for September 27 in the attempt to secure a broader base among the petty bourgeoisie following the Kornilov revolt.—*Ed.*

Why must the Bolsheviks assume power right *now?*

Because the impending surrender of Petrograd will make our chances a hundred times worse.

But to prevent the surrender of Petrograd while the army is headed by Kerensky and Co. is not in our power.

To "wait" for the Constituent Assembly would be wrong. By surrendering Petrograd, Kerensky and Co. can always *destroy* the Constituent Assembly. Only our party, having assumed power, can secure the convocation of the Constituent Assembly; and, after assuming power, it could blame the other parties for delaying it and could substantiate its accusations.

A separate peace between the English and German imperialists must and can be prevented, but only by quick action.[82]

The people are tired of the vacillations of the Mensheviks and S.-R.'s. Only our victory in the capitals will draw the peasants after us.

What we are concerned with is not the "day" of the uprising, not the "moment" of the uprising in the narrow sense of the word. This will be decided by the common voice of those who are in contact with the workers and soldiers, with the *masses.*

What matters is that now, at the Democratic Conference, our party has practically *its own congress,* and this congress must (whether it wishes to do so or not) decide the *fate of the revolution.*

What matters is that we must make the *task* clear to the party, place on the order of the day the *armed uprising* in Petrograd and Moscow (including their regions), the conquest of power, the overthrow of the government. We must think of *how* to make propaganda in favour of this without committing ourselves in the press.

We must recall and ponder the words of Marx on uprising: "*Uprising is an art,*" etc.

It would be naïve to wait for a "formal" majority on the side of the Bolsheviks; no revolution ever waits for *this.* Kerensky and Co. are not waiting either, but are preparing the surrender of Petrograd. It is just the miserable vacillations of the Democratic Conference that must and will cause the patience of the workers of Petrograd and Moscow to end in a violent outburst! History will not forgive us if we do not assume power now.

No apparatus? There is an apparatus: the Soviets and democratic organisations. The international situation *just now*, on the *eve* of a separate peace between the English and the Germans, is *in our favour*. It is precisely now that to offer peace to the people means to *win*.

Assume power at once in Moscow and in Petrograd (it does not matter which begins; perhaps even Moscow may begin); we will win *absolutely and unquestionably*.

N. Lenin.

Written September 25-27, 1917.
First published in the magazine *Proletarskaya Revolyutsiya*, No. 2, 1921.

MARXISM AND UPRISING

LETTER TO THE CENTRAL COMMITTEE OF THE SOCIAL-DEMOCRATIC LABOUR PARTY

AMONG the most vicious and perhaps most widespread distortions of Marxism practiced by the prevailing "Socialist" parties, is to be found the opportunist lie which says that preparations for an uprising, and generally the treatment of an uprising as an art, is "Blanquism." *

Bernstein, the leader of opportunism, long since gained sad notoriety by accusing Marxism of Blanquism; and our present opportunists, by shouting about Blanquism, in reality do not in any way improve or "enrich" the meagre "ideas" of Bernstein.

To accuse Marxists of Blanquism for treating uprising as an art! Can there be a more flagrant distortion of the truth, when there is not a single Marxist who denies that it was Marx who expressed himself in the most definite, precise and categorical manner on this score; that it was Marx who called uprising nothing but an *art*, who said that uprising must be treated as an art, that one must *gain* the first success and then proceed from success to success without stopping the *offensive* against the enemy and making use of his confusion, etc., etc.? [83]

To be successful, the uprising must be based not on a conspiracy, not on a party, but on the advanced class. This is the first point. The uprising must be based on the revolutionary upsurge of the people. This is the second point. The uprising must be based on the *crucial point* in the history of the maturing revolution, when the activity of the vanguard of the people is at its height, when the *vacillations* in the ranks of the enemies, and *in the ranks of the weak, half-hearted, undecided friends of the revolution are at their highest point*. This is the third point. It is in pointing out these three conditions as the way of approaching the question of an uprising, that Marxism differs from Blanquism.

---

* The teachings of the French revolutionist, Auguste Blanqui (1805-1881), favouring the overthrow of the ruling power through secret plotting of revolutionists rather than through preparation and organisation of the masses led by a revolutionary party.—*Ed.*

But once these conditions exist, then to refuse to treat the uprising *as an art* means to betray Marxism and the revolution.

To show why this very moment must be recognised as the one when it is obligatory for the party to recognise the uprising as placed on the order of the day by the course of objective events, and to treat uprising as an art—to show this, it will perhaps be best to use the method of comparison and to draw a parallel between July 16-17 and the September days.*

On July 16-17 it was possible, without trespassing against the truth, to put the question thus: it would have been more proper to take power, since our enemies would anyway accuse us of revolt and treat us as rebels. This, however, did not warrant a decision to take power at that time, because there were still lacking the objective conditions for a victorious uprising.

1. We did not yet have behind us the class that is the vanguard of the revolution. We did not yet have a majority among the workers and soldiers of the capitals. Now we have a majority in both Soviets. It was created *only* by the history of July and August, by the experience of ruthless punishment meted out to the Bolsheviks, and by the experience of the Kornilov affair.

2. At that time there was no general revolutionary upsurge of the people. Now there is, after the Kornilov affair. This is proven by the situation in the provinces and by the seizure of power by the Soviets in many localities.

3. At that time there were no *vacillations* on a serious, general, political scale among our enemies and among the undecided petty bourgeoisie. Now the vacillations are enormous; our main enemy, the imperialism of the Allies and of the world (for the "Allies" are at the head of world imperialism), has begun to vacillate between war to a victory and a separate peace against Russia. Our petty-bourgeois democrats, having obviously lost their majority among the people, have begun to vacillate enormously, rejecting a bloc, *i.e.*, a coalition with the Cadets.

4. This is why an uprising on July 16-17 would have been an error: we would not have retained power either physically or politically. Not physically, in spite of the fact that at certain moments Petrograd was in our hands, because our workers and soldiers would not have *fought and died* at that time for the sake of holding Petro-

* The strikes and demonstrations in July and the defeat of the Kornilov revolt in September.—*Ed.*

grad; at that time people had not yet become so "brutalised"; there was not in existence such a burning hatred both towards the Kerenskys and towards the Tseretelis and Chernovs; and our own people were not yet hardened by the experience of the Bolsheviks being persecuted, while the Socialist-Revolutionaries and Mensheviks took part in the persecuting.

We could not have retained power July 16-17 politically, for, *before the Kornilov affair*, the army and the provinces could and would have marched against Petrograd.

Now the picture is entirely different.

We have back of us the majority of a *class* that is the vanguard of the revolution, the vanguard of the people, and is capable of drawing the masses along.

We have back of us a *majority* of the people, for Chernov's resignation, far from being the only sign, is only the most striking, the most outstanding sign showing that the peasantry *will not receive land* from a bloc with the S.-R.'s, or from the S.-R.'s themselves. And in this lies the essence of the popular character of the revolution.

We are in the advantageous position of a party which knows its road perfectly well, while *imperialism as a whole*, as well as the entire bloc of the Mensheviks and the S.-R.'s, is vacillating in an extraordinary manner.

Victory is assured to us, for the people are now very close to desperation, and we are showing the whole people a sure way out, having demonstrated to the whole people the significance of our leadership during the "Kornilov days," and then having *offered* the bloc politicians a compromise which they *rejected* at a time when their vacillations continued uninterruptedly.

It would be a very great error to think that our compromise offer has *not yet* been rejected, that the *"Democratic Conference"* * *still* may accept it. The compromise was offered from *party* to *parties*. It could not have been offered otherwise. The *parties* have rejected it. The Democratic Conference is nothing but a *conference*. One must not forget one thing, namely, that this conference does not represent the *majority* of the revolutionary people, the poorest and most embittered peasantry. One must not forget the self-evident truth that this conference represents a *minority of the people*. It would

* Called by the Kerensky government in the attempt to secure a broader base among the petty bourgeoisie following the Kornilov revolt.—*Ed.*

be a very great error, a very great parliamentary idiocy on our part, if we were to treat the Democratic Conference as a parliament, for even *if* it were to proclaim itself a parliament, the sovereign parliament of the revolution, it would not be able to *decide* anything. The decision lies *outside* of it, in the workers' sections of Petrograd and Moscow.

We have before us all the objective prerequisites for a successful uprising. We have the advantages of a situation where *only* our victory in an uprising will put an end to the most painful thing on earth, the vacillations that have sickened the people; a situation where *only our* victory in an uprising will *put an end* to the game of a separate peace against the revolution by openly offering a more complete, more just, more immediate peace *in favour of* the revolution.

Only our party, having won a victory in an uprising, *can* save Petrograd, for if our offer of peace is rejected, and we obtain not even a truce, then *we* shall become "defensists," then we shall place ourselves *at the head of the war parties*, we shall be the most "warring" party, and we shall carry on a war in a truly revolutionary manner. We shall take away from the capitalists all the bread and all the shoes. We shall leave them crumbs. We shall dress them in bast shoes. We shall send all the bread and all the shoes to the front.

And then we shall save Petrograd.

The resources, both material and spiritual, of a truly revolutionary war are still immense in Russia; there are ninety-nine chances in a hundred that the Germans will at least grant us a truce. And to secure a truce at present means to conquer the *whole world*.

Having recognised the absolute necessity of an uprising of the workers of Petrograd and Moscow for the sake of saving the revolution and of saving Russia from being "separately" divided among the imperialists of both coalitions, we must first adapt our political tactics at the conference to the conditions of the maturing uprising; secondly, we must prove that we accept, and not only in words, the idea of Marx about the necessity of treating uprising as an art.

At the conference, we must immediately consolidate the Bolshevik fraction without worrying about numbers, without being afraid of leaving the vacillators in the camp of the vacillating: they are more useful *there* to the cause of revolution than in the camp of the resolute and courageous fighters.

We must compose a brief declaration in the name of the Bolsheviks in which we sharply emphasise the irrelevance of long speeches, the irrelevance of "speeches" generally, the necessity of quick action to save the revolution, the absolute necessity of breaking completely with the bourgeoisie, of completely ousting the whole present government, of completely severing relations with the Anglo-French imperialists who are preparing a "separate" partition of Russia, the necessity of all power immediately passing into the hands of *revolutionary democracy headed by the revolutionary proletariat.*

Our declaration must be the briefest and sharpest formulation of this conclusion; it must connect up with the points in the programme of peace to the people, land to the peasants, confiscation of scandalous profits, and a halt to the scandalous damage to production done by the capitalists.

The briefer, the sharper the declaration, the better. Only two more important points must be clearly indicated in it, namely, that the people are tired of vacillations, that they are tortured by the lack of decisiveness on the part of the S.-R.'s and Mensheviks; and that we are definitely severing relations with these *parties* because they have betrayed the revolution.

The other point. In offering an immediate peace without annexations, in breaking at once with the Allied imperialists and with all imperialists, we obtain either an immediate truce or a going over of the entire revolutionary proletariat to the side of defence, and a truly just, truly revolutionary war will then be waged by revolutionary democracy under the leadership of the proletariat.

Having made this declaration, having appealed for *decisions* and not talk; for *actions*, not writing resolutions, we must *push* our whole fraction *into the factories and barracks:* its place is there; the pulse of life is there; the source of saving the revolution is there; the moving force of the Democratic Conference is there.

In heated, impassioned speeches we must make our programme clear and we must put the question this way: either the conference accepts it *fully*, or an uprising follows. There is no middle course. Delay is impossible. The revolution is perishing.

Having put the question this way, having concentrated our entire fraction in the factories and barracks, *we shall correctly estimate the best moment to begin the uprising.*

And in order to treat uprising in a Marxist way, *i.e.*, as an art, we must at the same time, without losing a single moment, organise the staff of the insurrectionary detachments; designate the forces; move the loyal regiments to the most important points; surround the Alexander Theatre; occupy Peter and Paul Fortress; [84] arrest the general staff and the government; move against the military cadets, the Wild Division, etc., such detachments as will die rather than allow the enemy to move to the centre of the city; we must mobilise the armed workers, call them to a last desperate battle, occupy at once the telegraph and telephone stations, place *our* staff of the uprising at the central telephone station, connect it by wire with all the factories, the regiments, the points of armed fighting, etc.

Of course, this is all by way of an example, to *illustrate* the idea that at the present moment it is impossible to remain loyal to the revolution *without treating uprising as an art.*

N. LENIN.

Written September 26-27, 1917.
First published in the magazine *Proletarskaya Revolyutsiya*, No. 2, 1921.

THE RUSSIAN REVOLUTION AND CIVIL WAR

THEY ARE TRYING TO FRIGHTEN US WITH CIVIL WAR

FRIGHTENED by the fact that the Mensheviks and Socialist-Revolutionaries have refused to join a coalition with the Cadets, that perhaps democracy will be perfectly able to form a government without them and to govern Russia against them, the bourgeoisie is doing everything possible to intimidate democracy.[85]

Frighten them all you can! This is the slogan of the whole bourgeois press. Frighten them with all your might! Lie, slander, but frighten them!

The *Birzhevka* does it by fabricating news about the Bolshevik activities. They all do it by spreading rumours about Alexeyev's resignation, and about the imminent German offensive against Petrograd, as if it has not been proven by facts that it is the Kornilov generals (to whom Alexeyev undoubtedly belongs) who are capable of opening the front to the Germans both in Galicia and near Riga, as well as near Petrograd, and that it is the Kornilov generals that are arousing the greatest hatred in the army against General Headquarters.[86]

To give this method of frightening democracy a most "solid" and convincing appearance, they all refer to the danger of a "civil war." Of all the species of intimidation, frightening with civil war is perhaps the most widespread. This is how the Rostov-on-the-Don Committee of the People's Freedom Party, in its resolution of September 14 (*Ryech*, No. 210) formulated this widespread idea, which is very welcome in philistine circles:

> The Committee is convinced that civil war may sweep away all the gains of the revolution and drown in rivers of blood our young, not yet consolidated freedom; it is therefore the opinion of the Committee that an energetic protest against deepening the revolution as proposed by the unrealisable Socialist Utopias is necessary in order to save the gains of the revolution. . . .[87]

Here, in the clearest, most precise, well considered and substantial form, is expressed the fundamental idea which is to be met with innumerable times in the editorial articles of the *Ryech*, in the articles of Plekhanov and Potresov, in the editorials of Menshevik papers, etc., etc. It will therefore be useful to dwell on this idea more in detail.

First of all, let us try to analyse the civil war question a little more concretely, among other things also on the basis of the half year's experience of our revolution.

This experience, in full accord with the experience of all the European revolutions, from the end of the eighteenth century on, shows us that civil war is the sharpest form of the class struggle, it is that point in the class struggle when clashes and battles, economic and political, repeating themselves, growing, broadening, becoming acute, turn into an armed struggle of one class against another class. Most often—one may say almost always—there is to be observed in all more or less free and advanced countries a civil war between those classes whose contradictory position towards each other is created and deepened by the entire economic development of capitalism, by the entire history of modern society the world over, namely, between the bourgeoisie and the proletariat.

During the past half year of our revolution, we have thus, on May 3-4 and July 16-17, gone through very strong spontaneous outbursts which closely approach the beginning of civil war on the part of the proletariat. On the other hand, the Kornilov revolt represented a military conspiracy supported by the landowners and capitalists, and led by the Cadet Party, a revolt which has already brought about an actual beginning of the civil war on the part of the bourgeoisie.

Such are the facts. Such is the history of our own revolution. We must learn most of all from this history, we must ponder most of all on its course and its class meaning.

Let us try to compare the beginnings of the proletarian and of the bourgeois civil war in Russia from the standpoint of: (1) the spontaneous nature of the movement; (2) its aims; (3) the consciousness of the masses participating in it; (4) the forces in the movement; (5) its tenacity. We think that if all the parties which are now "recklessly spreading" the words "civil war" were to approach the question in this way, and make an attempt actually to study the beginnings of the civil war, the class-consciousness of the entire Russian Revolution would gain a very great deal.

Let us begin with the spontaneous nature of the movement. For the July 16-17 movement we have the testimony of such witnesses as the Menshevik *Rabochaya Gazeta* and the S.-R. *Dyelo Naroda*, which have recognised the fact that the movement sprang up spontaneously. This testimony I quoted in an article published in the *Proletarskoye Dyelo*, and issued as a separate leaflet entitled *An Answer*. For obvious reasons, however, the Mensheviks and the S.-R.'s, in defending themselves and their part in persecuting the Bolsheviks, officially continue to deny the spontaneous nature of the outburst of July 16-17.

Let us put aside for the present the controversial matter. Let us take what is undisputed. The spontaneous nature of the May 3-4 movement is denied by no one. This spontaneous movement was joined in by the Bolshevik Party under the slogan of "All Power to the Soviets"; it was joined in independently of the Bolsheviks by the late Linde, who led 30,000 armed soldiers into the street ready to arrest the government. (The coming out of these troops, by the way, has not been investigated and studied. If it is examined closely, and May 3 is placed in the historic sequence of events, *i.e.*, looked upon as a link in the chain which extends from March 12 to September 11, it becomes clear that the fault and the error of the Bolsheviks lies in the *insufficient* revolutionism of their tactics, and by no means in excessive revolutionism, of which the philistines accuse us.)

The spontaneous nature of the movement leading to the beginning of civil war on the part of the proletariat is thus beyond doubt. On the other hand, there is not even a trace of anything resembling spontaneity in the Kornilov affair: that was only a conspiracy of generals who hoped to carry part of the army by fraud and by the force of military command.

That the spontaneity of the movement is proof of its depth among the masses, of the firmness of its roots, of its inevitability, is beyond doubt. The proletarian revolution is firmly rooted, the bourgeois counter-revolution is without roots—this is what the facts prove if looked upon from the point of view of the spontaneous nature of the movement.

Let us now look at the aims of the movement. The movement of May 3-4 was very close to adopting the Bolshevik slogans, whereas that of July 16-17 directly advanced under these slogans, under their influence and guidance. Of the dictatorship of the proletariat and the poorest peasantry, of peace and an immediate offer of peace, of confiscating the landowners' lands—of all these chief *aims* of the proletarian civil war, the party of the Bolsheviks spoke perfectly openly, definitely, clearly, precisely, in everybody's hearing, in its papers and in verbal propaganda.

Of the aims of the Kornilov affair we all know, and no one among the democratic elements disputes that they consisted in a dictatorship of the landowners and the bourgeoisie, dispersal of the Soviets, preparation for the restoration of the monarchy. The Cadet Party, this main Kornilovist party (by the way, it ought to be called from now on the Kornilov Party), while possessing a large press and greater forces for propaganda than the Bolsheviks, has never dared and does not dare openly to tell the people either about the dictatorship of the bourgeoisie or about the dispersal of the Soviets, or about the Kornilovist aims in general!

As for the aims of the movement, the facts tell us that the proletarian civil war can come out with an open exposition of its final aims before the people, thus winning the sympathies of the toilers, whereas the bourgeois civil war can attempt to lead part of the masses only by concealing its aims; hence a tremendous difference as far as the class-consciousness of the masses is concerned.

Objective data concerning this question seem to exist only in relation to party affiliation and elections. There seem to be no other facts which would allow a clear judgment about the class consciousness of the masses. That the proletarian-revolutionary movement is represented by the Bolshevik Party, and the bourgeois counter-revolutionary movement by the Cadet Party, is clear and can hardly be disputed after the half year's experience of the revolution. Three comparisons of a factual nature can be made concerning the question under consideration. A comparison of the May elections to the borough councils in Petrograd with the August elections to the city council shows a decrease in Cadet votes and a tremendous increase in Bolshevik votes. The Cadet press admits that, as a rule, where masses of workers are concentrated, the strength of Bolshevism is to be observed.

In the absence of any statistics concerning the fluctuation of party members, the attendance of meetings, etc., the conscious participation of the *masses* in the parties, may be judged only from published data concerning cash collections for the party. These data show a tremendous mass heroism of the Bolshevik workers in collecting money for the *Pravda*, for the papers that were suppressed, etc. The reports of such collections have always been published. Among the Cadets we see nothing of the kind: their party work is being obviously "fed" by contributions from the rich. There is not a trace of active aid on the part of the masses.

Finally, a comparison between the movements of May 3-4 and July 16-17 on the one hand and the Kornilov affair on the other shows that the Bolsheviks directly point out to the masses their enemy in the civil war, namely, the bourgeoisie, the landowners, and the capitalists. On the other hand, the Kornilov affair has already shown that the army that followed Kornilov was *directly deceived*, a fact made obvious by the first meeting of the "Wild Division" and the Kornilov detachments with the Petrograd masses.

Furthermore, what are the data concerning the *strength* of the proletariat and the bourgeoisie in the civil war? The strength of the Bolsheviks lies only in the numbers and class consciousness of the proletarians, in the sympathy of the S.-R. and Menshevik "rank and file" (*i.e.*, workers and poorest peasants), with the Bolshevik slogans. It is a fact that it was these slogans that actually won over the *majority* of the active revolutionary masses in Petrograd on May 3-4, July 1, and July 16-17.

A comparison of the data concerning "parliamentary" elections with the data concerning the above-named mass movements, fully corroborates, as far as Russia is concerned, an observation often made in the West, namely, that the *strength* of the revolutionary proletariat, from the point of view of influencing the *masses* and drawing them into the struggle, is incomparably larger in the *extra-parliamentary* than in the parliamentary struggle. This is a very important observation as regards civil war.

It is quite clear why all the circumstances and all the environment of parliamentary struggle and elections minimise the strength of the oppressed classes in comparison with the strength which they actually can develop in civil war.

The strength of the Cadets and the Kornilov movement lies in the power of *wealth*. That the Anglo-French capitalists and imperialists are *in favour* of the Cadets and the Kornilov movement is proven by a long series of political actions and by the press. It is common knowledge that the entire "Right Wing" of the Moscow Conference of August 25 was wild in its support of Kornilov and Kaledin. It is common knowledge that the French and the English bourgeois press "aided" Kornilov. There are indications that he was aided by the *banks*.

All the power of wealth stood behind Kornilov—yet what a miserable and sudden collapse! The social forces that may be detected among the Kornilovists are, besides the wealthy, only two: the "Wild Division" and the Cossacks. In the first instance we have *only* the power of ignorance and deception. This force is the more formidable the longer the press remains in the hands of the bourgeoisie. After a victory in the civil war, the proletariat would undermine *this* source of "strength" once and for all.

As to the Cossacks, we deal here with a layer of the population consisting of rich, small or middle landowners (the average area of land owning is about 135 acres) in one of the outlying regions of Russia, where the population has retained many mediæval traits in its way of living, economy, and customs. We can detect here the social-economic basis for the Russian Vendée.* But what have the *facts* related to the Kornilov-Kaledin movement proved? *Not even* Kaledin, the "beloved leader" supported by the Guchkovs, Milyukovs, Ryabushinskys and Co., has created a mass movement!! Kaledin marched towards civil war much more "directly," much more unhesitatingly than did the Bolsheviks. Kaledin directly "went to arouse the Don." Still, Kaledin has not aroused a mass movement in his "home" region, in a Cossack region far removed from the general Russian democracy! On the contrary, we observe on the part of the proletariat spontaneous outbursts of a movement in the centre of influence and power of the anti-Bolshevik, all-Russian democracy.

Objective data on the attitude of various strata and economic groups of the Cossacks towards democracy and the Kornilov affair are lacking. There are only indications to the effect that the majority of the poor and middle Cossacks are rather inclined towards democracy and that only the officers and the top layer of the well-to-do Cossacks are entirely in favour of Kornilov.

However that may be, the extreme weakness of a mass Cossack movement in favour of a bourgeois counter-revolution appears historically proven after the experience of September 8-13.

There remains the last question—as to the *tenacity* of the movement. As far as the Bolshevik, proletarian-revolutionary movement is concerned, we have the undisputed fact that the struggle against Bolshevism has been conducted for the half year of the

---

* The region where the peasants, under the influence of the church, supported the nobles during the French Revolution in 1793.—*Ed.*

existence of a republic in Russia both as an ideological struggle, with a *gigantic* prevalence of press organs and propaganda forces on the side of the opponents of Bolshevism (even if we risk classing as "ideological" struggle the campaign of slander), and as a struggle *by means of repressions,* with hundreds arrested, our main printing plant demolished, and the chief newspaper and a number of other papers suppressed. The result is shown in facts: a tremendous growth of Bolshevism in the August Petrograd elections, a strengthening of the internationalist and "Left" trends in both the S.-R. and Menshevik Parties—trends that are approaching Bolshevism. This means that the tenacity of the proletarian-revolutionary movement in republican Russia is very great. The facts tell us that the combined efforts of the Cadets and the S.-R.'s and Mensheviks *have not succeeded* in weakening that movement in the least. On the contrary, it was the coalition of the Kornilovists with "democracy" that *strengthened* Bolshevism. There can be no other means of struggle against the proletarian-revolutionary trend than ideological influence *and* repressions.

Data concerning the tenacity of the Cadet-Kornilov movement are still lacking. The Cadets have suffered no persecution at all. Even Guchkov has been set free; Maklakov and Milyukov have not even been arrested. The *Ryech* has not been suppressed. The Cadets are being spared. The Cadet-Kornilovists are being *courted* by Kerensky's government. Let us put the question this way: assuming that the Anglo-French and Russian Ryabushinskys will give millions and millions more to the Cadets, the *Yedinstvo,* the *Dyen,* etc., to conduct a new election campaign in Petrograd; is it probable that now, after the Kornilov affair, the number of their votes will increase? The answer to this question can hardly be anything but negative, judging by meetings, etc.

Summing up the results of our analysis where we compared the data furnished by the history of the Russian Revolution, we arrive at the conclusion that the beginning of the civil war on the part of the proletariat has revealed the strength, the class-consciousness, the deep-rootedness, the growth, and the solidity of the movement. The beginning of the civil war on the part of the bourgeoisie has revealed no strength, no class-consciousness among the masses, no depth whatsoever, no chance of victory.

The union of the Cadets with the S.-R.'s and Mensheviks against the Bolsheviks, *i.e.*, against the revolutionary proletariat, has been tried in practice for a number of months, and that union of the temporarily dissembling Kornilovists with "democracy" has led in fact not to a weakening but to a strengthening of the Bolsheviks, to a collapse of the "coalition," to strengthening the "Left" opposition also among the Mensheviks.

A union of the Bolsheviks with the S.-R.'s and Mensheviks against the Cadets, against the bourgeoisie, *has not yet been tried;* or, to be more precise, such a union *has been tried at one front only*, for *five days* only, September 8-13, the time of the Kornilov affair, and this union yielded at that time, with an ease never yet achieved in any revolution, a victory over the counter-revolution, such a crushing suppression of the bourgeois, landowners', capitalist, Allied-imperialist and Cadet counter-revolution, that the civil war *from that side* crumbled to dust, turned into nothing at the very beginning, disintegrated before any "battle" had taken place.

In the face of this historic fact the entire bourgeois press with all its helpers (the Plekhanovs, Potresovs, Breshkovskayas, etc.) is shouting with all its might that a union of the Bolsheviks with the Mensheviks and S.-R.'s "threatens" the horrors of civil war!

This would be funny, if it were not so sad. It is sad indeed that such an open, self-evident, glaring absurdity, such a mockery of the facts of the whole history of our revolution, can still find listeners. . . . This only proves how widespread still is the selfish bourgeois lie (a phenomenon that cannot be avoided as long as the press is monopolised by the bourgeoisie), a lie that drowns and shouts down the most undoubted, palpable, and undisputed lessons of the revolution.

If there is an absolutely undisputed lesson of the revolution, one absolutely proven by facts, it is that only a union of the Bolsheviks with the S.-R.'s and Mensheviks, only an immediate passing of all power to the Soviets would make civil war in Russia impossible. For no civil war begun by the bourgeoisie against such a union, against the Soviets of Workers', Soldiers', and Peasants' Deputies is thinkable; such a "war" would not even live to see one battle: the bourgeoisie, for the second time after the Kornilov affair, would not find even a "Wild Division," not even the former number of Cossack detachments to move against the Soviet government!

The peaceful development of any revolution is, generally speaking, an extremely rare and difficult thing, for a revolution is the maximum sharpening of the sharpest class contradictions; but in a peasant country at a time when a union of the proletariat with the peasantry *can* give *peace* to the masses that are worn out by a most unjust and criminal war, when such a union can give the peasantry *all the land*, in such a country, at such an exceptional historic moment, a peaceful development of the revolution is *possible* and *probable* if all power passes to the Soviets. Within the Soviets the struggle of parties for power may proceed peacefully, with the Soviets fully democratised, with "petty thefts" and defrauding of democratic principles eliminated—such as giving the soldiers one representative to every five hundred, while the workers have one representative to every thousand voters. In a democratic republic such petty thefts are doomed to disappear.

Against Soviets that have given all the land to the peasants without compensation and offer a just peace to all the peoples, against such Soviets a union of the English and French with the Russian bourgeoisie, Kornilovs, Buchanans, Ryabushinskys, Milyukovs, Plekhanovs, and Potresovs, presents no dangers at all; it is completely impotent.

The resistance of the bourgeoisie against giving over the land to the peasants without compensation, against similar reforms in other realms of life, against a just peace and a break with imperialism, is, of course, unavoidable. But in order that such resistance may reach the stage of civil war, *masses* of some kind are necessary, masses capable of fighting and vanquishing the Soviets. Such masses the bourgeoisie does *not* have, and cannot get anywhere. The sooner and the more resolutely the Soviets take all power, the sooner both the "Wild Divisions" and the Cossacks will split, dividing into an insignificant minority of conscious Kornilovists and a tremendous majority of those in favour of a democratic and *Socialist* (for it is with Socialism that we shall deal at that time) union of workers and peasants.

Once power has passed to the Soviets, the resistance of the bourgeoisie will result in *scores and hundreds* of workers and peasants "watching," supervising, controlling, and testing *every single* capitalist, for the interests of the workers and peasants will demand struggle against the capitalists' deception of the people. The forms and methods of this testing and control have been developed and simplified by capitalism itself, by such creations of capitalism as the banks, the large factories, the trusts, the railroads, the post office, the consumers' societies, and the trade unions. It will be quite sufficient for the Soviets to punish those capitalists who evade the most detailed accounting or who deceive the people, by confiscating all their property and arresting them for a short time, to break all resistance of the bourgeoisie by these bloodless means. For it is through the banks, once they are nationalised, through the unions of employees, through the post office, the consumers' societies, the trade unions, that the control and the accounting will become universal, all-powerful, ubiquitous, and invincible.

And the Russian Soviets, the union of the Russian workers with the poorest peasants, are not alone in their *steps* towards Socialism. If we were alone, we should not be able to accomplish this task peacefully and completely, for this task is essentially an international one. But we have enormous reserves, the armies of the most advanced workers in other countries, where the break of Russia with imperialism and the imperialist war will inevitably accelerate the rising workers' Socialist revolution.

Some speak about "rivers of blood" in a civil war. This is mentioned in the resolution of the Cadet-Kornilovists quoted above. This phrase is repeated in a thousand ways by all the bourgeois and opportunists. After the Kornilov affair all the class-conscious workers are laughing and will laugh and cannot help laughing at it.

However, the question of "rivers of blood" in the war-time we are going through now can and must be placed on the basis of an approximate accounting of forces, consequences, and results; it must be taken seriously and not as an empty, stock phrase, not as simply an hypocrisy of the Cadets, who have done *everything* in their power to enable Kornilov to flood Russia with "rivers of blood," restore a dictatorship of the bourgeoisie, the power of the landowners, and the monarchy.

"Rivers of blood," they say. Let us analyse *this* side of the question as well.

Let us assume that the vacillations of the Mensheviks and S.-R.'s continue; that these parties do *not* give over power to the Soviets; that they do *not* overthrow Kerensky; that they restore the old rotten compromise with the bourgeoisie in a somewhat different form (say "non-partisan" *Kornilovists* instead of Cadets); that they do not replace the apparatus of state power by the Soviet apparatus; that they do not offer peace; that they do not break with imperialism, and do not confiscate the land of the landowners. Let us assume that this is the outcome of the present vacillations of the S.-R.'s and Mensheviks, of this present "September."

The experience of our own revolution tells us most clearly that the consequence of this would be a still further weakening of the S.-R.'s and Mensheviks, a further break between them and the masses, an incredible growth of indignation and bitterness among the masses, a tremendous growth of sympathy with the revolutionary proletariat, with the Bolsheviks.

Under such conditions, the proletariat of the capital will be still closer to a Commune, to a workers' uprising, to the conquest of power, to a civil war in its highest and most decisive form, than it is at present; after the experience of May 3-4 and July 16-17 such a result must be recognised as historically unavoidable.

"Rivers of blood," cry the Cadets. But such rivers of blood would give the victory to the proletariat and the poorest peasantry, and there are ninety-nine chances out of a hundred that this victory would yield *peace* instead of the imperialist war, *i.e.*, that it would save the lives of *hundreds of thousands* of men who are now shedding their blood for the sake of a division of spoils and seizures (annexations) by the capitalists. If May 3-4 had ended by the passing of all power to the Soviets, and within the Soviets the Bolsheviks allied with the poorest peasantry had won, then even if it had cost "rivers of blood," it would have saved the lives of the *half million* Russian soldiers who certainly perished in the battles of July 2.

This is how every class-conscious Russian worker and soldier figures, this is how he must figure, if he weighs and analyses the question of civil war now raised everywhere; and, of course, such a worker or soldier, who has lived and thought many things, will not be frightened by the cries of "rivers of blood" raised by persons, parties, and groups willing to sacrifice *more millions* of Russian soldiers for the sake of Constantinople, Lemberg, Warsaw, and "victory over Germany."

No "rivers of blood" in an internal civil war can even approximately equal those *seas* of blood which the Russian imperialists have shed since July 2 (in spite of the very great chances of avoiding this by giving over the power to the Soviets).

While this war is going on, you, Messrs. Milyukovs, Potresovs, and Plekhanovs, be careful about your arguments against "rivers of blood" in civil war, for the soldiers have seen *seas* of blood and know what they mean.

The international situation of the Russian Revolution now, in 1917, the fourth year of a terrifically burdensome and criminal war, that has worn out the peoples, is such that an offer of a just peace on the part of the Russian proletariat victorious in the civil war would have ninety-nine chances out of a hundred to achieve a truce and a peace *without the shedding of further seas of blood.*

For a combination of the warring Anglo-French and German imperialisms *against* the proletarian-Socialist Russian republic is *impossible* in practice, while a combination of the English, Japanese, and American imperialisms against us is extremely difficult of realisation and is not dangerous to us at all, due to Russia's geographic situation. On the other hand, the existence of revolutionary and Socialist proletarian masses within *all* the European states is a fact; the maturing and the inevitability of the world-wide Socialist revolution is beyond doubt, and such a revolution can be seriously aided, not by delegations and not by playing at Stockholm conferences * with the foreign Plekhanovs or Tseretelis, but only by pushing forward the Russian Revolution.

The bourgeoisie wails about the inevitable defeat of a Commune in Russia, *i.e.,* defeat of the proletariat if it were to conquer power. These are false, selfish class wailings.

Having conquered power, the proletariat will have *every* chance of retaining it and of leading Russia until a victorious revolution in the West.

For, firstly, we have learned much since the Commune, and we would not repeat its fatal errors, we would not leave the banks in the hands of the bourgeoisie, we would not confine ourselves to defending our line against being disrupted by the Versailles ** (the same as the Kornilovists), but we would take the offensive against them and crush them.

Secondly, the victorious proletariat will give Russia peace, and no power on earth will be able to overthrow a government of *peace,*

---

* A conference initiated by the Scandinavian Socialist parties and inspired by the German pro-war Socialists.—*Ed.*

** The counter-revolutionary elements who made their headquarters in Versailles during the Paris Commune of 1871.—*Ed.*

a government of an honest, sincere, just peace, after all the horrors of more than three years' butchery of the peoples.

Thirdly, the victorious proletariat will give the peasantry the land immediately and without compensation. And a tremendous majority of the peasantry—worn out and embittered by the "playing around with the landowners" practised by our government, particularly the "coalition" government, particularly the Kerensky government—will support the victorious proletariat absolutely, unreservedly, with every means in its power.

You, Messrs. Mensheviks and S.-R.'s, are all talking about the "heroic efforts" of the people. Only recently I have come across this phrase over and over again in the leading articles in your *Izvestiya* of the Central Executive Committee. With you this is a *mere* phrase. But the workers and peasants read it and *ponder* it, and such deliberation—reinforced by the experience of the Kornilov affair, by the "experience" of Peshekhonov's ministry, by the "experience" of Chernov's ministry, *and so forth*—every such deliberation inevitably leads to the conclusion that this "heroic effort" is nothing but confidence of the poorest peasantry in the city workers as their most faithful allies and leaders. The heroic effort is nothing but the victory of the Russian proletariat over the bourgeoisie in civil war, for such a victory alone will save the country from painful vacillations, it alone will show the way out, it alone will give land, will give peace.

If it is possible to effect a union of the city workers with the poorest peasantry through an immediate passing of power to the Soviets, so much the better. The Bolsheviks will do *everything* to secure this *peaceful* course of development of the revolution. Without this, even the Constituent Assembly, by itself, will not save the situation, for even there the S.-R.'s may continue their "playing" at collaboration with the Cadets, with Breshko-Breshkovskaya and Kerensky (wherein are they better than the Cadets?), and so on, and so forth.

If even the experience of the Kornilov affair has taught the "democracy" nothing, and it continues the destructive policy of vacillation and compromise, then we say: nothing destroys the proletarian revolution more than these vacillations. That being the case, do not frighten us, gentlemen, with civil war: civil war is inevitable, if you do not wish to break with Kornilovism and the "coalition" right now, once and for all; and this war will bring victory over the exploiters, it will give the land to the peasants, it will give peace to the peoples, it will open the right road to the victorious revolution of the world Socialist proletariat.

N. LENIN.

Rabochy Put, No. 12, September 29, 1917.

HEROES OF FRAUD

THE so-called Democratic Conference is over. Thank God, one more comedy is left behind. We are moving forward in spite of everything, if the book of fate says that our revolution must pass through no more than a definite number of comedies.

In order correctly to judge the political results of the conference, we must attempt to ascertain its precise class significance as indicated by objective facts.

Further decomposition of the government parties, of the Socialist-Revolutionaries and Mensheviks; their obvious loss of a majority in revolutionary democracy; one more step towards a brazen consolidation of the Bonapartism of both Mr. Kerensky and Messrs. Tsereteli, Chernov and Co.—such is the class meaning of the conference.

In the Soviets, the S.-R.'s and Mensheviks have lost their majority. They therefore have had to resort to a fraud: to violate their pledge to call a new congress of the Soviets after three months; to shirk the report they would have to give to those who elected the Central Executive Committee of the Soviets; to fix up a "Democratic" Conference. Of this fraud the Bolsheviks spoke at the conference, and the results fully confirmed their correctness. The Liberdans * and Messrs. Tseretelis, Chernovs and Co. saw that their majority in the Soviets was melting away, therefore they resorted to fraud.

Arguments like that which says that the co-operatives "have already gained great importance among the democratic organisations" or that this applies also to "properly" elected city and *Zemstvo* representatives, are so flimsy that only crass hypocrisy can advance them seriously. First of all, the Central Executive Committee was elected by the Soviets, and to refuse to deliver a report and relinquish its offices to *them*, is a Bonapartist . . . fraud; second, the Soviets represent revolutionary democracy in so far as they are joined by those who wish to fight in a revolutionary way. Their doors are not closed to members of the co-operatives and city

* A contraction of the names of two leading Mensheviks, Liber and Dan. —*Ed.*

dwellers. Those same S.-R.'s and Mensheviks were masters in the Soviets.

Those who remained *only* in the co-operatives, *only* within the limits of municipal (city and *Zemstvo*) work, voluntarily singled themselves out from the ranks of revolutionary democracy, thereby counting themselves among the reactionary or neutral democrats. Everybody knows that co-operative and municipal work is done *not only* by revolutionists, but also by reactionaries; everybody knows that people are elected to co-operatives and municipalities primarily for work that is *not* of general political scope and importance.

Secretly to bring up reserves from among the adherents of the *Yedinstvo* and "non-partisan" reactionaries, was the aim of the Dans, Tseretelis, Chernovs and Co. when they fixed up the conference. Therein consisted their fraud. Therein consists their Bonapartism, which unites them with the Bonapartist Kerensky.

They stole from democracy while hypocritically retaining a democratic appearance—this is the essence of the matter.

Nicholas II stole from democracy large sums, so to speak: he convened representative institutions but gave the landowners a hundredfold greater representation than the peasants. The Dans, Tseretelis, and Chernovs steal from democracy petty amounts; they convoke a "Democratic Conference" where *both* the workers and the peasants point with full justice to the curtailment of their representation, to *lack* of proportionality, to discrimination in favour of the elements closest to the bourgeoisie (and reactionary democracy)—the co-operatives and municipal councils.

Messrs. Libers, Dans, Tseretelis and Chernovs have broken with the masses of the poor workers and peasants. They saved themselves through a fraud, by which "their" Kerensky is also being supported.

The lines between classes are being drawn ever more sharply. Within the S.-R. and Menshevik Parties a protest is growing, a direct split is ripening in consequence of the "leaders'" betrayal of the interests of the majority of the population. The leaders are basing themselves on a *minority*, in defiance of the principles of democracy. Hence the *inevitability* of their frauds.

Kerensky is revealing himself as a Bonapartist more and more. He was considered a "Socialist-Revolutionary." Now we know that he is only a "March" Socialist-Revolutionary who ran over to them from the Trudoviks "for advertising purposes." He is an adherent of Breshko-Breshkovskaya, this "Mrs. Plekhanov" among the S.-R.'s, or "Mrs. Potresov" in the S.-R. *Dyen*. The so-called "Right" Wing of the so-called "Socialist" parties, the Plekhanovs, Breshkovskayas, Potresovs—this is where Kerensky *belongs*; this wing, however, differs in nothing substantial from the Cadets.

Kerensky is praised by the Cadets. He pursues *their* policies; *behind the back of the people* he confers with them and with Rodzyanko; he has been exposed by Chernov and others as conniving with Savinkov, a friend of Kornilov's. Kerensky is a *Kornilovist*; by sheer *accident* he has had a quarrel with Kornilov himself, but he remains in the most intimate union with other Kornilovists. This is a *fact*, proven both by the revelations of Savinkov and the *Dyelo Naroda* and by the continuation of the political game, the "ministerial leap-frog" of Kerensky with the Kornilovists disguised under the name of the "commercial and industrial class."

Secret pacts with the Kornilovists, secret hobnobbing (through Tereshchenko and Co.) with the imperialist "Allies"; secret obstruction and sabotage of the Constitutent Assembly; secret deception of the peasants in order to serve Rodzyanko, *i.e.*, the landowners (by doubling the price of bread)—this is what Kerensky does *in practice*. This is his *class* policy. This is what his Bonapartism consists in.

In order to shield him at the conference, the Libers, Dans, Tseretelis and Chernovs had to resort to a fraud.

The Bolshevik participation in this hideous fraud, in this comedy, had no other justification than had our participation in the Third Duma: even in a "pigsty" we must defend our course, even from a "pigsty" we must issue material exposing the enemy for the instruction of the people.

The difference, however, is this, that the Third Duma was created when the revolution was obviously ebbing, while at present there is an obvious rising of a *new revolution;* of the extent and the pace of this rising, however, we unfortunately know very little.

The most characteristic episode at the conference was, in my opinion, Zarudny's speech. He tells us that as soon as Kerensky "as much as hinted" at reorganising the government, all the Ministers began to hand in their resignations. "The following day," continues the naïve, childishly naïve (even better if *only* naïve) Zarudny, "the following day, notwithstanding our resignations, we were called, we were consulted, and finally we were prevailed upon to stay."

"General laughter in the hall," remarks at this point the official *Izvestiya*.

Gay folk, those participants of the Bonapartist deception of the people by the republicans. We are all revolutionary democrats—no joking!

> From the very beginning—says Zarudny—we heard two things: we were to strive to make the army capable of fighting, and to hasten peace on a democratic basis. Well, as far as peace is concerned, I do not know whether, during the month and a half that I was a member of the Provisional Government, the Provisional Government did anything in this respect. I noticed nothing of the kind. [Applause and a voice from the audience: "It did nothing," the *Izvestiya* remarks.] When I, as a member of the Provisional Government, inquired about it, I received no reply. . . .[88]

Thus speaks Zarudny, according to the report of the official *Izvestiya*. And the conference listens silently, tolerates such things, does not stop the orator, does not interrupt the session, does not raise the question of the immediate resignation of Kerensky and the government! How could that be? These "revolutionary democrats" are hand and foot for Kerensky!

Very well, gentlemen, but then, wherein does the term "revolutionary democrat" differ from the term "lackey"?

It is natural that the lackeys are capable of laughing gaily when "their" Minister, distinguished by rare naïveté or rare stupidity, tells them how Kerensky drives away the Ministers (in order to come to terms with the Kornilovists behind the back of the people and "in full privacy"). It is not surprising that the lackeys keep silent when "their" Minister, who seems to have taken the general peace phrases seriously without understanding their hypocrisy, admits that he did not even receive a reply to his question as to the real steps for peace. Such is the destiny of lackeys, to allow themselves to be fooled by the government. But what has this to do with revolution, what has it to do with democracy??

And now I come to the errors of the Bolsheviks. To confine themselves to ironic applause and exclamations at such a moment was an error.

The people are weary of vacillations and delays. Dissatisfaction is obviously growing. A new revolution is approaching. The whole interest of the reactionary democrats, the Libers, Dans, Tseretelis, etc., is to *divert* the attention of the people towards the "conference" comedy, to *"entertain"* the people by this comedy, to *cut* the Bolsheviks from the masses, to keep the Bolshevik delegates at such an unworthy occupation as sitting and listening to the Zarudnys! And the Zarudnys are more sincere than the others!

The Bolsheviks should have left the conference as a protest and in order to avoid the trap of diverting the attention of the people, through the conference, from serious questions.

Ninety-nine hundredths of the Bolshevik delegation ought to have gone to the factories and barracks; that was their place, those delegates who came from all the ends of Russia and who, after Zarudny's speech, saw all the abyss of S.-R. and Menshevik rottenness. There, closer to the masses, in hundreds and thousands of meetings and talks, they ought to have discussed the lessons of this conference comedy.

Ten converted soldiers or workers from a backward factory *are worth a thousand times more* than a *hundred* delegates fraudulently picked by the Liberdans. Utilising parliamentarism, particularly in revolutionary times, does not at all consist in wasting precious time on the representatives of rottenness, but in *utilising the example of rottenness to teach the masses.*

N. LENIN.

Rabochy Put, No. 19, October 7, 1917.

FROM A PUBLICIST'S DIARY [89]

THE MISTAKES OF OUR PARTY

Friday, October 5, 1917.

THE more one reflects on the meaning of the so-called Democratic Conference, and the more attentively one observes it with detachment—and it is said that detachment helps one to see more clearly—the more firmly convinced one becomes that our party has committed a mistake by participating in it. We should have boycotted it. One may ask: of what use is it to analyse such a question? The past cannot be remedied. Such an objection against criticising the tactics of yesterday, however, would be clearly unfounded. We have always condemned, and as Marxists we are obliged to condemn, the tactics of those who live "from day to day." Temporary successes are insufficient for us. Plans calculated for a minute or a day are insufficient for us. We must constantly test ourselves, *studying* the chain of political events in their entirety, in their causal connection, in their results. By analysing the errors of yesterday, we learn to avoid errors today and tomorrow.

A new revolution is obviously growing in the country, a revolution of *other* classes (compared with those which carried out the revolution against tsarism). At that time it was a revolution of the proletariat, the peasantry and the bourgeoisie in alliance with Anglo-French finance capital against tsarism.

Now there is growing a revolution of the proletariat and the majority of the peasants, the poorest peasantry, against the bourgeoisie, against its ally, Anglo-French finance capital, against its governmental apparatus headed by the Bonapartist Kerensky.

At present we shall not dwell on the facts which testify to the rise of a new revolution, since, judging by the articles of our central organ *Rabochy Put*, the party has already made clear its views on this point. The rise of a new revolution seems to be a phenomenon commonly recognised by the party. Of course, it will still be necessary to summarise the data concerning this process of rising, but they must form the subject of other articles.

At the present moment it is more important to call the closest attention to the class differences between the old and the new revolution, to take account of the political situation and our tasks from the point of view of this fundamental phenomenon, the correlation of classes. At that time, in the first revolution, the vanguard was formed by the workers and soldiers, *i.e.*, by the proletariat and the advanced strata of the peasantry.

This vanguard *carried along* not only many of the worst, the vacillating elements of the petty bourgeoisie (remember the indecision of the Mensheviks and Trudoviks concerning a republic), but also the monarchist party of the Cadets, and the liberal bourgeoisie, which by this token turned republican. Why was such a transformation possible?

Because economic domination is to the bourgeoisie everything, while the form of the political domination is of very little importance; because the bourgeoisie can dominate just as well under a republic, its domination being even more secure under the latter, in the sense that the republican political order, no matter what changes take place in the composition of the government or in the composition and the grouping of the ruling parties, does not infringe upon the bourgeoisie.

Of course, the bourgeoisie stood and will stand for a monarchy, because the most brutal, the military, defence of capital by monarchist institutions is more obvious and "closer" to all the capitalists and landlords. However, under a strong pressure "from below," the bourgeoisie has always and everywhere "reconciled" itself to a republic, if only it maintains its economic domination.

Now the proletariat and the poorest peasantry, *i.e.*, the majority of the people, have placed themselves in such a relation to the bourgeoisie and to "Allied" (and world) imperialism that it is *impossible* for them to "*carry along*" the bourgeoisie. Moreover, the upper strata of the *petty* bourgeoisie and the more well-to-do strata of the *democratic* petty bourgeoisie are obviously against a new revolution. This fact is so obvious that it is not necessary to dwell on it at present. Messrs. Liberdans, Tseretelis, Chernovs illustrate this most clearly.

The interrelation of classes has changed. This is the crux of the matter.

Not those classes stand now "on the one and the other side of the barricade."

This is the main thing.

This, and this *alone*, is the *scientific* foundation for speaking of a *new* revolution which—arguing purely theoretically, taking the question in the abstract—could be accomplished legally if, for instance, the Constituent Assembly, convoked by the bourgeoisie, gave a majority that is opposed to the bourgeoisie, gave a majority to the parties of the workers and poorest peasants.

The objective interrelation of the classes, their rôle (economic and political) outside and inside of certain representative institutions; the rise or the fall of the revolution; the interrelation between extra-parliamentary and parliamentary means of struggle—these are the chief, the fundamental objective data which must be taken into account if the tactics of boycott or participation are to be deduced not arbitrarily, not according to our "sympathies," but in a Marxist way.

The experience of our revolution clearly demonstrates how to approach the boycott question in a Marxist way.

Why did the boycott of the Bulygin Duma * prove correct tactics?

Because it corresponded to the objective correlation of social forces in their development. It gave to the rising revolution a slogan for the overthrow of an old order which, to distract the people from the revolution, was convoking a clumsily adulterated institution (the Bulygin Duma) which did not open perspectives of an earnest "anchoring" in parliamentarism. The extra-parliamentary means of struggle of the proletariat and the peasantry were stronger. These are the elements that went into shaping the correct tactics of boycotting the Bulygin Duma, tactics which took account of the objective situation.

Why did the tactics of boycotting the Third Duma prove incorrect?

Because they were based only on the "sharpness" of the boycott slogan and on the repulsion felt towards the brutal reaction of the June 16 "pigsty." ** The objective situation, however, was such that on the one hand the revolution was in a state of collapse and going down fast. To help it rise, a parliamentary base (even inside a "pigsty") became of tremendous political importance, since extra-

---

* Minister of Interior Bulygin proposed in the summer of 1905 the calling of a Duma with consultative powers and based upon limited suffrage.—*Ed.*

** On June 16, 1907, the Second Duma was dissolved and a new suffrage law promulgated which assured the control of the Duma to the feudal and industrial interests.—*Ed.*

parliamentary means of propaganda, education and organisation were almost non-existent or extremely weak. On the other hand, the most brutal reaction of the Third Duma did not prevent it from being an organ of a real interrelation of classes, namely, the Stolypin combination of the monarchy with the bourgeoisie. This new interrelation of classes the country had to outlive.

These are the elements that went into the shaping of the tactics of participation in the Third Duma, tactics which correctly took account of the objective situation.

It is sufficient to examine more closely these lessons from experience, the conditions of a Marxist approach to the question of boycott or participation, to become convinced of the absolute incorrectness of the tactics of participating in the "Democratic Council" or pre-parliament.

On the one hand, a new revolution is growing. The war is on the up-grade. The extra-parliamentary means of propaganda, agitation and organisation are tremendous. The importance of the "parliamentary" tribune in the given pre-parliament is insignificant. On the other hand, this pre-parliament neither expresses nor serves a new interrelation of classes; for instance, the peasantry is here more poorly represented than in the already existing organs (Soviets of Peasant Deputies). The parliament is in substance a Bonapartist *fraud,* not only in the sense that the filthy gang of the Liberdans, Tseretelis and Chernovs, together with Kerensky and Co., *have stacked the cards,* have falsified the composition of this Tsereteli-Bulygin Duma, but also in that deeper sense that it is the only aim of the pre-parliament to trick the masses, to deceive the workers and peasants, to distract them from the new rising revolution, to dazzle the eyes of the oppressed classes by a new dress for the *old,* long tried out, bedraggled, threadbare "coalition" with the bourgeoisie (*i.e.,* the transforming by the bourgeoisie of Messrs. Tsereteli and Co. into clowns helping to subordinate the people to imperialism and the imperialist war).

"We are weak now," says the Tsar in August, 1905, to his feudal landowners. "Our power is shaking. A wave of workers' and peasants' revolution is rising. We must trick the 'plain man,' we must dangle something before his eyes. . . ."

"We are weak now," says the present "tsar," the Bonapartist Kerensky, to the Cadets, the non-party shop-keepers, Plekhanovs, Breshkovskayas and Co. "Our power is shaking. A wave of workers' and peasants' revolution against the bourgeoisie is rising. We must trick democracy. For this we must repaint with new colours that clown costume which the Socialist-Revolutionary and Menshevik 'leaders of revolutionary democracy,' our dear friends the Tseretelis and Chernovs, have been wearing since May 19, 1917, to fool the people. We can easily dangle before their eyes a 'pre-parliament.' "

"We are strong now," says the Tsar to his feudal landowners in June, 1907. "The wave of workers' and peasants' revolution is receding, but we cannot maintain ourselves as of old; deception alone will not suffice. We must have a new policy in the village, we must have a new economic and political bloc with the Guchkovs-Milyukovs, with the bourgeoisie."

Thus it is possible to present the three situations, of August, 1905, September, 1917, and June, 1907, in order more clearly to demonstrate the objective foundations of the boycott tactics, their connection with the interrelation of classes. The deception of the oppressed classes by the oppressors is always present, but the meaning of this deception is different at different historic moments. Tactics cannot be based on the bare fact that the oppressors deceive the people; tactics must be shaped after analysing the interrelation of classes in its entirety and the development of both extra-parliamentary and parliamentary struggle.

The tactics of participating in the pre-parliament are *incorrect*. They do not correspond to the objective interrelation of classes, to the objective conditions of the moment.

We should have boycotted the Democratic Conference; we all erred by not doing so, but mistakes are bound to occur. We shall correct the mistake only when we sincerely wish to take up the revolutionary struggle of the masses, when we think earnestly of the objective foundations of our tactics.

We must boycott the pre-parliament. We must leave it and go to the Soviets of Workers', Soldiers', and Peasants' Deputies, to the trade unions, to the masses in general. We must call them to struggle. We must give *them* a correct and clear slogan: disperse the Bonapartist gang of Kerensky with *his* forged pre-parliament, with this Tsereteli-Bulygin Duma. The Mensheviks and Socialist-Revolutionaries, even after the Kornilov affair, refused to accept our compromise of peacefully giving over the power to the Soviets (in which we had *no* majority *then*); they have again sunk into the morass of filthy and mean bargains with the Cadets. Down with the Mensheviks and S.-R.'s! Struggle against them ruthlessly. Expel them ruthlessly from all revolutionary organisations. No negotiations, no communication with those *friends of the Kishkins,* the friends of the Kornilovist landlords and capitalists.

Saturday, October 6.

Trotsky was for the boycott. Bravo, Comrade Trotsky!

Boycottism was defeated in the fraction of the Bolsheviks who came to the Democratic Conference.

Long live the boycott!

We cannot and must not reconcile ourselves to participation under any condition. A fraction in one of the conferences is not the highest organ of the party; even the decisions of the highest organs are subject to revision on the basis of life's experiences.

We must at all costs strive to have the boycott question solved in the plenum of the Central Committee and at an extraordinary party congress. The boycott question must now be made the platform for elections to the congress and for *all* elections inside the party. We must draw the *masses* into discussing this question. It is necessary that the enlightened workers should take the matter into their hands, should organise the discussion and exert pressure on the *"top."*

There is not the slightest doubt that in the "top" of our party we note vacillations that may become *ruinous,* because the struggle is developing; under certain conditions, at a certain moment, vacillations are capable of *ruining* the cause. Before it is too late, we must begin the struggle with all our forces, we must defend the correct line of the party of the revolutionary proletariat.

Not all is well at the "parliamentary" top of our party; more attention must be paid to it, more vigilance of the workers over it; the jurisdiction of parliamentary fractions must be more strongly defined.

The mistake of our party is obvious. There is no danger in mistakes for the fighting party of the advanced class. There is danger, however, in persisting in a mistake, in false pride which refused to admit and correct a mistake.

Sunday, October 7.

The Congress of Soviets has been postponed till November 2. At the tempo of Russian life at present, this almost means postponing it to the Greek Calends. The comedy staged by the S.-R.'s and Mensheviks after May 3-4 is repeated for the second time.

Written October 5-7, 1917.
First published in the magazine *Proletarskaya Revolyutsiya*, No. 3 (26), 1924.

THE TASKS OF THE REVOLUTION

Russia is a petty-bourgeois country. A gigantic majority of the population belongs to this class. Its vacillations between the bourgeoisie and the proletariat are inevitable. Only when it joins the proletariat is the victory of the cause of the revolution, of the cause of peace, freedom, and land for the toilers secured—easily, peacefully, quickly, and smoothly.

The course of our revolution shows us the existence of such vacillations in practice. Let us then not harbour any illusions concerning the parties of the Socialist-Revolutionaries and Mensheviks; let us stick firmly to our class-proletarian road. The poverty of the poorest peasants, the horrors of the war, the horrors of hunger—all these show to the masses more and more clearly the correctness of the proletarian road, the necessity of supporting the proletarian revolution.

The "peaceful" petty-bourgeois hopes for a "coalition" with the bourgeoisie, for agreements with it, for the possibility of waiting "calmly" for the "speedy" convocation of the Constituent Assembly, etc.—all this is mercilessly, cruelly, implacably destroyed by the course of the revolution. The Kornilov affair was the last cruel lesson, a lesson on a large scale, supplementing thousands upon thousands of small lessons, consisting of the workers and peasants being deceived locally by the capitalists and landowners, lessons consisting of the soldiers being deceived by the officers, etc., etc.

The discontent, the revolt, the bitterness in the army, among the peasantry, among the workers, are growing. The "coalition" of the S.-R.'s and Mensheviks with the bourgeoisie, promising everything and carrying out nothing, is irritating the masses, is opening their eyes, is pushing them towards an uprising.

The opposition of the "Lefts," among the S.-R.'s (Spiridinova and others) and among the Mensheviks (Martov and others), is growing—an opposition that has already reached forty per cent of the "Council" and "Congress" of these parties. And down *below*, among the proletariat and the peasantry, particularly the poorest sections, the *majority* of the S.-R.'s and Mensheviks belong to the "Lefts."

The Kornilov affair is instructive. The Kornilov affair has proved very instructive.

It is impossible to know whether the Soviets will be able to go further than the leaders of the S. R.'s and Mensheviks, and thus secure a peaceful development of the revolution, or whether they will continue to mark time, thus making a proletarian uprising inevitable.

We cannot know this.

Our business is to help do everything possible to secure the "last" chance for a peaceful development of the revolution, to help this by presenting our programme, by making clear its general, national character, its absolute harmony with the interests and demands of an enormous majority of the population.

The following lines are an attempt at presenting such a programme.

Let us go with it more to those below, to the masses, to the office employees, to the workers, to the peasants, not only to our own, but particularly to those who follow the S.-R.'s, to the non-party elements, to the unenlightened ones. Let us raise them to an independent judgment, to passing their own decisions, to sending *their own* delegations to the conference, to the Soviets, to the government. Then our work will not have been in vain, *no matter* what the outcome of the conference. Then this will prove useful for the conference, for the elections to the Constituent Assembly, and for every other political activity in general.

Life teaches us that the Bolshevik programme and tactics are correct. Between May 3 and the Kornilov affair "so little time has passed, so much has happened!"

The experience of the *masses*, the experience of the *oppressed* classes has yielded them a very great deal during that time; the leaders of the S.-R.'s and Mensheviks have entirely parted ways with the masses. This will most assuredly reveal itself in the discussion of our concrete programme, if it will be possible to bring it to the masses.

Agreements with the Capitalists Are Disastrous

1. To leave in power the representatives of the bourgeoisie, even in a small number, to leave such notorious Kornilovists as Generals Alexeyev, Klembovsky, Bagration, Gagarin, and others, or such as

have proved their complete powerlessness in face of the bourgeoisie, and their ability of acting Bonaparte-fashion like Kerensky—this means to open the door wide, on the one hand, to famine and the inevitable economic catastrophe which the capitalists are purposely accelerating and intensifying; on the other hand, to a military catastrophe, since the army hates General Headquarters and cannot enthusiastically participate in the imperialist war. Besides, the Kornilovist generals and officers remaining in power will undoubtedly *open the front to the Germans on purpose,* as they have done in Galicia and near Riga. This can be prevented only by the formation of a new government on a new basis, as expounded below. To continue any kind of agreements with the bourgeoisie after all that we have gone through since May 3 would be, on the part of the S.-R.'s and Mensheviks, not only an error but a direct betrayal of the people and the revolution.

Power to the Soviets

2. All power in the state must pass exclusively to the representatives in the Soviets of Workers', Soldiers', and Peasants' Deputies on the basis of a definite programme and under the condition of the power being fully responsible to the Soviets. New elections to the Soviets must be held immediately, both in order to give expression to the experiences of the people during the recent weeks of the revolution, which were particularly full of content, and in order to eliminate crying injustices (lack of proportional representation, unequal elections, etc.) which have here and there remained uncorrected.

All power locally, wherever there are not yet in existence democratically elected institutions, as well as in the army, must pass exclusively to the local Soviets and to commissars and other institutions elected by them, but only such as have been really elected.

The arming of the workers and of the revolutionary troops, *i.e.,* such as have in practice shown their ability to suppress the Kornilovists, must be realised absolutely and everywhere with the full support of the state.

Peace to the Peoples

3. The Soviet government must *immediately* offer to *all* the belligerent peoples (*i.e.,* simultaneously both to their governments and

to the worker and peasant masses) the conclusion of an immediate general peace on democratic conditions, as well as the conclusion of an immediate truce (even if only for three months).

The main condition for a democratic peace is the renunciation of annexations (seizures)—not only in the incorrect sense that all powers get back what they have *lost*, but in the only correct sense that *every* nationality without any exceptions both in Europe and in the colonies shall obtain the freedom and the possibility to decide for itself whether it is to form a *separate* state or whether it is to enter into the composition of any other state.

In offering the conditions of peace, the Soviet government must itself immediately take steps towards their fulfilment, *i.e.*, it must publish and repudiate the secret treaties by which we have been bound up to the present time, which were concluded by the Tsar and promise the Russian capitalists the pillaging of Turkey, Austria, etc. Then we are obliged immediately to satisfy the demands of the Ukrainians and the Finns. We must secure for them, as well as for all the other non-Russian nationalities in Russia, full freedom, including the freedom of secession, applying the same to all of Armenia, making it our duty to evacuate it as well as the Turkish lands occupied by us, etc.

Such conditions of peace will not meet with the good will of the capitalists, but they will be met by all the peoples with such tremendous sympathy and will cause such a great world-historic outburst of enthusiasm and general indignation against the continuation of the predatory war that it is extremely probable that we shall at once obtain a truce and a consent to open peace negotiations. For the workers' revolution against the war is irresistibly growing everywhere, and it can be spurred on not by phrases about peace (with which the workers and peasants have been deceived by all the imperialist governments including our own, Kerensky government) but by a break with the capitalists and by the offer of peace.

If the least probable thing happens, *i.e.*, if not a single belligerent state accepts even a truce, then the war on our part becomes truly forced upon us, it becomes a truly just and defensive war. The very consciousness of this fact among the proletariat and the poorest peasantry will make Russia many times stronger even militarily, especially after a complete break with the capitalists who are robbing the people, not to speak of the fact that under such conditions the war on our part would be, not in words but in deeds, a war in league with the oppressed classes of all countries, a war in league with the oppressed peoples of the whole world.

The people must be particularly cautioned against an assertion made by the capitalists, and which sometimes influences the frightened, the philistines, namely, that in case we break with the present predatory alliance with the English and other capitalists, they are capable of causing serious damage to the Russian Revolution. Such an assertion is false through and through, for the "financial aid of the Allies," while enriching the bankers, "supports" the Russian workers and peasants even as the rope supports the hanged man. There is plenty of bread, coal, oil and iron in Russia; it is only necessary to free ourselves from the landowners and the capitalists who rob the people, and we shall be able to distribute those products properly. As to the possibility of a military threat to the Russian people on the part of its present allies, the supposition that the French and Italians are capable of combining their armies with the Germans and of moving them against Russia, once the latter offers a just peace, is an obviously absurd assumption. As to England, America, and Japan, even were they to declare war against Russia (which for them is extremely difficult, both in view of the unpopularity of such a war among the masses and in view of the divergence of material interests of the capitalists of those countries as to the partition of Asia, particularly the robbing of China), they could not cause Russia one-hundredth part of the damage and misery which the war with Germany, Austria, and Turkey causes it.

Land to the Toilers

4. The Soviet government must immediately declare private ownership in land abolished without compensation and turn over all these lands to be managed by peasant committees pending the solution of this problem by the Constituent Assembly. These peasant committees are also to be given the management of all the landowners' stock and implements, with the proviso that it be placed at the disposal of the poorest peasants for use before anybody else, and absolutely free of charge.

Such measures, which have long been demanded by an immense majority of the peasantry, both in resolutions of its congresses and in hundreds of instructions from local peasants (as may be seen, among others, from a summing up of 242 instructions made by the

Izvestiya of the Soviet of Peasant Deputies), are absolutely necessary and urgent. No further procrastinations, like those under which the peasantry suffered during the "Coalition" Cabinet, are admissible.

Any government which hesitated in introducing those measures would have to be recognised as a government *hostile to the people*, worthy of being overthrown and crushed by an uprising of the workers and peasants. On the other hand, only a government that has realised those measures will be a government of all the people.

Struggle Against Famine and Economic Ruin

5. The Soviet government must immediately introduce workers' control, on a general state scale, of production and consumption. As has been shown by the experience of May 19, in the absence of such a control all the promises of reforms and attempts at introducing them are powerless, and famine, with unprecedented catastrophe, menaces the whole country more and more every week.

It is necessary immediately to nationalise the banks and the insurance business, as well as the most important branches of industry (oil, coal, metallurgy, sugar, etc.), and at the same time, to abolish commercial secrets and to establish unrelaxing vigilance by the workers and peasants over the negligible minority of capitalists, who wax rich on government contracts and evade accounting and just taxation of their profits and properties.

Such measures, without depriving either the middle peasants or the Cossacks or the small artisans of a single kopeck, are absolutely just, in so far as they distribute the burdens of the war equitably, and are absolutely necessary for the struggle against famine. Only after the marauding by the capitalists has been curbed, and a stop put to their intentional sabotaging of production, will it be possible to achieve an increase in the productivity of labour, to establish universal labour duty, to introduce the proper exchange of grain for industrial products, and to effect a return to the treasury of the many billions of paper money now hoarded by the rich.

Without such measures, the abolition of property in the landowners' lands without compensation is also impossible, for the landowners' lands are, in their major part, mortgaged to the banks, so that the interests of the landowners and capitalists are inseparably linked up.

The last resolution of the Economic Section of the All-Russian

Central Executive Committee of the Soviets of Workers' and Soldiers' Deputies (*Rabochaya Gazeta*, No. 152) recognises not only the *"severity"* of the government's measures (like the raising of bread prices for the enrichment of the landowners and kulaks), not only "the fact of the *complete inactivity* on the part of the central organs created by the government for the regulation of economic life," but also the *"violation of the laws"* by this government. This admission on the part of the ruling parties, the S.-R.'s and Mensheviks, proves once more the criminal nature of the policy of conciliation with the bourgeoisie.

Struggle Against the Counter-revolution of the Landowners and Capitalists

6. The Kornilov and Kaledin uprising was supported by the entire class of the landowners and capitalists, with the party of the Cadets ("People's Freedom" Party) at their head. This has already been fully proven by the facts published in the *Izvestiya* of the Central Executive Committee.

However, nothing has been done either for the complete suppression of this counter-revolution or even for investigating it, and nothing serious can be done without the power passing to the Soviets. No commission is capable of conducting a full investigation, of arresting the guilty, etc., unless it is in possession of state power. Only a Soviet government can and must do this. Only this government, by arresting the Kornilovist generals and the heads of the bourgeois counter-revolution (Guchkov, Milyukov, Ryabushinsky, Maklakov, and Co.), by disbanding the counter-revolutionary unions (State Duma, the officers' unions, etc.), by placing their members under the surveillance of the local Soviets, by disbanding the counter-revolutionary armed units, will be able to make Russia secure against the inevitable repetition of "Kornilov" attempts.

Only this government can create a commission to make a full and public investigation of the actions of the Kornilovists as well as of all the other actions started even by the bourgeoisie; and the party of the Bolsheviks, in its turn, would appeal to the workers to give full obedience and co-operation only to such a commission.

Only a Soviet government could successfully combat such a flagrant injustice as the seizure by the capitalists, with the aid of millions squeezed out of the people, of the largest printing plants and the majority of the papers. It is necessary to suppress the bourgeois counter-revolutionary papers (*Ryech, Russkoye Slovo*, etc.), to confiscate their printing plants, to declare private advertisements in the papers a state monopoly, to transfer them to the paper published by the Soviets and telling the peasants the truth. Only in this way can and must the powerful weapon of unpunished lies and slanders, of deceit of the people, of misleading the peasantry, of preparing a counter-revolution, be wrested from the hands of the bourgeoisie.

Peaceful Development of the Revolution

7. Before the democracy of Russia, before the Soviets, before the S.-R. and Menshevik Parties, there opens now a possibility very seldom to be met with in the history of revolutions, namely, a possibility of securing the convocation of the Constituent Assembly at the appointed date without new delays, a possibility of securing the country against a military and economic catastrophe, a possibility of securing a peaceful development of the revolution.

If the Soviets now take the state power into their hands, fully and exclusively, with the purpose of carrying out the programme set forth above, they will secure not only the support of nine-tenths of the population of Russia, the working class and a tremendous majority of the peasantry, but they will secure also the greatest revolutionary enthusiasm of the army and the majority of the people, an enthusiasm without which a victory over the famine and the war is impossible.

There could be no question of any resistance to the Soviets if there were no vacillations on their part. No class will dare start an uprising against the Soviets, and the landowners and capitalists, chastened by the experience of the Kornilov affair, will give up their power peacefully upon the categorical demand of the Soviets. To overcome the resistance of the capitalists to the programme of the Soviets, it will be sufficient to exercise the supervision of the workers and peasants over the exploiters and to use such measures of punishing the recalcitrants as confiscation of the whole property coupled with a short term of arrest.

Having seized power, the Soviets could still at present—and this is probably their last chance—secure a peaceful development of the revolution, peaceful elections of the deputies by the people, a peaceful struggle of parties inside of the Soviets, a testing of the programmes of various parties in practice, a peaceful passing of power from one party to another.

If this possibility is allowed to pass by, then the entire course of the development of the revolution, from the movement of May 3 to the Kornilov affair, indicates the inevitability of the bitterest civil war between the bourgeoisie and the proletariat. The inevitable catastrophe will bring this war nearer. It will culminate, if all data and considerations accessible to human reason do not deceive, in a complete victory of the working class, in its being supported by the poorest peasantry for the purpose of carrying out the above programme. Still it may prove very difficult, bloody, costing the lives of tens of thousands of landowners, capitalists, and officers who sympathise with them. The proletariat will stop before no sacrifices to save the revolution, which is impossible without the programme set forth above. On the other hand, the proletariat would support the Soviets in every way if they were to make use of their last chance for securing a peaceful development of the revolution.

N. K.

Rabochy Put, Nos. 20-21, October 9 and 10, 1917.

LETTER TO I. T. SMILGA [90]

I AM taking this good opportunity to talk with you in more detail.

1.

The general political situation causes me great anxiety. The Petrograd Soviet and the Bolsheviks have declared war on the government. But the government has an army, and is preparing itself *systematically*. (Kerensky at General Headquarters is obviously entering into an understanding—and a business-like understanding—with the Kornilovists about using the troops for the suppression of the Bolsheviks.)

And what do we do? We only pass resolutions. We lose time. We set "dates" (November 2, the Soviet Congress—is it not ridiculous to put it off so long? Is it not ridiculous to rely on that?). The Bolsheviks do *not* conduct systematic work to prepare their *own* military forces for the overthrow of Kerensky.

Events have fully proven the correctness of the motion I made during the Democratic Conference, namely, that the party *must* put the armed uprising on the order of the day.* Events *compel* us to do so. History has made the *military* question now the fundamental *political* question. I am afraid that the Bolsheviks forget this, being steeped in "day to day events," in petty current questions, and *"hoping"* that "the wave will sweep Kerensky away." Such hope is naïve; it is the same as relying on chance. On the part of the party of the revolutionary proletariat this may prove a crime.

It is my opinion that we must make propaganda within the party for an earnest attitude towards the armed uprising; for this purpose this letter should be typed and delivered to the Petrograd and Moscow comrades.

2.

Now about your rôle. It seems to me that the only things that we can have *completely* at our disposal and that can play a *serious* military rôle, are the troops in Finland and the Baltic fleet. I think

---

* See p. 221.—*Ed.*

you must utilise your high position, shift to the assistants and secretaries all the petty routine work without wasting time on "resolutions," but giving *all your attention* to the *military* preparation of the troops in Finland plus the fleet for the impending overthrow of Kerensky. You must create a *secret* committee of *trustworthy* military men, together with them discuss matters *thoroughly*, collect (and *personally* verify) the most accurate data concerning the composition and the location of troops near and in Petrograd, the transfer of the troops in Finland to Petrograd, the movement of the navy, etc.

If we do not do this, we may turn out to be ridiculous fools: in possession of beautiful resolutions and Soviets, but *without power!!* I think it is possible for you to select really reliable and informed military men, to make a trip to Ino [91] and other most important points, to weigh and study the matter *earnestly*, not relying on the boastful general phrases *all too common* with us.

It is obvious that we can *under no circumstances* allow the troops to be transported from Finland. Better do anything, better decide on an uprising, on the seizure of power, later to be transferred to the Congress of Soviets. I read in the papers today that in two weeks the danger of a naval occupation will be nil.[92] Obviously, you have very little time left for preparation.

3.

Now something else. We must utilise our "power" in Finland to conduct systematic propaganda among the Cossacks now stationed in Finland. Kerensky and Co. purposely removed some of them from Vyborg, for instance, fearing "bolshevisation," and placed them in Usikirko and Perkyarvi, between Vyborg and Terioki, in Bolshevik-proof isolation.[93] We must study all information about the location of the Cossacks, and must organise the despatch of *propaganda groups* from among the best forces of the sailors and soldiers in Finland. This is imperative. Do the same thing about literature.

4.

And now another point. Of course, both sailors and soldiers go home on furloughs. Out of these men we must form a unit of propagandists to travel over the provinces systematically and to carry on in the villages both general propaganda and propaganda in favour of the Constitutent Assembly. Your situation is exceptionally good because you are in a position immediately to *begin* the realisation of that bloc with the Left Socialist-Revolutionaries which alone can give us stable power in Russia and a majority in the Constitutent Assembly. Without much ado, organise such a bloc immediately in your place, organise the publication of leaflets (find out what you can do for it technically as well as in the matter of transporting them into Russia.) It will then be necessary for each propaganda group intended for the village to include not less than two persons: one from the Bolsheviks, another from the Left S.-R.'s. The "firm" of the S.-R.'s still reigns in the village, and we must utilise your luck (you have Left S.-R.'s) to realise in the village *in the name* of this "firm" a bloc of the Bolsheviks with the *Left* S.-R.'s, with the peasants and workers, not with the capitalists.

5.

It seems to me that, in order correctly to prepare the minds, we must immediately put forward the following slogan: all power to the Petrograd Soviet *now*, later to be transferred to the Congress of Soviets. Why should we tolerate three more weeks of war and Kerensky's "Kornilovist preparations"?

Propaganda in favour of this slogan by the Bolsheviks and Left S.-R.'s in Finland can be nothing but useful.

6.

Since you are vested with "power" in Finland, it is incumbent upon you to do one more very important, though in itself modest piece of work, namely, to organise the illegal transportation of literature from Sweden. Without this all talk of an "International" is a *phrase*. This can be easily done, first, by creating our own organisation of soldiers at the frontier; second, if this is impossible, by organising *regular trips* of at least one reliable man to a certain place where I began to organise the transport *with the aid of the person in whose house I lived for one day* before entering Helsingfors (Rovio knows him). Perhaps we must help with some money. By all means do it!

7.

I think we must see each other to talk all these things over. You could come here; it would take you less than a day, if you come *only* to see me; have Rovio ask Huttunen on the telephone whether Rovio's "wife's sister" (meaning you) may see Huttunen's "sister" (meaning myself). For I may have to leave suddenly.

Do not fail to notify me of the receipt of this letter (*burn it*) by the comrade who will bring it to Rovio *and who will soon go back*.

In case I stay here longer, we must organise mail connections. You *could help us* by sending envelopes through railway workers to the Vyborg *Soviet* (inside envelope: "for Huttunen").

8.

Send me by the same comrade a certificate (as formal as possible: on the stationery of the Regional Committee with the signature of the president, and stamped, either typewritten, or *in very clear handwriting*) in the name of Konstantin Petrovich Ivanov, to the effect that the president of the Regional Committee vouches for comrade so and so and requests *all Soviets*, the *Vyborg* Soviet of Soldiers' Deputies as well as others, to give him *full confidence*, aid and support.

I need it for *any* emergency, since a "conflict" and a "meeting" are possible.

9.

Have you a copy of the Moscow collection of articles *On the Revision of the Programme?* [94] Try to find one among the comrades in Helsingfors and send it to me by the same comrade.

10.

Have in mind that Rovio is a splendid man, but *lazy*. He must be looked after and *reminded* of things twice a day. Else he won't do them.

Greetings,
K. IVANOV.*

Written October 10, 1917.
First published in *Pravda*, No. 255 (3186), November 7, 1925.

* A name used by Lenin in this case for conspirative purposes.—*Ed.*

POSTSCRIPT TO THE BOOK *THE AGRARIAN PROGRAMME OF THE SOCIAL-DEMOCRACY IN THE FIRST RUSSIAN REVOLUTION, 1905-1907* *

THIS work was written at the end of 1907. In 1908 it was printed in St. Petersburg, but the tsarist censorship seized and destroyed it. Only one copy was saved, with the last part missing (after p. 269 of the present edition); this last part has now been added.

At present the revolution has rendered the agrarian question infinitely wider, deeper and sharper than it was in 1905-1907. Acquaintance with the history of our party programme during the first revolution will, I hope, help more correctly to understand the tasks of the present revolution.

The following must be particularly stressed. The war has caused the belligerent countries such unheard-of miseries, and at the same time has hastened the development of capitalism so tremendously by transforming monopoly capitalism into state monopoly capitalism, that neither the proletariat nor revolutionary petty-bourgeois democracy can confine itself to the framework of capitalism.

Life has already proceeded far beyond this framework, putting on the order of the day regulation of production and distribution on a nation-wide scale, universal labour duty, compulsory trustification (organisation into associations), etc.

Under such conditions, both nationalisation of the land and the agrarian programme must inevitably be approached in a new way. Nationalisation of the land is not only "the last word" of a bourgeois revolution, but it is *a step towards Socialism*. It is impossible to struggle against the war sufferings without taking such steps.

The proletariat, leading the poorest peasantry, is compelled on the one hand to shift the centre of gravity from the Soviets of Peasant Deputies to the Soviets of Deputies of agricultural workers, on the other hand to demand the nationalisation of the livestock and implements of landowners' estates as well as the formation of model farms out of those estates under the control of the last-named Soviets.

Of course, I cannot expand here on these important questions, and

---

* See V. I. Lenin, *Collected Works*, Vol. XI.—*Ed.*

I must refer the interested reader to the current Bolshevik literature and to my pamphlets: *Letters on Tactics* and *Tasks of the Proletariat in Our Revolution (Proposed Platform of a Proletarian Party).**

Written September 28, 1917.
Printed in the book *The Agrarian Programme of the Social-Democracy in the First Russian Revolution, 1905-1907.*

* See V. I. Lenin, *The Revolution of 1917, Collected Works*, Vol. XX, Book I, pp. 118 and 130.—*Ed.*

THE CRISIS HAS MATURED [95]

I

THERE is no doubt that the beginning of October has brought us to the greatest turning point in the history of the Russian and, according to all appearance, also of the world revolution.

The world workers' revolution started with the actions of individuals who, by their unswerving courage, represented everything honest that has survived the decay of official "Socialism," which is in reality social-chauvinism. Liebknecht in Germany, Adler in Austria, MacLean in England—these are the best known names of those individual heroes who took upon themselves the difficult rôle of forerunners of the world revolution.

A second stage in the historic preparation for this revolution was a broad mass ferment which assumed the form of a split in the official parties, the form of illegal publications and of street demonstrations. The protest against the war grew—and the number of victims of governmental persecutions also grew. The prisons of countries famed for their lawfulness and even for their freedom, Germany, France, Italy, England, began to be filled with scores and hundreds of internationalists, opponents of the war, advocates of a workers' revolution.

Now the third stage has come, which may be called the eve of the revolution. Mass arrests of party leaders in free Italy, and particularly the beginning of mutinies in the German army, are undoubted symptoms of the great turning point, the symptoms of *the eve of revolution* on a world scale.

There is no doubt that even before this, there were in Germany individual cases of mutiny in the army, but those cases were so small, so isolated, so weak, that it was possible to hush them up, to pass over them in silence—and this was the main thing required to check *the mass contagion* of seditious actions. Finally, such a movement in the navy matured that it became *impossible* either to hush it up or to pass over it in silence, notwithstanding the severity of the German military prison régime, elaborated with unheard-of astuteness and followed with unbelievable pedantry.

There is no room for doubts. We are on the threshold of a world proletarian revolution. And since we, Russian Bolsheviks, alone out of all the proletarian internationalists of all countries, enjoy comparatively great freedom, since we have an open party, a score or so of papers, since we have on our side the Soviets of Workers' and Soldiers' Deputies in the capitals, since we have on our side the *majority* of the masses of the people in revolutionary times, to us may and must truly apply the famous dictum: he who has been given much shall have to account for more.

II

In Russia, the turning point in the revolution has undoubtedly come.

In a peasant country, under a revolutionary republican government enjoying the support of the Socialist-Revolutionary and Menshevik Parties that only yesterday held sway among the petty-bourgeois democracy, *a peasant uprising* is growing.

It is incredible, but it is a fact.

We Bolsheviks are not surprised by this fact; we have always maintained that the government of the famed "coalition" with the bourgeoisie is a government of *betrayal* of democracy and revolution, a government of *imperialist* slaughter, a government *guarding* the capitalists and landowners *against* the people.

Thanks to the deceptions of the S.-R.'s and Mensheviks, there has been and still remains in Russia, under a republic and during a revolution, a government of capitalists and landowners side by side with the Soviets. Such is the bitter and formidable reality. Is there any wonder that at the time when the prolongation of the imperialist war and its consequences are causing the people unheard-of misery, a peasant uprising has begun and is developing?

Is it any wonder that the opponents of the Bolsheviks, the leaders of the official S.-R. Party, the same party that has supported the "coalition" all along, the same party that up to the last days or last weeks had the majority of the people on its side, the same party that continues to blame and to hound the "new" S.-R.'s who have realised that the coalition policy is betraying the interest of the peasants—is it any wonder that these leaders of the official S.-R. Party, in an editorial of their official organ, the *Dyelo Naroda*, October 12, wrote as follows:

Almost nothing has been done up to the present time to do away with the bondage relations that still prevail in the village, particularly in Central Russia. . . . The law regulating the land relations in the village, a law that has long been introduced into the Provisional Government, and has even passed the purgatory of the Judicial Conference, has been hopelessly buried in some quagmire of a bureau. . . . Are we not right in asserting that our republican government is far from having freed itself of the old habits of the Tsar's administration, that the dead grip of Stolypin is still strongly felt in the methods of the revolutionary Ministers? [96]

This is written by the official S.-R.'s! Just think of it: the adherents of a coalition are *forced* to admit that, in a peasant country, seven months after the revolution, "almost nothing has been done to do away with the bondage relations" of the peasants, with their being enslaved by the landowners! These S.-R.'s are *forced* to call their colleague Kerensky, and all his band of Ministers, *Stolypinists*.

Can there be found more eloquent testimony coming from the camp of our opponents to corroborate not only the fact that the coalition has collapsed, not only the fact that the official S.-R.'s who tolerate Kerensky have become an *anti-national, anti-peasant, counter-revolutionary party*, but also that the whole Russian Revolution has reached a turning point?

A peasant uprising in a peasant country against the government of Kerensky, the S.-R., of Nikitin and Gvozdev, the Mensheviks, and other Ministers, representatives of capital and of the landowners' interests! A suppression of this uprising by the republican government with *military measures!*

In the face of such facts can one be a conscientious partisan of the proletariat and at the same time deny that the crisis has matured, that the revolution is going through its greatest turning point, that the victory of the government over the peasant uprising at the present time would be the death knell of the revolution, the final triumph of Kornilovism?

III

It is self-evident that if matters have reached the point of a peasant uprising in a peasant country after seven months of a democratic republic, this proves beyond dispute that the revolution is suffering a collapse on a national scale, that it is passing through a crisis of unheard-of severity; that the counter-revolutionary forces are approaching the *last ditch*.

This is self-evident. In the face of such a fact as the peasant uprising, all the other political symptoms, even if they were to contradict this maturing of a national crisis, would have no significance whatsoever.

But all the symptoms, on the contrary, indicate just this—that the country-wide crisis has matured.

After the agrarian question, the national question is of the greatest importance in the national life of Russia, particularly for the petty-bourgeois masses of the population. And we see that at the "Democratic" Conference packed by Messrs. Tsereteli and Co. the "national" curia take the second place in radicalism, yielding only to the trade unions and *exceeding* the curia of the Soviets of Workers' and Soldiers' Deputies by percentage of votes cast *against* the coalition (40 out of 55). The government of Kerensky, a government suppressing the peasant uprising, is withdrawing the revolutionary troops from Finland, in order to strengthen the reactionary Finnish bourgeoisie. In the Ukraine, the conflicts of the Ukrainians in general and of the Ukrainian troops in particular, with the government are becoming more frequent.

Let us further look at the army, which in war time is of exceptional importance in the whole life of the state. We have seen that the Finnish army and the Baltic fleet have entirely *split* away from the government. We hear the testimony of the officer Dubasov, not a Bolshevik, speaking in the name of the whole front, and saying in a more revolutionary manner than the Bolsheviks that the soldiers will not fight any longer. We hear governmental reports saying that the morale of the soldiers is low, that it is impossible to guarantee "order" (*i.e.*, participation of these troops in suppressing the peasant uprising). We witness finally the vote in Moscow where fourteen thousand out of seventeen thousand soldiers voted for the Bolsheviks.

This voting in the elections to the borough councils in Moscow is one of the most striking symptoms of a very deep change taking place in the general mood of the nation. It is generally known that Moscow is more petty-bourgeois than Petrograd. It is a fact, many times corroborated and undisputed, that the Moscow proletariat has a vastly greater number of connections with the village, that it harbours more sympathies and is closer to the peasant village sentiment, than the Petrograd proletariat. And in Moscow the votes cast for the S.-R.'s and Mensheviks dropped from 70 per cent in June to 18 per cent at present. The petty bourgeoisie has turned away from the coalition; the people have turned away from it;

there can be no doubt of this. The Cadets have increased their strength from 17 to 30 per cent, but they remain a minority, a hopeless minority, notwithstanding the fact that they have been obviously joined by the "Right" S.-R.'s and the "Right" Mensheviks. The *Russkiye Vyedomosti* [97] says that the *absolute* number of votes cast for the Cadets fell from 67,000 to 62,000. But the number of votes cast for the Bolsheviks grew from 34,000 to 82,000. They received 47 per cent of the total number of votes.[98] There can be not the shadow of a doubt that, together with the Left S.-R.'s, we have at present a majority in the Soviets, in the army, and *in the country*.

Among the symptoms that serve not only as an indication but have a significance in themselves, must be counted the fact that the armies of the railroad men and postal employees, which are of an immense general economic, political, and military importance, continue to be engaged in a sharp conflict with the government, while even the Menshevik defensists are dissatisfied with "their own" Minister Nikitin, and the official S.-R.'s call Kerensky and Co. "Stolypinists." Is it not clear that such "support" given to the government by the Mensheviks and S.-R.'s has only a negative meaning, if any?

....*

V

Yes, the leaders of the Central Executive Committee are pursuing tactics whose sole logic is the defence of the bourgeoisie and the landowners. And there is not the slightest doubt that the Bolsheviks, were they to allow themselves to be caught in the trap of constitutional illusions, of "faith" in the Congress of Soviets and in the convocation of the Constituent Assembly, of "waiting" for the Congress of Soviets, etc.—that such Bolsheviks would prove *miserable traitors* to the proletarian cause.

They would be traitors to the cause, for they would have, by their behaviour, betrayed the German revolutionary workers who have started a mutiny in the fleet. To "wait" for the Congress of Soviets, etc., under such conditions means *betraying internationalism,* betraying the cause of the international Socialist revolution.

For internationalism consists not in phrases, not in protestations of solidarity, not in resolutions, but in *deeds*.

* Chapter IV of this article has thus far not been located.—*Ed.*

The Bolsheviks would be traitors to the *peasantry*, for to tolerate the suppression of the peasant uprising by a government which *even* the *Dyelo Naroda* compares with Stolypinists means to *destroy* the whole revolution, to destroy it forever and irrevocably. They shout about anarchy and about the increasing apathy of the masses. Why shouldn't the masses be apathetic in the elections when the peasantry has been driven to an *uprising*, while the so-called "revolutionary democracy" patiently tolerates the suppression of the peasants by military force!!

The Bolsheviks would prove traitors to democracy and freedom, for to tolerate the suppression of a peasant uprising at the present moment *means* to allow the elections to the Constituent Assembly to be fixed in *just the same way*—and even worse, more crudely—as the "Democratic Conference" and the "pre-parliament" have been fixed.

The crisis has matured. The whole future of the Russian Revolution is at stake. The whole honour of the Bolshevik Party is in question. The whole future of the international workers' revolution for Socialism is at stake.

The crisis has matured. . . .

N. LENIN.

Written October 12, 1917.

[Note by Lenin.—*Ed.*]

Publish up to here; what follows is to be *distributed* among the members of the Central Committee, The Petrograd Committee, the Moscow Committee, and the *Soviets*.

VI

What, then, is to be done? We must *aussprechen, was ist,* "say what is," admit the truth, that in our Central Committee and at the top of our party there is a tendency in favour of *awaiting* the Congress of Soviets, *against* the immediate seizure of power, *against* an immediate uprising. We must *overcome* this tendency or opinion.[99]

Otherwise the Bolsheviks would *cover themselves with shame forever;* they would be *reduced to nothing* as a party.

For to miss such a moment and to "await" the Congress of Soviets is either *absolute idiocy* or *complete betrayal*.

It is a complete betrayal of the German workers. Indeed, we must not wait for the *beginning* of their revolution!! When it begins, even the Liberdans will be in favour of "supporting" it. But it *cannot* begin as long as Kerensky, Kishkin and Co. are in power.

It is a complete betrayal of the peasantry. To have the Soviets of *both capitals* and to allow the uprising of the peasants to be suppressed means *to lose, and justly so,* all the confidence of the peasant; it means to become in the eyes of the peasants equal to the Liberdans and other scoundrels.

To "await" the Congress of Soviets is absolute idiocy, for this means losing *weeks,* whereas weeks and even days now decide *everything.* It means timidly to *refuse* the seizure of power, for on November 14-15 it will be impossible (both politically and technically, since the Cossacks will be mobilised for the day of the foolishly "appointed" * uprising).

To "await" the Congress of Soviets is idiocy, for the Congress *will give nothing, it can give nothing!*

The "moral" importance? Strange indeed! The "importance" of resolutions and negotiations with the Liberdans when we know that the Soviets are *in favour* of the peasants and that the peasant uprising *is being suppressed!!* Thus, we will reduce the *Soviets* to the rôle of miserable chatterers. First vanquish Kerensky, then call the Congress.

The victory of the uprising is now *secure* for the Bolsheviks: (1) we can ** (if we do not "await" the Soviet Congress) launch a *sudden* attack from three points, from Petrograd, from Moscow, from the Baltic fleet; (2) we have slogans whose support is guaranteed: down with the government that suppresses the uprising of the peasants against the landowners! (3) we have a majority *in the country;* (4) complete disorganisation of the Mensheviks and S.-R.'s; (5) we are technically in a position to seize power in Moscow (which might even be the one to start, so as to deal the enemy a surprise blow); (6) we have *thousands* of armed workers and soldiers in Petrograd who can seize *at once* the Winter Palace, the General Staff Building, the telephone exchange and all the largest printing establishments. They will not be able to drive us out from there, whereas there will be such propaganda *in the army* that it

---

* To "call" the Congress of Soviets for November 2, in order to decide upon the seizure of power—is there any difference between this and a foolishly "appointed" uprising? Now we can seize power, whereas November 2-11 you will not be allowed to seize it.

** What has the party done by way of *studying* the location of the troops, etc.? What has it done for the carrying out of the uprising as "an art"? Only talk in the Central Committee, etc.!!

will be *impossible* to fight against this government of peace, of land for the peasants, etc.

If we were to attack at once, suddenly, from three points, in Petrograd, Moscow, and the Baltic fleet, there are ninety-nine out of a hundred chances that we would gain a victory with fewer victims than on July 16-18, because *the troops will not advance* against the government of peace. Even if Kerensky has *already* "loyal" cavalry, etc., in Petrograd, when we attack from two sides and when the army is in sympathy *with us*, Kerensky will be compelled to *surrender*. If, with chances like the present, we do not seize power, then all talk of Soviet rule becomes a *lie*.

To refrain from seizing power at present, to "wait," to "chatter" in the Central Committee, to confine ourselves to "fighting for the organ" (of the Soviet), to "fighting for the Congress," means to *ruin the revolution*.

Seeing that the Central Committee has left *even without an answer* my writings insisting on such a policy since the beginning of the Democratic Conference, that the Central Organ *is deleting* from my articles references to such glaring errors of the Bolsheviks as the shameful decision to participate in the pre-parliament, as giving seats to the Mensheviks in the Presidium of the Soviets, etc., etc.—seeing all that, I am compelled to recognise here a "gentle" hint as to the unwillingness of the Central Committee even to consider this question, a gentle hint at gagging me and at suggesting that I retire.

I am compelled to *tender my resignation from the Central Committee*, which I hereby do, leaving myself the freedom of propaganda *in the lower ranks* of the party and at the Party Congress.

For it is my deepest conviction that if we "await" the Congress of Soviets and let the present moment pass, we *ruin* the revolution.

Written October 12. N. LENIN.

P.S. A whole series of facts has proven that even the Cossack troops will not move against the government of peace! And how many are they? Where are they? And will not the entire army delegate units in *our favour?*

Chapters I-III and V, published in the *Rabochy Put*, No. 30, October 20, 1917. Chapter VI published in 1925.

END OF BOOK I

EXPLANATORY NOTES

1. Members of the Constitutional-Democratic Party (Cadets)—Shingarev, Manuilov, Shakhovskoy and other Ministers in the first Coalition Cabinet of Prince Lvov—who demonstratively resigned on July 15, 1917, under the pretext of protesting against the Provisional Government's granting too great autonomy to the Ukraine: the Cadets wanted to postpone the solution of the Ukrainian question until the meeting of the Constituent Assembly. The resignation of the Cadets occurred simultaneously with the beginning of the revolutionary outbreak in Petrograd in July.

The article, "What Could the Cadets Count On When Leaving the Cabinet?" was apparently written by Lenin on July 16, 1917, in the village of Neivola, near the station Mustamyaki on the Finnish railroad, not far from Petrograd, before he received news from Petrograd about the events then beginning (the "July days"). The article was intended for the *Pravda*, but was not published because the *Pravda* was suppressed and its printing plant demolished. The article appeared somewhat later in the *Proletarskoye Dyelo*, Cronstadt, No. 2, July 28, 1917, without the signature of the author. The article has at the very end one extra paragraph, which is not in the original manuscript:

"But Tsereteli and Chernov preferred the road of compromise, and yielding to the counter-revolutionaries against the revolutionary class."

Whether this paragraph was actually written by Lenin has not been established.—p. 15.

2. *Proletarskoye Dyelo*, a daily Bolshevik paper published in 1917 by the Cronstadt Committee of the R. S.-D. L. P., began to appear during the July days after the Provisional Government suppressed the *Cronstadt Pravda*. The first number of *Proletarskoye Dyelo* appeared on July 27, 1917.—p. 16.

3. The "July days" were prepared by the whole course of the Russian Revolution. From the second half of June, 1917, the dissatisfaction of the masses against the reactionary policies of the Provisional Government was growing. At the demonstration on July 1, the masses came out with the slogans: "Down with the ten capitalist Ministers!" "All Power to the Soviets!" The failure of the offensive undertaken by Kerensky at the front on July 1 and the sacrifices offered to satisfy the Allies still further revolutionised the masses. The reserves—men over 40 years of age—demanded immediate demobilisation. Minister of Justice Pereverzev sharpened the conflict when he tried by military force to oust the Anarchists and some trade unionists from the Durnovo estate, which had been occupied by the workers. The Petrograd regiments were aroused because the government, in violation of its agreement of March 12 with the Executive Committee of the Petrograd Soviet, wanted to send them to the front to free the capital from the troops loyal to the revolution. The counter-revolutionary generals threatened to surrender the capital to the Germans. The resignation of the Cadet Ministers gave further

EXPLANATORY NOTES

impetus to the movement that had already begun. According to Stalin's report at the Sixth Congress of the R. S.-D. L. P., events developed in this fashion: on July 16, one of the first to act was the machine gun regiment, a delegation of which came to Kshesinskaya's house, to the Bolshevik City Conference, which had the municipal question under consideration, to inform them that their regiment had sent delegates to all the military units, calling them to mutiny, and to ask the help of the Bolsheviks. The Conference refused their request, considering the movement premature. In the evening two regiments came to Kshesinskaya's house with the slogan on their banners: "All Power to the Soviets!" Somewhat later a workers' demonstration arrived, with the same slogans against the coalition. When the Central Committee met at 10 o'clock that night, taking into consideration the mood of the masses, it issued the slogan calling for a peaceful demonstration. The Workers' Section of the Petrograd Soviet by a two-thirds vote decided in favour of an uprising and elected a temporary committee of 15 members to carry on the work. The appeal to abstain from a premature uprising, which had been sent out during the day to the *Pravda*, was deleted at night by order of the C.C. and was cut out from the mat; the intention was to substitute for it the new slogans of a peaceful demonstration, but this could not be done, as it was too late, so that the *Pravda* of July 17 appeared with a blank space. On July 16 Lenin was not in Petrograd and when notified of the events he was not able to come to town until the next day. On July 17 more than half a million workers and soldiers participated in the movement. The demonstrations all converged upon the Tauride Palace. Sailors arrived from Cronstadt. The Fortress of Peter and Paul was on the side of the demonstrators. Remarkable order reigned in the city. The masses seized no public buildings, used no violence. At the corner of Nevsky and Sadovaya the demonstrators were fired upon, and the workers and soldiers returned the fire. The demand that the Central Executive Committee of the Soviets, which was in the hands of the Mensheviks and S.-R.'s, should assume power, met with a refusal. The movement came to an impasse. Part of the soldiers returned to the barracks, part of them remained in the streets. On July 18, in the name of Alexinsky and Pankratov, documents were published which had been fabricated by the counter-revolutionary investigating committees with the purpose of demoralising the masses; in them it was claimed that Lenin's actions were dictated by the German General Staff. Towards evening the counter-revolutionary troops which had been brought from the front by Kerensky, and the military cadets from the environs of Petrograd, occupied the city, dismantled the bridges and took to arresting, searching and pillaging. The movement was suppressed. The July events were the turning point on the road of the revolution from February to October. The essence of the turning point consisted in that the peaceful transfer of power to the proletariat had been exhausted. The July demonstration of the workers and soldiers, according to Lenin, "was the last attempt, by means of demonstrations, to cause the Soviets to take power."—p. 17.

4. *Zhivoye Slovo*, which appeared in Petrograd in 1916, a small newspaper of the boulevard variety calculated to appeal to the less cultured strata of the city's population, appeared after the February Revolution with the sub-

heading: "The Paper of Non-Partisan Socialists." During the July days it conducted a reactionary agitation. In August it was suppressed. Later, it reappeared for a few weeks under the names *Slovo* and *Novoye Slovo*.

The slanderous allegations of Alexinsky and Pankratov were published in the *Zhivoye Slovo*, No. 51 (404), July 18, 1917, under the heading, "Lenin, Hanecki and Co.—Spies." The text of this statement, fabricated with the help of the General Staff and the secret service, is as follows:

The following letter, signed in their own handwriting, was submitted by G. Alexinsky and the former inmate of the Schlüsselburg prison, V. Pankratov, members of the Second State Duma, to the Committee of Journalists attached to the Provisional Government:
"We, the undersigned, Gregory Alexeyevich Alexinsky, former member of the Second State Duma representing the workers of the city of Petrograd, and Vasily Semyonovich Pankratov, member of the Socialist-Revolutionary Party, who spent fourteen years in the Schlüsselburg prison at hard labour, believe it to be our revolutionary duty to publish extracts from documents just received by us, from which the Russian citizens will see how and from what direction are endangered Russian liberty, the revolutionary army and the Russian people who won this liberty with their blood. We demand an immediate investigation. G. Alexinsky, V. Pankratov, July 17, 1917, Petrograd."
In a letter dated May 16, 1917, under the number 3719, the Chief of Staff of the Supreme Command sent the Minister of War the record of the examination, April 28, of Ensign Yermolenko of the 16th Siberian infantry regiment. From his statements to the chief of the Investigating Division of the General Staff the following is established: on May 8 of this year he was dispatched to us behind the lines of the Sixth Army, to agitate for the speediest conclusion of a separate peace with Germany. This commission was accepted by Yermolenko at the insistence of the comrades. Officers of the German General Staff, Schiditzki and Lübers, had told him that propaganda of a similar kind was being carried on in Russia by the chairman of the Ukrainian Section of the Union for the Liberation of the Ukraine, A. Skoropis-Yoltukhovsky, and Lenin. Lenin was commissioned to use every means in his power to undermine the confidence of the Russian people in the Provisional Government. Money for the propaganda is being received through a certain Svedson, employed in Stockholm at the German embassy. Money and instructions were forwarded through trusted persons.
In accordance with the information just received, these trusted persons in Stockholm were: the Bolshevik Jacob Fürstenberg, better known under the name of "Hanecki," and Parvus (Dr. Helfand); in Petrograd: the Bolshevik attorney, M. U. Kozlovsky, a woman relative of Hanecki—Sumenson, engaged in speculation together with Hanecki, and others. Kozlovsky is the chief receiver of German money, which is transferred from Berlin through the "Disconto-Gesellschaft" to the Stockholm "Via Bank," and thence to the Siberian Bank in Petrograd, where his account at present has a balance of over 2,000,000 rubles. The military censorship has unearthed an uninterrupted exchange of telegrams of a political and financial nature between the German agents and Bolshevik leaders (Stockholm-Petrograd).

The letter was accompanied by the following note by G. Alexinsky and V. Pankratov: "Owing to technical considerations the original documents will be published by us later as a supplement."—p. 18.

5. The "Union for the Liberation of the Ukraine" was a Ukrainian ultra-nationalist organisation of German orientation, springing into existence at the beginning of the imperialist war from groups which had earlier been con-

nected with the Ukrainian Social-Democracy. At the head of the Union were: Basok-Melenevsky and A. Skoropis-Yoltukhovsky, former directors of the "Spilka," a Ukrainian Social-Democratic union, which had been connected with the R. S.-D. L. P., close in its general tendencies to the Mensheviks, and A. Isuk, V. Doroshenko and P. Benzi, former members of the Ukrainian S.-D. Labour Party (a separate organisation from the Spilka). The "Union for the Liberation of the Ukraine," issuing its slogans for the independence of the Ukraine, and securing the help of German-Austrian imperialism, was really nothing more than an agency of the latter. The Union was broadly subsidised by the German government, with its money conducted propaganda in Germany among the Ukrainian prisoners of war, and tried, besides, without much success, to evoke in the Ukraine a corresponding nationalistic movement. The Union published the *Robitnichi Prapor (Labour Banner)*.—p. 18.

6. The *Pravda Bulletin* appeared on July 19, 1917, two pages in size, in place of the *Pravda*, which had been raided by the military cadets. In the *Pravda Bulletin* were published the proclamation of the C.C., the Petrograd Committee, the Military Organisation of the Bolsheviks and the Interborough Committee of United Social-Democratic Internationalists, to the workers and soldiers, calling upon them to discontinue the demonstration; the short leading article "Struggling for What?"; articles by Lenin (unsigned): "Where Is Power and Where Is Counter-revolution?," "Hideous Slanders by the Black Hundred Papers and Alexinsky," "Dreyfusade," "Calumny and Facts," "Close to the Real Issue"; and the letter of M. Kozlovsky.—p. 21.

7. Lenin quotes from the article "The Shooting on the Nevsky" (*Birzheviye Vyedomosti*, No. 16317, July 17, 1917, evening edition).—p. 24.

8. N. V. Chaikovsky, People's Socialist, at a joint meeting of the C.E.C. of Soviets of Workers' and Soldiers' Deputies and the C.C. of the Soviets of Peasant Deputies on July 17, 1917, participating in the discussion on the question "The Government Crisis," said:

The threatening thing in our situation consists in that we conduct a world war from which we cannot turn away, and at the same time willy-nilly we must carry out a social revolution. In Petrograd the war is forgotten; at the front the social revolution is forgotten. The war requires money, it demands not only military power but also financial power. If the Socialists take power into their hands, they will be bankrupt in a month. This means that then would come hunger, anarchy . . . and a German dictator would appear (*Izvestiya*, No. 109, July 18, 1917).—p. 25.

9. Lenin's article "Dreyfusade" was intended for *Pravda* but could not be published, as that newspaper was suppressed by the Provisional Government and its printing plant wrecked.—p. 26.

10. A letter by M. U. Kozlovsky to "the chairman of the Central Committee of Soviets" (so it is in the text), dated July 18, 1917, and made public by M. Kozlovsky on the same day at the meeting of the C.E.C., was published in the *Pravda Bulletin* on July 19, 1917. In the letter M. Kozlovsky, among other things, declared:

... Without entering into a political estimate of this shameful slander, I consider it necessary, as a member of the C.C. of the Soviet of W. and S. D. to make the following statement:

1. There have been no relations whatever between me and the agents of the German General Staff.
2. I never had a balance to my account of two million rubles in the Siberian or any other bank. The total amount of my balances on current accounts does not exceed a few thousand rubles.
3. I never received "German money from Berlin through Stockholm" or through any other channels.
4. I did not send or receive any telegrams of "a political or monetary nature" from German agents.

Addressing the C.C. of Soviets of W. and S. D., through you as the vice-chairman, I wish at the same time to state that I am ready at any time to give a suitable and exhaustive explanation to the Central Committees of the Socialist-Revolutionaries and Social-Democrats in case it should be found necessary. —p. 26.

11. While returning from Switzerland to Russia via Germany and Sweden, Lenin and the other Bolsheviks, on April 14, 1917, met at Stockholm with the Left Swedish Socialists headed by Lindhagen.—p. 27.

12. The article "Three Crises" was written by Lenin for *Pravda*, but did not appear until August 3 in the Cronstadt *Proletarskoye Dyelo*, No. 7, with insignificant changes in the text of a purely editorial character. At the beginning of the article, Lenin, having in mind its publication in *Pravda*, referred to "the article printed below, which gives documentary evidence that on July 15 the Bolsheviks carried on propaganda *against* the demonstration" . . . ; it is evident that the article mentioned did not appear in *Proletarskoye Dyelo*. (This article was not preserved.)

The article "Three Crises" was published for the first time from the manuscript in *Pravda*, No. 93, 1924.—p. 29.

13. The proclamation starting "Fellow workers and soldiers of Petrograd," signed by "C.C., R. S.-D. L. P., P. C., R. S.-D. L. P., Interborough Committee, R. S.-D. L. P., Military Organisation of the C.C., R. S.-D. L. P. and Commission of the Workers' Section of the Soviet of W. and S. D." (See "Documents and Materials," No. 1), was released the morning of July 17, 1917, and reprinted in *Dyelo Naroda*, No. 92, July 18.—p. 29.

14. The article "The Moment Obliges" (*Dyelo Naroda*, No. 93, July 19), evaluating the July movement and in full accord with the Provisional Government in crushing it, says among other things: "It is not our rule to close our eyes to facts, or try to evade their eloquent testimony. The dissatisfaction with the coalition government is a fact; it made its appearance some time ago and continues to grow. . . ."—p. 29.

15. Lenin quotes from the leading article of *Dyelo Naroda*, No. 93, July 19, 1917.—p. 31.

16. Excerpt from Plekhanov's article, "Two Weeks for Reflection," *Yedinstvo*, No. 83, July 20, 1917; the article is devoted to the resolution of the

Executive Committee of the Soviets of W., S. and P. D. of July 17, 1917, ordering the convocation within two weeks of a joint plenary session of the Executive Committee with local representatives to decide the question of the reconstruction of the government, brought on by the July crisis and the withdrawal of the Cadet Ministers from the Cabinet.—p. 31.

17. There was vacillation among a part of the members of the C.C. on the question of whether Lenin and G. Zinoviev should appear in court. V. Nogin regarded it as necessary that the leaders of the party give themselves up and appear in court for the purpose of an open struggle with the slanderous and lying accusations. J. Stalin and S. Orjonikidze decidedly objected to this, fearing a lynching party of the counter-revolutionary military cadets or secret murder in jail. After a consultation with Lenin and Zinoviev, Nogin and Orjonikidze, at the insistence of Lenin, set out for the C.E.C. to clear up the situation, and, in the case of voluntary appearance, to secure a guarantee of safety. At the negotiations with the members of the C.E.C., Anisimov (Menshevik worker) explained that it was impossible to secure such a guarantee, as the actual power after the July days had passed into the hands of the counter-revolutionary militarists. Anisimov's statement finally overcame the hesitation of the individual members of the C.C., and the question of the appearance in court was decided in the negative. At the Sixth Conference of the R. S.-D. L. P., the question of appearance in court was again submitted for consideration, and the Conference decisively came out against it, in view of the absence of a guarantee of the personal safety of the accused. For the resolution of the Conference on this question, see "Documents and Materials," No. 4 (9).—p. 34.

18. In the article "The Political Situation" Lenin for the first time after the February Revolution raises the question of the preparation of an armed uprising. With the purpose of making possible the appearance of the article in the legal press, Lenin replaced every mention in the manuscript of the words "armed uprising" by the words "decisive struggle." Due to the suppression of the Bolshevik press, the article was not made public in time. Its principal proposals were included in the article "On Slogans" (p. 43) and in "On Constitutional Illusions" (p. 62).

The last paragraph of the article was deleted in the manuscript.—p. 36.

19. In Nizhni-Novgorod there was a mutiny of the soldiers, coinciding in time with the July events in Petrograd. The movement began on July 17, 1917, with a peaceful demonstration of the soldiers evacuated from the front, against whom the military command sent out the military cadets. The evacuated soldiers were supported by two infantry regiments. After an armed clash, the advantage proved to be with the revolutionary detachments. The municipal government fell into the hands of the revolutionary democracy. On July 20 the movement was liquidated by a punitive expedition which arrived from Moscow.—p. 36.

20. The letter to the editors of the *Novaya Zhizn*, appearing in the issue of July 24, 1917, was reprinted on July 26 in the newspaper of the Moscow Com-

EXPLANATORY NOTES

mittee of the Bolsheviks, *Sotsial-Demokrat*, No. 106. The text of this letter as it appears in the latter paper is worded somewhat differently than that appearing in *Novaya Zhizn*. Apparently these changes were made by the editors of the *Sotsial-Demokrat*.—p. 39.

21. For the purpose of informing the foreign internationalists about the Russian Revolution, *Pravda* issued a bulletin in Stockholm in foreign languages. The German bulletin bore the headline: "Russische Korrespondenz 'Prawda'. Herausgegeben von der ausländischen Vertretung des Zentralkomitees der Russ. Soz-Dem. Arbeiterpartei (Bolschewiki). Erscheint in Stockholm 2 Mal wöchentlich." ("Russian bulletin of the *Pravda*, issued by the foreign representation of the Central Committee of the R. S.-D. L. P. (Bolsheviks). Appears in Stockholm twice a week"). Thirty-three numbers appeared from June 16 to November 16, 1917.—p. 39.

22. The letter to the editors of *Proletarskoye Dyelo*, published on July 28, 1917, was later reprinted in the newspaper of the Moscow Committee of the Bolsheviks, *Sotsial-Demokrat*, No. 110, July 31. The text of the *Sotsial-Demokrat* differs somewhat from that of the *Proletarskoye Dyelo*: several of the typographical errors that appeared in the *Proletarskoye Dyelo* were corrected, and after the signatures of N. Lenin and G. Zinoviev was added the signature of L. Kamenev, who at that time was already arrested. In the present edition the original text of the *Proletarskoye Dyelo* is used, as undoubtedly nearer to the original, although it has several defects in style, for example, the not entirely clear sentence: "There can be at present no legal basis in Russia, not even such constitutional guarantees as exist in bourgeois, Social-Democratic, orderly countries." In the sentence preceding the one quoted, the words "simply in vain" (so it reads in the *Proletarskoye Dyelo*)— the editors considering them an obvious typographical error—were changed into the word "simply."—p. 41.

23. Lenin refers to "P. N. Pereverzev's Reply to N. V. Nekrasov and M. I. Tereshchenko" (*Novoye Vremya*, No. 14822, July 22, 1917).—p. 41.

24. The reference is to Friedrich Engels' book, *The Origin of the Family, Private Property and the State*. The first German edition appeared in 1884. For greater detail about the state and "detachments of armed men," see "State and Revolution" in the present volume, Book II, Chapter I, paragraphs 1 and 2.—p. 47.

25. The communication under the heading: "Documents about Lenin and Co. Data of the investigation (from the public prosecutor of the Petrograd Supreme Court)" was published in *Novoye Vremya*, No. 14833, August 4, 1917. —p. 51.

26. On July 16, 1917, during the day, an appeal to abstain from an uprising was turned over by the Central Committee to the *Pravda* for publication, but by evening the movement had spontaneously assumed a mass character, and

the C.C. composed a new statement calling for a peaceful demonstration. At that late hour the proclamation of the C.C. could not be published in the *Pravda*, and it appeared as a separate leaflet. The statement prepared during the day was cut out of the mat of *Pravda*, which appeared on July 17 with a blank space on the first page.

During the night of July 17, the C.C. prepared a new proclamation with an appeal to end the demonstration. The proclamation was published in the *Pravda* on July 18; however, this number was distributed only to the extent of several hundred copies, as the printing establishment was wrecked by military cadets during the work. In the *Pravda Bulletin* appearing on July 19, a third proclamation of the C.C. was published, also proposing that the demonstration be stopped. See "Documents and Materials," Nos. 1 and 2.—p. 52.

27. Lenin refers to the correspondence of N. Andreyev, "Counter-revolution on the Streets of Petrograd, July 17," published in *Rabochaya Gazeta*, No. 100, July 20, 1917.—p. 53.

28. Lenin refers to the short article in *Rabochaya Gazeta*, No. 100, July 20, 1917, "Troubled Days. An Impression of July 17," signed "Sh."—p. 53.

29. The lists of dead and wounded during the July days were published in the columns of the Petrograd newspapers. In *Dyelo Naroda*, No. 96, July 22, 1917, was a list of "Killed and Wounded," mentioning the names of the victims and their social or official position. In *Ryech*, No. 156, July 19, was published "Communication of the Chief of Militia to the City Duma"; in No. 159, July 22, a short article "Victims"; in No. 161, July 28, "Information About 700 Victims." All this data was very fragmentary and incomplete.—p. 56.

30. The text of the article "On Constitutional Illusions," first published in the newspaper *Rabochy i Soldat*, Nos. 11 and 12, August 17 and 18, 1917, and soon after re-issued as a separate pamphlet with the sub-heading "The Present Situation," differs somewhat from the text of the manuscript. The editor of *Rabochy i Soldat*, with the purpose of softening the sharpest places, made some changes in the article.—p. 62.

31. In *Pravda*, No. 92, July 10, 1917, in a note under the heading "The Bolsheviks Are Guilty" is inserted a reprint from the Moscow *Sotsial-Demokrat*, No. 84, June 30, of a news item from the newspaper *Vlast Naroda* [*Power of the People*] to the following effect: "We are informed that the Provisional Government published in good time a decree about the date of the convening of the Constituent Assembly, in view of the fact that the Bolsheviks planned to come out with the accusation against the Provisional Government that it has intentionally been delaying the convening of the Constituent Assembly."—p. 65.

32. The note under the heading "The Delay in the Convening of the Constituent Assembly" reads:

It is stated that in the negotiations of the Provisional Government with the candidates for the ministerial posts in the new coalition government, the ques-

EXPLANATORY NOTES 287

tion was raised about the date of convening the Constituent Assembly. These candidates, as representatives of the People's Freedom Party, persistently pointed out that to convoke the Constituent Assembly on September 30 was impossible. The members of the Provisional Government, including I. G. Tsereteli, pointed out that the Provisional Government was forced to fix the convocation of the Constituent Assembly for September 30, but that if the near future should show the impossibility of assuring the regular convocation of the Constituent Assembly at the appointed time, it would be postponed. It is proposed to postpone the convocation of the Constituent Assembly for two months, fixing it for November 20 (*Volya Naroda*, No. 67, July 29, 1917). —p. 65.

33. *Rabochaya Gazeta*, central organ of the Mensheviks, called the future All-Russian Constituent Assembly the "Russian National Convention" in a leading article in No. 112, August 2, 1917, "The Dismissal of the Diet."—p. 66.

34. Speaking of the "Social-Democrats" of 1848, Lenin has in mind the French petty-bourgeois party headed by Ledru-Rollin, which also called itself, by analogy with 1793, the "Mountain," and constituted the Left opposition in the Constituent Assembly of 1848, in which the monarchists were in the majority. The party was based upon the city petty bourgeoisie, part of the peasantry and some strata of the proletariat. See the estimate of its activity and class analysis by Karl Marx in *The Eighteenth Brumaire of Louis Bonaparte*.—p. 66.

35. The Peasant Wars—a series of peasant risings in Germany in 1524-1525 caused by the heavy oppression of serfdom and requisitions by the nobility. The principal demands of the peasants were the abolition of serfdom, the abrogation of feudal dues and privileges, elected courts, etc. Concerning the peasant wars in Germany, see Engels' *The Peasant War in Germany*.—p. 69.

36. Lenin here refers to the article in *Dyelo Naroda*, No. 92, July 18, 1917, entitled "To Sum Up."—p. 73.

37. *The State Conference* was called in Moscow in the Bolshoi Theatre on August 25 to 28, 1917, for the purpose of strengthening the position of the government, which had been shaken by the July events of the Petrograd proletariat. To the conference were invited mainly representatives of bourgeois organisations, of the generals and other army officers; the representatives of that part of the Soviet democracy which favoured national defence were in the minority. According to the approximate data of the Moscow municipal council, the delegates were distributed according to the following groups: members of the four State Dumas—488; peasants—100; from the Soviets and social organisations—129; from the municipal councils—129; zemstvos—118; zemstvo and town unions—18; trade-industrial circles and banks—150; educational organisations—99; professional people—83; army and navy—117; clergy—24; national organisations—58; food supply committees—90; agricultural societies—51; co-operatives—313; trade unions—176; government commissars—33; military departments—16; institutions of the Estates—4; members of the government—15; etc. Representatives of the capital and provincial Soviets were not admitted. In the name of the Soviets a delegation

of the C.E.C. appeared, composed of Mensheviks and S.-R.'s and carefully
purged of Bolsheviks. The trade unions received a small representation, and
in their name D. B. Ryazanov made a Bolshevik declaration. The Conference
was opened with an introductory address by Kerensky, who declared the
fundamental tasks of the government to be the continuation of the war, the
establishment of order in the army and in the country, and the organisation
of a firm power. "I . . . will set limits to the attempts to make use of the
great Russian calamity . . . and whatever ultimatum should be presented to
me, and whoever should present it, I will be able to subject them to the
supreme authority and to myself, as its supreme head." After Tsereteli's
speech supporting the demand for a firm government, attention was concentrated mainly on the address of the commander-in-chief, General Kornilov,
who at this time, with the aid of the Cadet leaders and bankers, was openly
preparing a dictatorship by himself. "As heritage from the old régime free
Russia received the army. . . . This army was in good fighting condition,
steady and ready for self-sacrifice. . . . By a whole series of legislative measures . . . this army was transformed into a maddened mob." "Iron discipline"
at the front and a "firm power" in the rear are therefore necessary. "The
measures adopted at the front" (*i.e.*, capital punishment), "should also be
adopted at the rear. . . . There should be no difference between front and
rear with regard to the degree of severity which is necessary to save the country. . . . It cannot be permitted that order in our rear should be secured at
the expense of the loss of Riga by us and that order on the railroads should
be re-established at the price of the cession of Moldavia and Bessarabia."
General Kaledin, speaking in the name of the Don Cossacks and supporting
the demands of Kornilov, put forth the following programme: (1) The army
must stay out of politics; (2) it is necessary to abolish the Soviets and army
committees; (3) the Declaration of Rights of the soldiers must be abolished;
(4) full power must be given to the officers. The speeches of Kornilov and
Kaledin were applauded by the Right Wing of the Conference. The "Left"
confined itself to a declaration of the usual conciliatory type, published in the
name of the C.E.C. of the Soviets by Chkheidze. The Conference did not
increase the authority of the Provisional Government, but helped the country
to differentiate between the parties, and revealed the counter-revolutionary designs of the bourgeoisie. The working class, having succeeded in recovering
from the July defeat, took a sharply negative attitude towards the attempt to
deceive the country by means of a *Zemsky Sobor* (National Assembly), replacing by that substitute the Constituent Assembly. The Moscow Bureau of
Trade Unions, which was already in the hands of the Bolsheviks, on the day
of the opening of the State Conference ordered a one-day protest strike in the
city, which became general.—p. 74.

38. *Rabochy i Soldat*, central organ of the Bolsheviks, appeared from August
5 to 22, 1917, instead of *Pravda* and *Soldatskaya Pravda*, which had been suppressed. In all, 15 numbers appeared.—p. 75.

39. The second Coalition Cabinet of the Provisional Government (or the
third after the February Revolution) was formed after the July days, under

the chairmanship of A. F. Kerensky and the vice-chairmanship of N. V. Nekrasov. The Cabinet was composed of the Mensheviks, M. I. Skobelev and A. M. Nikitin; S.-R.'s, N. D. Avksentyev and V. M. Chernov; People's Socialists, A. V. Peshekhonov and A. S. Zarudny; the non-party Left, C. N. Prokopovich; Cadets and representatives of the property owning bourgeoisie, F. F. Kokoshkin, A. V. Kartashov, S. F. Oldenburg, P. I. Yurenev, I. N. Efremov, M. V. Tereshchenko and M. F. Bernatsky. Kerensky kept for himself the Ministries of War and Navy, with B. V. Savinkw and V. I. Lebedev as vice-secretaries.—p. 76.

40. The declaration of the Provisional Government of July 22, 1917, published by the second Coalition Cabinet, stated that ". . . the Provisional Government considers as its first and principal task the straining of all its forces for the struggle with the foreign enemy and for the safeguarding of the new state order from all monarchist and counter-revolutionary attempts, not stopping at the most determined measures of authority. . . ." In the business part of the declaration they promised the convocation of an inter-Allied conference not later than August "for the determination of the general character of foreign policies of the Allies and for co-ordinating their activities in the carrying out of the principles proclaimed by the Russian Revolution"; to convoke the Constituent Assembly September 30, 1917; the early introduction of local self-government on the basis of the four-point formula; the abolition of the Estates system and of civil ranks and orders; the organisation of an Economic Council and Chief Economic Committee for the purpose of combating economic ruin; freedom to strike and form trade unions; labour legislation; and also a series of preparatory measures necessary for the solution by the Constituent Assembly of the land problem with a view of transferring the land to the peasants, provided, however, that the most decisive struggle be undertaken against "land seizures and similar unauthorised local methods for the solution of the land problem, that are in contradiction to the principle of a general state plan for future land reform."—p. 76.

41. In an article in the *Izvestiya* of the Petrograd Soviet of W. and S. D., No. 126, August 7, 1917, entitled "The Government Crisis," it was argued that "the general composition of the government indubitably displays a substantial turn to the Left."

In an article in No. 128, August 9, of the same newspaper, "In Defence of Justice," hopes were expressed in the loyalty of the Minister of Justice Zarudny and in the beneficial influence of the Soviets on the government.—p. 77.

42. *Rabochy*—central organ of the R. S.-D. L. P. (Bolsheviks), which appeared instead of *Proletary* from September 7 to 15, 1917. In all, 12 numbers appeared, including the evening editions.—p. 93.

43. The question of the Stockholm Conference (see *The Revolution of 1917, Collected Works*, Volume XX, Book I, notes 165 and 177, and also Lenin's address at the All-Russian April Conference of the R. S.-D. L. P. and the resolution of the conference—*Ibid.*, Book I, p. 315 and Book II, p. 401) was

considered at the C.E.C. on August 19, 1917 on the basis of a report of the Menshevik Rozanov. *Novaya Zhizn*, No. 95, August 21, 1917, reports as follows the speech of Kamenev, who took part in the debate:

In his speech U. Kamenev says that the Bolshevik Party had hitherto maintained a negative attitude towards the Stockholm Conference, as peace could be attained not by way of the Stockholm Conference or diplomatic negotiations even by representatives of democracy, but only as the result of the world proletarian revolution. But now when our revolution has retreated to the second line of trenches, it is fitting to support this conference. Now, when the Stockholm Conference has become the banner of the struggle of the proletariat against imperialism, when Tereshchenko has submitted to the order of Buchanan and come out against it, we naturally must support it. In spite of the fact that the Soviet arrests our comrades, we must strengthen it, and the success of the Stockholm Conference will strengthen the authority of the Soviet. But we must go to the Stockholm Conference with clean hands.

Further on *Novaya Zhizn* mentions that the representative of the Bolsheviks (Starostin), who spoke later, pointed out that Kamenev had spoken in his own name and that the Bolshevik fraction would not change its attitude to the Conference and would not participate in it.—p. 94.

44. *Proletary*—central organ of the R. S.-D. L. P., appearing instead of the suppressed *Rabochy i Soldat* from August 26 to September 6, 1917. In all, 10 numbers appeared.—p. 96.

45. N. Bukharin's article "Towards Revision of the Party Programme," published in the Moscow Bolshevik journal *Spartak*, No. 4, August 23, 1917, says, among other things:

The Party conference which has just been concluded acknowledged in principle that the programme of the R. S.-D. L. P. must be revised. For this purpose a special conference will be called, a narrower one in its composition, and strictly business in purpose. In this way, the necessity of revising the programme was officially recognised by the Party.

Spartak—the popular theoretical journal of the Moscow District Bureau, the Moscow Committee and (beginning with No. 2) the Moscow Regional Committee of the R. S.-D. L. P., appearing in Moscow in the summer of 1917 under the editorship of N. I. Bukharin. In all, 10 numbers appeared (No. 1, June 2, to No. 10, November 11). The chief collaborators of the journal were: M. Olminsky, I. Stepanov, V. Smirnov, N. Osinsky, E. Yaroslavsky, M. Ovsyannikov, N. Meshcheryakov and others.—p. 97.

46. The speech of L. Martov at the session of the C.E.C., August 17, 1917, was published in *Novaya Zhizn*, No. 93, August 18, 1917.—p. 98.

47. At all the elections taking place in the year 1917, the Cadet Party was the furthest Right of all the social groups that put up independent tickets. The Octobrists, the Union of Russian People and other Right parties decided not to put up their own candidates, and voted for the Cadets. This was the case, for instance, in the elections to the district Dumas in Petrograd in May,

1917, and the same thing repeated itself in June in Moscow at the elections of the Central City Duma; in the latter case the Octobrists and the Black Hundreds figured in the Cadet tickets under the name of "non-partisan."—p. 102.

48. A short article in the *Novaya Zhizn*, No. 103, August 30, 1917, under the heading: "Rumours of a Conspiracy" in general correctly reported the facts that took place in Moscow during the period of the State Conference. For the purpose of preparing a counter-revolutionary overturn by the Kornilovists, a Cossack regiment was actually called away from the front and sent to Moscow, but was detained on the way. The Menshevik-S.-R. Moscow Soviet of W. and S. D., having learnt the news about the preparation of an overturn, took a number of measures for the defence of the city, turning at the same time for help to the Bolsheviks, whom they asked to hold meetings among the soldiers on August 25 to 29 (for a month and a half before this the Bolsheviks had been forbidden to enter the Moscow barracks). At the same time, in case of a possible rising, an unofficial military revolutionary body was organised by the Moscow Soviet, consisting of two Bolsheviks (Nogin and Muralov), two Mensheviks (Khinchuk and Matveyev), two S.-R.'s (Gavronsky and Shubnikov) and a representative of the Moscow military region. The result was that the Kornilovists postponed their attack for some time—till September 8. —p. 104.

49. The Sixth Congress of the R. S.-D. L. P. (Bolsheviks) took place in Petrograd semi-legally on August 8 to August 16, 1917. The sessions were held on the Vyborg side of town and at the Nevsky gate, practically in conspiratorial surroundings. As the "Interboroughites" had decided to join the Party, the congress was called in the name of the Organisation Bureau, which consisted of two Bolsheviks and two "Interboroughites." At the congress were present 157 delegates with the right to vote, from 112 organisations with a membership of 177,000. Lenin, who was compelled at that time to remain in hiding, was not present at the meetings. The congress elected him honorary chairman. The main questions on the agenda were: political and organisational report of the C.C. (reporters: Stalin and Sverdlov), local reports, the present situation (Bukharin and Stalin), economic conditions (Milyutin), organisation question, preparation for elections to the Constituent Assembly, trade union movement (Yurenev), fusion of parties, etc. The congress appointed a group to revise the party programme, but it did not pass any resolution on this question and postponed the revision of the programme. For the resolutions which were adopted, see *Documents and Materials*, No. 4.—p. 105.

50. The words are Nekrasov's (Lenin did not quote him quite correctly), from his poem "Blessed Be the Gentle Poet" (1852). The verse referred to runs as follows:

> "Obloquy pursues him,
> He hears the sounds of approbation
> Not in the dulcet sounds of praise,
> But in the roar of irritation."—p. 110.

51. Slander, as a weapon of struggle against Bolshevism, was made use of after the July days not only in relation to Lenin and Zinoviev, but also to L. B. Kamenev, who at that time was the representative of the Bolsheviks in the C.E.C. On August 23, in *Izvestiya* of the C.E.C., No. 140, and also in other papers, was published a communication supposedly issued by the Ministry of Justice about relations of Kamenev to the political police in prerevolutionary times. Kamenev immediately issued a statement to the Minister of Justice in which he wrote: ". . . I request you, as Attorney-General, to ascertain on which of the members of the Ministry of Justice lies the responsibility for publishing the mentioned statement, in order to give me the possibility of calling to trial those guilty of publishing the slanderous and lying statements about me." On that same day, August 23, the C.C. of the R. S.-D. L. P. (Bolsheviks), for its part, carried a resolution in which, regarding the slander against Kamenev as a continuation of a counter-revolutionary campaign against the Bolsheviks, it demanded "the strictest investigation of the conditions of publishing this data" and insisted on "expediting the conducting of the investigation, for the purpose of which the C.C. appoints a member of the C.C. to the commission on this matter" (*Novaya Zhizn*, No. 98, August 24, 1917). On August 25, Kamenev made a statement to the C.E.C. of the Soviets in which, among other things, he said: ". . . in order to make easier the work of the commission and to safeguard from slanderous attacks the political institutions in which I worked, I am refraining from all social activity until the end of the commission's work. I express the conviction that in the nearest future the commission of the C.E.C. will succeed in shedding full light on the inventions of Messrs. gendarmes and their assistants. . . ." On September 13, the Ministry of Justice was compelled to state that ". . . neither by the Ministry of Justice nor by any authorised member of the Ministry of Justice was the statement issued to any of the papers. The editorial office of the *Izvestiya* of the S. of W. and S. D., it seems, was led into error in publishing a forged statement that supposedly came from the Ministry of Justice. . . ."—p. 112.

52. Tsereteli in his speech on capital punishment at the session of the Petrograd Soviet of W. and S. D. on August 31, 1917 (*Ryech*, No. 194, September 1, 1917), spoke as follows:

Who would have thought at the beginning of the revolution that the death penalty would be re-introduced? Even Guchkov himself did not dream of this, but there came terrible days and the revolution had to re-introduce this institution, which had seemed forever buried. None of your resolutions will help. What is needed is not paper resolutions, but concrete actions. It is necessary to prevent the possibility of repeating those events which compelled us again to introduce capital punishment. Wasn't there treason at the front? Weren't the regiments that advanced betrayed? . . .

The last sentences of Tsereteli refer to the refusal of some detachments to go into attack in the offensive of July 1.—p. 114.

53. Paragraph 3 of the resolution of the Petrograd Soviet of W. and S. D. of August 31, 1917, reads:

EXPLANATORY NOTES   293

"(3). Re-introduced under the pretence of fighting traitors, capital punishment under the new régime appears clearly to be a measure for terrorising the masses of soldiers, with a view to enslaving them to the commanding staff. . . ."
—p. 115.

54. The German Independent Social-Democratic Party, formed during the war, split off from the official Social-Democracy on the question of the attitude towards the war. Its nucleus consisted of 18 Deputies to the Reichstag who were opposed to granting war credits. Officially the party was organised in April, 1917. At the head of the party stood Haase, Ledebour, Kautsky and Hilferding. The Communist Spartacus League found itself at one time organisationally connected with it for tactical reasons. After the November (1918) Revolution in Germany, the Independents together with the Scheidemannists entered the Provisional Government of the German republic. At the Congress in Halle in 1920 the party split; its majority, merging with the Communists, entered the Communist Party of Germany, while the minority for some time preserved its independent existence, joining the Second-and-a-Half Vienna International; later, however, they fused with the official S.-D. Party of the Second International. Ledebour's insignificant group continues an independent existence, as a fragment of the independent Social-Democracy.
—p. 120.

55. Lenin quotes from the leading article of *Novaya Zhizn*, No. 97, August 23, 1917, under the heading, "The Bolsheviks and Stockholm."—p. 121.

56. *Izvestiya* of the All-Russian Soviet of Peasant Deputies, the official organ of the Soviet of P. D., appeared in Petrograd beginning May 22, 1917, under the editorship of N. J. Bykhovsky. The newspaper was in the hands of the Right Wing of the Socialist-Revolutionaries (the representative of the Soviet of P.D. was the Right S.-R. Avksentyev), reflecting their political coalition with the bourgeoisie and opportunism on the agrarian question, which amounted to a negation of their own programme ("not to take the land before the Constituent Assembly"), and social-patriotism.—p. 127.

57. "The sample instructions comprising 242 instructions presented by local delegates at the First All-Russian Congress of the Soviets of Peasant Deputies in Petrograd in the year 1917" formulated the 6th and 11th paragraphs of the peasants' demands in the following way:

. . . (6) In the republic of Russia there must be established the election and responsibility of all officials, not excluding deputies and judges.
. . . (11) At the end of the war a standing army in the Russian republic must be forever abolished and must be replaced by a people's militia.—p. 128.

58. In the article "The Peasant Question in France and Germany," which was first published in *Neue Zeit*, No. 10, in 1894, Friedrich Engels says:

In the first place, the following attitude of the French programme is absolutely right: we see beforehand the inevitable ruin of the small peasant, but in no way are we called upon to hasten it with any kind of interference on our part. And secondly, it is also clear to us that being in possession of state power, we would not think of forcefully expropriating the small peasant (with compensation or without is immaterial) as we would be forced to do with the big landowner. Our aim in regard to the small peasant consists first of all, in transferring his small-scale production and private property into collective ones, though not by force, but through example and by proposing public help for that purpose.—p. 133.

59. In the article "The Union for the Liberation of the Ukraine," published in *Ryech*, No. 195 (3937), September 2, 1917, without the author's signature, it is stated:

In the possession of the War Ministry there is considerable material in regard to the organisation of the "Union for the Liberation of the Ukraine," which proves the participation of the Austro-Hungarian and German governments in the organisation. . . . The German Government instructed Lenin to agitate for peace and to try with all his might to undermine the confidence of the people in the Provisional Government and to aim under all circumstances to replace those Ministers who come out against the German aims to conclude peace. . . . There were two gatherings of Socialists in Berlin in which Lenin and Yoltukhovsky participated.—p. 135.

60. Lenin's letter to the Central Committee of the R. S.-D. L. P. with regard to the Kornilov revolt was written in Helsingfors. Lenin's appraisal of the situation which was created by the Kornilov revolt coincided in principle with the line of the C.C., which was in constant communication with Lenin. The letter was of a conspiratorial character and was known to few members of the Party besides the members of the C.C.

V. Milyutin ("V. M-n") and V. Volodarsky ("V-sky"), who are mentioned at the end of the article, took a very close part in the central Bolshevik organ which appeared under the general direction of J. Stalin. In Nos. 1-6 of *Rabochy* there appeared a series of articles written by them. In particular, the articles "The Victories of Messrs. Fusionists" and "Petrograd and Russia" were written by Volodarsky; "A Half Year's Result of Bourgeois Policies" and "The Directory" were written by Milyutin. In *Rabochy*, No. 2, was published "A Letter to the Editor," by Volodarsky, in which he refutes the incorrect account by *Novaya Zhizn* and other papers of a speech of his at the session of the C.E.C., which apparently served as a pretext for a rebuke to Lenin. The "Letter to the Editors" cleared up the misunderstanding that had arisen, as is related by Lenin.—p. 137.

61. The Kornilov revolt was prepared by the high command of the army and the Cadet leaders. Kornilov, who was appointed Commander-in-Chief, had already spoken at the Moscow State Conference as the leader of the approaching counter-revolution and future dictator, demanding the re-establishment of "iron discipline" in the army, threatening otherwise to surrender Riga and lay open the way to Petrograd. At the same time, Kornilov had several conferences with the Cadet leaders and Moscow industrialists. On September 8, following a secret agreement with the Provisional Government, which was in need of the support of loyal army detachments in Petrograd, Kornilov, using the excuse of an expected attack by the Bolsheviks, moved one of the army corps, some Cossack detachments, and the so-called "Wild Division" from the

front to the capital. Through V. N. Lvov, Kornilov simultaneously presented Kerensky with a number of demands which meant the proclamation of Kornilov as dictator and the creation of a new government able to smother the revolution. The agreement between Kornilov and the Provisional Government did not materialise, however, and Kerensky was forced to declare Kornilov, behind whom stood the big bourgeoisie and the Cadet Party, which was his political mentor, a traitor to the state. The bourgeois press, headed by the *Ryech*, supported the Kornilov revolt. The Petrograd and Moscow Soviets of Workers' Deputies took the lead in the defence. In the workers' sections of Petrograd, detachments of Red Guards were organised. The Bolshevik organisations of both capitals, especially the military ones, played a deciding rôle during the Kornilov revolt, organising the masses and holding enormous mass meetings in the barracks and factories. The influence of the Bolsheviks grew tremendously within these few days. Agitators and revolutionary troops were sent to meet the Kornilov detachments. His troops were demoralised under the influence of revolutionary agitation before reaching Petrograd, and proved useless for a counter-revolutionary overturn. General Krymov, who commanded the corps sent against Petrograd, shot himself; Kornilov and several other generals were placed under arrest by the Provisional Government, but later succeeded in escaping, taking the Cossack detachment guarding them along with them. The Kornilov revolt revolutionised even the most backward masses, and hastened the victory of the revolution in October.—p. 137.

62. The Fourth State Duma, which was dissolved on March 12, 1917, by decree of Nicholas II, refused to obey the order and appointed from its midst a Provisional Committee of the State Duma. The Provisional Government did not officially dissolve the State Duma, and it continued to meet under the name "Conferences of Members of the State Duma," exerting a very strong influence on the policies of the Provisional Government. The Cadet Party placed serious hopes in the State Duma, as its support, hoping under favourable circumstances to set it up in opposition to the Constituent Assembly, the convocation of which was purposely delayed. In this way, in spite of the fall of tsarism, there continued to exist a bourgeois-landowner body which was elected on the basis of the census [property-qualification] election law of tsarist days. The Provisional Government decided on the formal dissolution of the State Duma only after the Kornilov revolt.—p. 138.

63. Lenin quotes from N. Sukhanov's article "On the Liquidation of the Struggle for Peace" (*Novaya Zhizn*, No. 106, September 2, 1917).—p. 140.

64. The "Unity Congress of the R. S.-D. L. P." called by the "Central Commission," and to which came: Mensheviks (O. C.), "*Novaya Zhizn*-ists," the Martov group, the Moscow "unificationists," Bundists and representatives of the Caucasian regional organisations, took place in Petrograd on September 1 to 6, 1917. The Congress ended by uniting the various mentioned currents and electing a Central Committee, which included representatives of all the different trends of opinion at the Congress. (Tsereteli, Dan, Chkheidze, Martov, Rozhkov, Yakhontov, Abramovich, etc.)—p. 140.

65. General Kaledin in a speech at the State Conference in Moscow on August 27, 1917, among other things, said: ". . . accusations of counter-revolution were not made until after the Cossack regiments, saving the revolutionary government, *at the call* of the Socialist Ministers, on July 16 came to the defence of the government against anarchy and treason. . . ." (*Ryech*, No. 190, August 28, 1917.)—p. 145.

66. The elections to the Petrograd municipal Duma, September 2. 1917, strengthened the Bolsheviks a great deal as compared with the elections to the regional Duma that had taken place in May. The Bolsheviks received 33% of all the votes (as against 20% in May); the S.-R.—Menshevik bloc of conciliators, 44% (instead of 58%), and the Cadets, 23% (instead of 22%). The municipal council consisted of Socialist-conciliators and Cadets, who immediately entered a coalition; the Right Socialist-Revolutionary Schroeder was elected Mayor.—p. 147.

67. The question of the relation to Zimmerwald was discussed at the All-Russian April (May) Conference. Acting on the report of Zinoviev, May 12, 1917, on the situation in the International and the tasks of the Russian Social-Democratic Labour Party, the Conference declared for participation in the Third Zimmerwald Conference, which was at that time planned for May 31. In the resolution by Zinoviev, adopted by the April Conference, a point was made about the opportunism of the majority of Zimmerwald, but at the same time it was proposed to stay in the Zimmerwald bloc, fighting within for the tactic of the Zimmerwald Left and undertaking the necessary steps for the formation of a Third International. Lenin proposed "to stay only for information purposes," but this proposition was rejected.

While the Zimmerwald Conference was in preparation, preparations were also made for a conference of the Socialist parties, which was being organised by the social-chauvinists, to take place in Stockholm. About September, 1917, the representatives to the Zimmerwald Conference and the delegates to the Stockholm Conference came to Stockholm. The Stockholm Conference did not take place: the English government refused passports to the delegates, and the French Socialist Party refused to sit together with the delegates of the German Social-Democrats.

From the end of May to September, a series of conferences of the delegates to the Zimmerwald Conference took place at Stockholm; at these conferences the question of the Stockholm Conference was considered. Several of the Zimmerwaldists spoke in favour of participation in the Stockholm Conference. This gave Lenin the opportunity to address a letter to the C.C. of the party against the further connection of the Russian Bolsheviks with the Zimmerwald union.

"The Stockholm representatives" of which Lenin speaks were the delegates of the C.C. of the Bolsheviks to the Third Zimmerwald Conference, V. Vorovsky and N. Semashko.—p. 150.

68. The articles by Engels "Programme of Blanquists-Communists" and "Blanquists" appeared in a special collection in 1894 under the title: "Inter-

nationales aus dem *Volksstaat"* (1871-1875). ("On International Subjects from the *Volksstaat"*) *Vorwärts* publishing house, Berlin.—p. 152.

69. *Rabochy Put,* central organ of the R. S.-D. L. P., appeared instead of the suppressed *Rabochy* from September 16 to November 8, 1917, when, after the victory of the revolution, *Pravda,* which had been suppressed during the July days by the Kerensky government, again began to come out. Altogether 46 numbers of *Rabochy Put* appeared.—p. 157.

70. "Draft Resolution on the Political Situation" was apparently written by Lenin September 16, 1917, after the Kornilov revolt, when the question was raised about the convocation of the so-called Democratic Conference. The draft was planned for submission to the Central Committee of the party. However, in the minutes of meetings of the C.C. of the R. S.-D. L. P. which have been preserved, as published in *Proletarskaya Revolyutsiya,* No. 10, 1927, there are no indications that this draft was discussed by the Central Committee.—p. 158.

71. Minister of Agriculture Chernov resigned on September 8, 1917. Soon after, another representative of the Narodniks—Minister of Supplies Peshkhonov—also resigned. The resignations were due to the Provisional Government's refusal to put into effect Chernov's agrarian bills, which were intended to pave the way for agrarian reform, and also due to the doubling of the price of bread, which the Provisional Government did in the interests of the big landowners.—p. 162.

72. The Council of the Socialist-Revolutionary Party (a "party council" was with the S.-R.'s something in between a C.C. plenum and a conference) took place on August 19 to 23, 1917. At the council was represented a considerable Left Wing, consisting primarily of those elements who later, in November, 1917, broke away and formed the party of "Left Socialist-Revolutionaries-Internationalists." The basic resolution on the present situation, which approved the policy of the C.C. and came out for unqualified support of the Provisional Government (Rosenblum's resolution), received 54 votes; the opposing resolution of the opposition, which criticised the activities of the Provisional Government, demanded resistance to its counter-revolutionary measures and declared for the transfer of power to the revolutionary democracy, "responsible to the Soviets" (Steinberg's resolution), received 35 votes. The report and the resolutions of the party council are published in *Dyelo Naroda,* Nos. 121-125, August 21-25, 1917.—p. 163.

73. Lenin refers to the editorial in *Dyelo Naroda,* No. 147, September 19, 1917, entitled "The Problem of Power and the Constituent Assembly."—p. 164.

74. From the article by I. Prilezhayev, "The Crisis in the Provisioning Policy of the Ministry of Supplies," published in *Dyelo Naroda,* No. 147, September 19, 1917.—p. 169.

75. The Democratic Conference, convoked by the Provisional Government because of the changed interrelationship of social forces brought about by the Kornilov revolt, and which had as its purpose the widening of the social base supporting the government and the strengthening of its position, took place in Petrograd in the Alexander Theatre, September 27 to October 5, 1917. The municipal governments, the *zemstvos* and the co-operatives were given greater representation, while the representation of the Soviets, army organisations, trade unions and factory committees was reduced. Of a very variegated composition, the Conference after long hesitation and repeated voting declared in favour of a coalition ministry, but without the participation of the Cadets. Kerensky, however, did not submit to the vote of the Conference and formed a cabinet with the participation of individual members of the Cadet Party, as well as of representatives of Moscow industrialists. The Conference chose from its own ranks a "Provisional Soviet of the Republic" ("pre-parliament"), which, supplemented by representatives of the "census" bourgeoisie, was to take the place of a (consultative) representative organ until the Constituent Assembly, the convocation of which was being delayed.

The Bolshevik fraction of the Conference worked out a detailed political declaration which was read at the October 1st Session (see *Documents and Materials*, No. 8).

The Democratic Conference, which did not carry any authority in the country, did not accomplish its purpose of strengthening the Provisional Government and broadening its base. Lenin in his letters to the C.C. proposed to "surround the Alexander Theatre" and disperse the Democratic Conference. The Democratic Conference "does not represent the *majority* of the revolutionary people," wrote Lenin, "but merely the conciliatory petty-bourgeois leadership. The pitiable hesitations of the Democratic Conference must exasperate and will exasperate the patience of the workers of Petrograd and Moscow" (see pp. 226-229).—p. 171.

76. *Russkoye Slovo*, a popular newspaper published in Moscow by I. Sytin, edited by Doroshevich and Blagov. Like the entire liberal press, *Russkoye Slovo* supported the revolt of General Kornilov and was an open counter-revolutionary organ. Soon after the victory of the October Revolution in Moscow, the Moscow Soviet suppressed the paper and confiscated its printing plant for labour publications. In 1918 Sytin's newspaper appeared for several months under the name *Nashe Slovo*.—p. 172.

77. In the decision of the Economic Department of the C.E.C. on the increase of bread prices by the Provisional Government, which was published in the *Izvestiya* of the C.E.C., No. 164, September 20, 1917, it was stated:

Recognising that raising the fixed prices of bread is a pernicious measure, dealing a violent blow to matters of provisioning as well as to the entire economic life of the country, the Economic Department considers it necessary to liquidate this measure, replacing it by a system of measures which will assure the most extensive supplying of the village with necessities at fixed prices on the basis of the general regularisation of the economic life.

In further recording "the absolute lack of activity on the part of the central organs created to work with the government for the regulation of economic life," the department considered it necessary to submit this decision for consideration to the C.E.C. together with a detailed report. Independently of this, the department instructed the delegates of the C.E.C. in the Supply Committee of the state and in the Economic Soviet to "urgently raise the question of encroachment on the rights of these institutions, rights which were guaranteed them by the law—this encroachment having found expression in the raising of the fixed prices without preliminary consideration by these organs."—p. 182.

78. Lenin quotes from M. Smith's article, "The Voice of Democracy" (*Svobodnaya Zhizn*, No. 1, September 15, 1917). *Svobodnaya Zhizn* appeared in place of *Novaya Zhizn*, which had been suppressed by the Provisional Government.—p. 205.

79. Political resolutions proposed by the Bolsheviks were first carried in the Soviets of the capitals: in Petrograd, September 13; in Moscow, September 18, 1917. In view of the submission of their resignation by the Menshevik-S.-R. presidiums, the presidium of the workers' section of the Petrograd Soviet was re-elected on September 8, consisting of 6 Bolsheviks, 3 S.-R.'s and 2 Mensheviks; on September 26 the presidium of the soldiers' section was re-elected; 9 Bolsheviks, 10 S.-R.'s, 3 Internationalists (Lefts) and 2 Mensheviks were elected. As chairman of the Petrograd Soviet Trotsky, instead of Chkheidze, was elected; as chairman of the Moscow Soviet, Nogin (instead of the Menshevik, Khinchuk), as chairman of the Moscow provincial Soviet, which was won by the Bolsheviks a week later, Vladimirsky. The Moscow Soviet of Soldiers' Deputies, which existed separately from the Soviet of Workers' Deputies, as well as the Moscow Soviet of Peasant Deputies, which remained in the hands of the S.-R.'s until the October Revolution, upon its re-election merged with the corresponding workers' Soviets.—p. 217.

80. The Seventh Petrograd Conference of Socialist-Revolutionaries, which was held on September 23, 1917, was devoted to the evaluation of the present situation (report by Chernov) and the re-election of the Petrograd Committee. The Conference was under the leadership of the Left Wing (Schroeder, Trutovsky, Kamkov, Spiridonova), which demanded the rejection of the policy of coalition and the organisation of a government based on the Soviets. The resolution adopted demanded: the homogeneity and responsibility of the government to the organs of the revolutionary democracy, the transfer of all the land to the management of the land committees, state control over production through factory committees, legislative sanction of the eight-hour day, maximum taxation of propertied classes, democratisation of the army, "decisive struggle against war," the carrying out of the principle of self-determination of nations, the dissolution of counter-revolutionary organisations, the State Duma and the State Soviet, the abolition of capital punishment at the front, investigation of the Kornilov affair, etc. The Conference re-elected the Petrograd Committee and gave the majority in this committee to the Lefts.—p. 217.

81. The letters of Lenin, "The Bolsheviks Must Assume Power" and "Marxism and Uprising" (p. 224), were discussed at the session of the Central

Committee of the Bolsheviks on September 28, 1917. The minutes of the C.C. contain the following entry:

Order of business. Letters of Lenin. Decided in the near future to call a meeting of the C.C. for the consideration of technical questions. Comrade Stalin proposes to send the letters to the most important organisations with the proposal that they discuss them. Decided to postpone decision till next meeting of the C.C. The question was put to a vote as to who favours that only one copy of the letters be kept. For, 6; against, 4; abstained, 6. Comrade Kamenev proposes for adoption the following resolution: "The C.C. having considered the letters of Lenin reject the practical propositions contained in them, calls upon all organisations to follow the instructions of the C.C., and again reaffirms that the C.C. finds that any actions on the streets are entirely inadmissible in the present situation. The C.C. at the same time addresses a demand to Comrade Lenin to develop in a special pamphlet the question raised in his letters about the evaluation of the present situation and the policy of the party." Resolution rejected. In conclusion the following decision is carried: "Members of the C.C. conducting the work in the Military organisation and in the Petrograd Committee are instructed to adopt measures to prevent any actions from developing in the barracks or in the factories" (Minutes of Central Committee of R. S.-D. L. P., *Proletarskaya Revolyutsiya*, No. 10, 1927).

At the same session for the first time appeared sharp differences of opinion within the C.C. on the question of the attitude towards an armed uprising; these differences of opinion, gradually increasing, led at the end of October to an open parting of the ways between Kamenev and Zinoviev on the one hand and Lenin and the majority of the C.C. on the other, and after the October Revolution ended by their demonstrative resignation from the C.C. and by a part of the people's commissars resigning from the Council of People's Commissars.—p. 221.

82. At the end of the summer of 1917 the German armies gained many important victories on the western front, and the submarines blockaded the British Isles with great success, which created conditions favourable for the conclusion of peace between several powers, especially between England and Germany, at the expense of Russia. Diplomats were already sounding out the ground for such an agreement. The entrance of the United States into the war and the American troops rushed to France changed the interrelationship of forces, assuring in 1918 victory to the Entente.—p. 222.

83. The definition of uprising as an art is given in *Revolution and Counterrevolution in Germany*; the book was written not by Marx, as was thought for a long time to be the case, but by Engels. The reference about uprising here mentioned is given by Lenin on page 52 of Book II of this volume.—p. 224.

84. The Alexander Theatre in Petrograd, where the Democratic Conference held its sessions; the Fortress of Peter and Paul on the Neva River in the centre of Petrograd opposite the Winter Palace, which served under tsarism as a jail for political prisoners.—p. 229.

85. Lenin's phrase "the Mensheviks and Socialist-Revolutionaries refused to join a coalition with the Cadets" refers to the vote of the Democratic Con-

ference, October 2, 1917, declaring in favour of coalition with the bourgeoisie, but without the Cadet Party (on the exclusion of the Cadets from the coalition 595 voted in favour, 493 against, and 72 abstained). But even such purely formal limitations were not carried out by the Provisional Government and the Mensheviks and S.-R.'s supporting it. After the Democratic Conference, Kerensky organised a cabinet with the participation of the Moscow industrialists and the leading members of the Cadet Party, with the provision, however, that the Cadets enter the Ministry not in the capacity of representatives of their party but in their personal capacity. Several Mensheviks and Narodniks also went into the cabinet. The most important portfolios were distributed as follows: A. F. Kerensky, Prime Minister; A. M. Nikitin (Menshevik), Internal Affairs; A. P. Konovalov, Commerce and Industry, and Vice-Premier; M. E. Tereshchenko, Foreign Affairs; A. V. Kartashov, Religion; N. M. Kishkin, Social Welfare; P. N. Malyantovich (Menshevik), Justice; S. A. Smirnov, State Control; M. V. Bernatsky, Finance; A. V. Liverovsky, Communication; S. N. Prokopovich, Supplies; S. S. Salazkin, Education; K. A. Gvozdev (Menshevik), Labour; A. I. Verkhovsky, War; Verderevsky, Navy; S. Tretyakov, Chairman of Economic Council.—p. 230.

86. On September 3, 1917, the German army, after having broken through the Russian lines, captured Riga. The Russian armies made energetic resistance, the Lettish regiment of marksmen especially fighting bitterly. In the press indications appeared that at Riga the Supreme Command purposely paralysed the resistance of the army with a view to creating a threat to revolutionary Petrograd, producing a panic in the country, exerting pressure on the Mensheviks and S.-R.'s and securing the withdrawal from Petrograd of the troops faithful to the revolution. The bourgeois press put the blame on the soldiers and Bolsheviks and made use of the surrender of Riga for counter-revolutionary propaganda, forecasting (and provoking) the advance of the Germans on Petrograd. Using the proximity of Petrograd to the front as a pretext, the Kerensky government was preparing to transfer the capital to Moscow, where it expected to have greater freedom from the pressure of the revolutionary masses.—p. 230.

87. The resolution of the Rostov-on-the-Don Committee of the Cadet Party on September 14, 1917, declared:

. . . as the final establishment of the new order is the inalienable right of the Constituent Assembly, any action against the Provisional Government and the programme proclaimed by it for the immediate future is a counter-revolutionary act. The further deepening of the revolution leads to the destruction of the economic and cultural life and threatens civil war. The Committee is convinced that civil war may sweep away all the gains of the revolution and drown in rivers of blood our young, not yet consolidated freedom, it is therefore the opinion of the Committee that an energetic protest against deepening the revolution as proposed by the unrealisable Socialist Utopias, is necessary, in order to save the gains of the revolution.

The Cadet committee therefore called upon all "vital forces" to rally around the Provisional Government (*Ryech*, No. 210, September 20, 1917).—p. 230.

88. A. Zarudny delivered this address at the Democratic Conference, September 29, 1917. Lenin quotes from the report in *Izvestiya* of the C.E.C., No. 175, October 2, 1917.—p. 247.

89. The article by Lenin, "From a Publicist's Diary: The Mistakes of Our Party," devoted to the difference of opinion in connection with the question of boycotting the Democratic Conference, was first published in 1924, in the magazine *Proletarskaya Revolyutsiya*, No. 3, together with a note by Comrade Tayezhnik (Mogilnikov), in which the latter stated that in September (old calendar), 1917, this article "went from hand to hand in the Vyborg district." The article was published from the manuscript which had been preserved by Comrade Tayezhnik.

On the question of boycotting the Democratic Conference and the pre-parliament created by it, two points of view struggled within the Bolshevik C.C.: that of Lenin, for boycott, and that of Kamenev, for participation. The question of withdrawing from the Democratic Conference was discussed by the C.C. on October 4, 1917. The minutes of the meeting contain the following entry:

On the question of the Democratic Conference it was decided not to withdraw, but merely to recall the members of our Party from the presidium. As to the pre-parliament, it was decided by a vote of 9 against 8 not to enter it. However, taking into consideration that the vote was divided almost equally, the final decision was left to the party conference, which was to be constituted immediately from the fraction of the Democratic Conference in session. Two reports were to be made: by Comrade Trotsky and Comrade Rykov.

The session of the Bolshevik fraction of the Democratic Conference took place on October 4. It was addressed by Stalin and Trotsky in favour of boycotting the pre-parliament, and by Kamenev and Rykov against the boycott. There is no report of the session at our disposal. In the minutes of the C.C. it is merely stated: "At the conference by a majority of 77 against 50 it was decided to participate in the pre-parliament. This decision has also been confirmed by the C.C." The question of boycotting the pre-parliament was again considered at the session of the C.C. on October 18. "After a discussion it was decided by all, with one exception, to withdraw from the pre-parliament on the very first day after the declaration had been read. The theses were adopted, but the preparation of the declaration was left to the editorial board of the central organ." Kamenev voted against the withdrawal from the pre-parliament, and attached to the minutes of the C.C. the following statement:

To the C.C. of the R. S.-D. L. P.:
Dear Comrades: I think that your decision to withdraw from the very first session of the "Soviet of the Russian Republic" predetermines the tactics of the Party during the next period in a direction which I personally consider quite dangerous for the Party. In submitting to the decision of the Party I at the same time beg the comrades to relieve me of the duties in the representative bodies (C.E.C., etc.) and give me some other work. October 5, 1917. Kamenev. (Minutes of the sessions of the C.C. of the R. S.-D. L. P., *Proletarskaya Revolyutsiya*, No. 10 (169), 1927.)

The Bolshevik fraction withdrew from the pre-parliament at its very first session, October 20, after the reading of the declaration by Trotsky.—p. 249.

90. The letter to I. T. Smilga, who at that time was the chairman of the Regional Committee of the Army, Navy and Workers of Finland (in Helsingfors), was written by Lenin, October 10, 1917, in Vyborg, where he had gone from Helsingfors in connection with the new upsurge of the revolution, in order to be nearer to Petrograd (about determination of the date of the letter, see note 92).
Lenin advised Smilga to burn this letter. Smilga kept the letter, only tearing from it the name of the sender, out of considerations of conspiracy.—p. 265.

91. Fort Ino on the Finnish coast of the Finnish Bay was a powerful fortification which, together with Cronstadt, defended the approaches to Petrograd. In April, 1918, during the landing of the German army in Finland, the fort was blown up in accordance with the decision of the Council of People's Commissars, since the territory of the fort was to be transferred to Finland.—p. 266.

92. The date of Lenin's letter to I. Smilga is determined with exactitude on the basis of the following words of the former. "I read in papers today that in two weeks the danger of a naval occupation will be nil." Lenin evidently refers to the following notice of the occupation in *Novaya Zhizn*, No. 138, October 10, in the section "Latest News":

In authoritative circles it is pointed out that a German landing in Finland is hardly possible. Sending the fleet and the landing party from Kiel to Finland will demand immense quantities of fuel, which Germany does not possess at present. Within two weeks all probability of a landing will be eliminated since the time has been lost which is necessary for the development of this operation.

Newspapers from Petrograd were received in Vyborg on the same day.—p. 266.

93. Usikirko and Perkyarvi are railroad stations in Finland on the line Petrograd (Leningrad)—Vyborg; Terioki is a country-place in Finland near Leningrad on the same railroad line.—p. 266.

94. "Materials for the Revision of the Party Programme" was a collection of articles by V. Milyutin, V. Sokolnikov, A. Lomov, V. Smirnov, published by the Moscow Regional Bureau, R. S.-D. L. P. (Bolsheviks), Moscow, 1917. For further details about it, see article by Lenin "Towards the Revision of the Party Programme," page 71, Book II of this volume.—p. 268.

95. The article "The Crisis Has Matured" was written by Lenin on October 12, 1917, in Vyborg; Chapters I-V were published in *Rabochy Put*, No. 30; Chapter IV was left out, and Chapter V was marked as the fourth; thus, Chapter IV remains unknown and in the present edition it is denoted by dots. Apparently Chapter IV was omitted by the editorial board of *Rabochy Put* out of considerations of a conspirative nature.—p. 271.

96. Lenin quotes the editorial from *Dyelo Naroda*, No. 167, October 12, 1917.—p. 273.

97. *Russkiye Vyedomosti*, a Cadet newspaper published in Moscow and very popular among the intelligentsia. The editorial board included several professors of Moscow University.—p. 275.

98. At the elections to the Moscow municipal Duma on July 8-11, 1917, according to official data, the Cadets received 109,000 votes and 34 councillors; the People's Socialists, 8,000 votes and 3 councillors; the S.-R.'s, 375,000 and 116 councillors, the Mensheviks and Internationalists—76,000 and 24 councillors, the Bolsheviks, 75,000 and 23 councillors, and the group *Yedinstvo* (the Plekhanovists) 1,500 votes and no councillors; altogether the Moscow municipal Duma had 200 councillors.

The elections to the district Dumas of Moscow, October 7 to 9, 1917, gave the Bolsheviks about 52% of all the votes cast in the city. The figures quoted by Lenin, 47%, 49% and 51% are not exact. Altogether according to the data of the Moscow municipal Duma, there were elected 350 Bolsheviks, 184 Cadets, 104 S.-R.'s, 31 Mensheviks and several non-partisans. The soldiers of the Moscow garrison voted solidly for the Bolshevik ticket. In all the district Dumas on the outskirts of the city and the district councils selected by them the Bolsheviks obtained full control.—p. 275.

99. In the Central Committee of the Bolsheviks two currents were struggling in the fall of 1917. One, under the leadership of Lenin, considered an uprising and overthrow of the Provisional Government as necessary; the other, headed by Kamenev and Zinoviev, was against an uprising, preferring "parliamentarian" ways of development and leaving for the Bolshevik Party the part of an extreme Left opposition in the coming Constituent Assembly. This same current objected to the boycott of the pre-parliament. During the decisive sessions of the C.C. on October 23 and 29, Kamenev and Zinoviev spoke against an armed uprising. Differences of opinion continued also after the victory of the October Revolution, but already in the form of a controversy about the formation of a coalition "Socialist" Ministry, from the Right S.-R.'s and Mensheviks to the Bolsheviks. The difference of opinion in the higher committees of the Party ended in the resignations of Kamenev, Zinoviev, Rykov and others from the C.C. and the Council of People's Commissars in November, 1917.—p. 276.